DRAWN TOGETHER

BLOOMSBURY RESEARCH IN ILLUSTRATION

The *Bloomsbury Research in Illustration Series* welcomes topics from the full remit of illustration – from materiality, practice and technologies, through to history, theory and beyond. The series is designed to bring together global research within illustration to form a cohesive body of literature unique to this discipline. The series is the place for scholars, researchers, students and authors to turn to for high quality discussion of contemporary and historical issues within illustration, providing a base from which to further disseminate discourse within the field.

In the series:

Illustration and Heritage
Rachel Emily Taylor

Illustration, Narrative and The Suffragette
Mireille Fauchon

Representations of Art and Art Museums in Children's Picture Books
Perry Nodelman

Illustrated Sheet Music in the U.S., 1830-1930
Theresa Leininger-Miller and Kenneth Hartvigsen

DRAWN TOGETHER

Illustration, Community and Collective World-Making

Luise Vormittag

BLOOMSBURY VISUAL ARTS
LONDON • NEW YORK • OXFORD • NEW DELHI • SYDNEY

BLOOMSBURY VISUAL ARTS
Bloomsbury Publishing Plc, 50 Bedford Square, London, WC1B 3DP, UK
Bloomsbury Publishing Inc, 1359 Broadway, New York, NY 10018, USA
Bloomsbury Publishing Ireland, 29 Earlsfort Terrace, Dublin, 2 D02 AY28, Ireland

BLOOMSBURY, BLOOMSBURY VISUAL ARTS and the Diana logo are trademarks of Bloomsbury Publishing Plc

First published in Great Britain 2026

Cover design by Europa

A catalogue record for this book is available from the British Library.

A catalog record for this book is available from the Library of Congress.

ISBN: HB: 978-1-350-25246-2
PB: 978-1-350-63474-9
ePDF: 978-1-350-25247-9
eBook: 978-1-350-25248-6

Series: Bloomsbury Research in Illustration

Typeset by Integra Software Services Pvt. Ltd.
Printed and bound in Great Britain

For product safety related questions contact productsafety@bloomsbury.com.

To find out more about our authors and books visit www.bloomsbury.com and sign up for our newsletters.

CONTENTS

FIGURES

PREFACE

The world has changed during the years I was writing this book. I started my research in 2015, after working on various commissions as an illustrator where I was asked to 'engage with the local community'. I greatly enjoyed these projects, but I couldn't shake the feeling that the intersection of community and illustration had more to offer than these commissions allowed me to explore. I decided to pursue these questions in an academic context. I started drawing on theoretical ideas about the political and used my practice as an illustrator to initiate community-focused projects (this time without the framework of a commission) to test things out and think things through. Once I had finished that, I promptly set off on a second round of pursuing these themes; this time taking in a broader range of other practitioners. This work spread itself, sometimes thickly, sometimes thinly, over a decade of my life. All the while, other things kept happening, too: I became a parent. I progressed in my academic career. The world went through the COVID-19 pandemic. New global conflicts erupted, and old ones reignited with new levels of atrocious violence. Meanwhile our digital devices continued to engage us with ever greater levels of persuasiveness, devouring our attention and warping our ambitions. But as I submit this manuscript for publication, it seems to me that the question of community, and more generally the themes of kinship, belonging and human connection, are – if anything – more urgent than ever.

We are losing common ground. Many people feel disconnected and abandoned and experience themselves as lacking both community and agency. The dizzying rise of social media that started in earnest during the 2010s has splintered our attentional commons. In the whirlwind of algorithmic configurations, we often find ourselves breathlessly, frantically, enmeshed with one another and simultaneously profoundly alone. Recently, there has been a steady increase of AI inserting itself in human relationships – either by taking on the 'arduous' task of drafting our written communications, or by replacing human connection entirely with digital companionship.

Of course, sending perfectly pitched messages is not really the way to cultivate connection. Part of the power of human relationships comes from the risks involved in revealing ourselves to another. But moments of disclosure need a counterpart who is at least *somewhat* able to receive what is being offered up. Sociologist Allison Pugh recently coined the term 'connective labour' to describe both the efforts and rewards involved in this type of receptive encounter (Pugh 2024). Her work reminds us of the importance of everyday interactions in civic life. We need to be seen by others outside our intimate circle to grasp who we are (and to help us work out who we might want to become). But not everyone is recognized in this way. Who is seen and who is not has political ramifications. Being repeatedly overlooked has dire consequences.

But what does all this mean for illustration? Can illustration provide an arena for this 'connective labour'? In this book I argue that it can, but it took me a while to reach this conclusion. I initially started this research with an idea that over time proved itself to be somewhat misguided. I assumed that as illustrators we could somehow visualize the collective imaginaries of a community. In one project where I worked with an organization that promotes the interest of migrant communities in South London, I attempted to visually represent how this group of people perceive and navigate their neighbourhood. But I soon realized that trying to retrieve collective imaginaries was not really getting me anywhere. (Do different people even truly imagine the same thing?) Nor was the presumption that communities were somehow simply 'out there' turn out to be particularly helpful. The question of whether either of these things (collective imaginaries or community) actually exist in any stable form was soon eclipsed by the simple realization that, whatever their ontological status, I did not have the ability to magically access and visualize them. Collective imaginaries proved elusive – I struggled to find a method to translate people's accounts of shared neighbourhoods into a coherent visual narrative that they might recognize as their own. And neither could I figure out how to illustrate community – a supposedly unified group of people – in a way that didn't bring me uncomfortably close to stereotypical tropes.

This was a sobering moment. But I soon came to understand that my problem was that I had been thinking of communities as something that simply exists. If, instead, community is understood as a kind of behaviour, as a group of people acting *towards* one another, new possibilities for the role of illustration start taking shape. I gradually realized that carefully considered participatory illustration projects, where people are invited to contribute to a gradually emerging visual document, can offer a space for community to unfold. Put another way, these projects can be a realm for individuals to see, and be seen by, others. This approach directs people's attention towards each other, as well as the things and concerns they hold in common. In the projects that followed, I found myself no longer trying to represent something or someone that already exists, instead acknowledging that my intervention would inevitably create a new scenario – one in which community could be enacted. My project with a group of older feminists offered them an arena to picture themselves as a group of individual women who had come together through their shared convictions and experiences, delighting in their plurality. Mitch Miller's work in Scotland involves gathering people around a large, gradually emerging illustration of a place they hold in common to negotiate what should be included in the work and how. In Argentina, Sidney Mann brings together a group of women to jointly create an embroidered map of their province, establishing new ties of connection and belonging.

In practice none of this is straightforward. Anyone who has ever tried to host a participatory art or design project will tell you that the majority of people will swiftly abscond if you suggest they pick up a pen and draw something. And even if you overcome this initial challenge, and you have successfully accumulated contributions from your group, drawings, inscriptions, stories or any other manner of responses, the question of how to coherently assemble and present this work is far from obvious. Quite the opposite – it is profoundly challenging. I rolled up my sleeves and worked through the details of it all. I anxiously reflected on my role (What was I: facilitator, translator, ethnographer, graphic designer?); I grappled with the slippery question of aesthetic appeal (Is it wrong to want to make a collective visual document look good? And who has the authority to say what is 'good'?); and I worked hard to devise projects where the individual contribution remains distinctly legible while also forming part of an eloquent whole. But I also came to realize that this was hard because being in community is, actually, hard. The challenges I was encountering in this work were, unsurprisingly perhaps, quite similar to the challenges of community: How can we find ways to structure our togetherness so that we don't just continuously trip over one another causing a big jumble? How can we form a group with bonds sufficiently strong to hold people together, but that is also, simultaneously, lose enough for everyone to remain recognizable as a singular being? How can we speak eloquently as an alliance, but also ensure everybody's individual voice is heard? How can we encounter one another in ways that allow us to jointly forge new ways of understanding our shared interests, see our mutual landscapes, and narrate our overlapping histories? Can we admit to and celebrate our interdependence; the ways in which we realize ourselves in our encounters with another? These challenges were reflected in the many hours that I and other illustrators and practitioners spent wrestling with our projects, devising structures, editing, assembling, arranging, consulting, circling in and drawing out. The results are necessarily partial and patchy, but then again, so is being in community.

Of course, community unfolds incessantly, everywhere, through innumerable actions and gestures, without the slightest need for illustrators to play any role in its manifestation. But one of the special contributions illustration can make with respect to community is that it is a practice that can record, with at least some degree of permanence, this process of collective becoming. To illustrate is to leave a trace. And, because as illustrators we tend to be hardwired for communication, the projects often continue beyond the immediate moment of their creation. They travel out into the world, seeking and addressing new audiences. They carry with them visions of collectively articulated common ground, ready for others to take up, revise, or contest. Illustration can draw us together here, in the present, but by leaving a trace, it draws us forward into potential futures, too.

ACKNOWLEDGEMENTS

This book has benefitted from the generosity of many people. I am deeply grateful to all my collaborators and participants who worked on the projects I undertook as part of the research for this book. Patria Roman, Santiago Peluffo and Natalia Perez at Latin Elephant were instrumental in shaping my project *Walking the Elephant*, thank you. Thank you also to the many participants who dropped in and took part in the workshops, as well as Cristina Errea, Daniel Hopkinson and Ana Rita Otsuka who helped me run them, and Mike Stevens and Lucy Maria from See, Also Studio, who worked on the digital output of this project with me. In *Write Women into History*, I am indebted to Anne-Marie Payne (City and Hackney Carers Centre), and, most of all, to the fourteen 'Hackney HOWLers' who made up the group. An especially warm thank you goes to Gail Chester and Celia Burgess-Macey, the two group facilitators. I am also grateful to Houman Momtazian, who kindly reviewed my layouts and my typographic choices in *Write Women into History* and Rich and Estelle at Duplikat Press. I would like to thank all walkers who took part in *Cracks in the Pavement*. I am indebted to the team at Panopus Print who operated a COVID-secure large-scale scanning service during the pandemic, which was essential for this project. I am also very grateful to Lydia Julien at the Hackney Archives, who hosted a thoughtful 'handing over ceremony' for the *Cracks in the Pavement* maps and documents and who has given them such a great new home at the archives.

I would like to thank Mitch Miller, Sidney Mann, Nina Sabnani, Jhinuk Sarkar, Billy Ash Sakula, Alaa Alsaraji, Grace Holliday, Rebecca Davies and Anna Francis. Thank you for the generosity of sharing your work and your time with me. Thank you to Valentina Zunino for helping me obtain the necessary image permissions for Grace Holliday's work.

I am grateful to my doctoral supervisory team Ian Horton, Alison Barnes and Lawrence Zeegen. Thank you for the many excellent conversations and for never allowing me to get away with a shoddy argument. Thank you also to my colleague Peter A. Hall who engaged with earlier versions of this manuscript in such thoughtful detail.

Thank you for insightful and enriching conversations: Toma Peiu, Patricia Markert, Franz Buhr, Sarah DeMott, Alexandra D'Onofrio, Lucy Hunt, CIELab members, Sergios Strigklogiannis, Karen Sung and Pat Wong.

I would like to thank my colleagues at UAL, especially the staff team and students in the illustration programme at Camberwell. Thank you to Rachel Emily Taylor and Stephanie Black for your encouraging friendship – your work has been an inspiration. And thank you to Annabelle Dance for going through the manuscript and adding your magic.

I am indebted to my parents who always trusted my endeavours and allowed me to pursue my interests, thank you for your support over the many years. Stewart, thank you for being by my side through all the ups and downs and for the seemingly never-ending supply of Jean-Luc Nancy books. And Malka, thank you for being the cool kid you are!

Earlier versions of some aspects of this research were published as: 'Walking the Elephant: Drawing as enactment of community', *Migration Studies*, Volume 12, Issue 2, June 2024; and 'Illustration as an announcement of a world', *Journal of Illustration*, Volume 11, Issue 1, November 2024.

ABOUT THE COVER DESIGN

The cover design for this book was developed in drawing workshops with the design studio Europa (Mia Frostner, Robert Sollis, William Jacobson) and their kids. These hands-on experiments – where they were literally drawing together – helped explore multiple ideas before choosing a single design for the cover.

FIGURE 0.1 Drawing Together. Photograph by Europa.

INTRODUCTION

When most people think of an illustrator, they envisage a solitary figure sequestered in their studio, assiduously labouring over their drawings. However, this represents, at best, a partial picture. Yes, numerous illustrators do spend many hours on their own working on their images, but even while doing so, they are embedded in a network of relations with other people, such as clients, agents, collaborators, editors, graphic designers and anticipated audiences. In her essay 'Making Meaning of Illustration' (2018), the US-American art historian Michele H. Bogart describes illustration as a 'collective, negotiated enterprise' and as 'collectively generated material culture' (Bogart 2018). Rather than focusing on individual practitioners or discrete images, Bogart suggests that scholarship should widen its scope and consider the multitude of other people, as well as historic, institutional, social and cultural forces, that impact an illustration's creation, distribution and reception.

While I share Bogart's view of illustration as a socially negotiated enterprise, the type of work she studies – American advertising images of the 1950s – differs considerably from the illustrative projects I am curious about. Most illustration, including the body of work surveyed by Bogart, does not highlight the multiple people and forces that contributed to its creation; in fact, quite the opposite is true, with many illustrators striving to develop 'a personal voice' in their work – a recognizable style that speaks of singular and identifiable authorship. In contrast, I am interested in illustrated documents that actually speak of heterogeneity and work hard to *foreground* the relational processes that led to their creation. This is the type of illustration I will explore in this book.

In the following chapters, I discuss my own illustration work with community groups alongside projects by other practitioners whose work and interests overlap with mine. This is not a coherent list of examples; while they all contain a dimension of community participation, they are as methodologically and conceptually diverse as the groups and individuals that contributed to them. But in gathering up this work, I identified an opportunity to think about ideas of sociality, community and multiplicity *through illustration*. This is a slippery undertaking. Neither the idea of community nor the discipline of illustration can be easily defined – quite the opposite. The precise meaning of both of these words is notoriously difficult to pin down. Nevertheless, it is my hunch that, in the kinds of encounters that arise through these projects, illustration can mark out a space for community to reveal and enact itself. I believe that reflecting on this work creates a space to question widely held assumptions about the nature of community and the political, as well as opening up new vistas for illustration itself.

My research on this topic arises from a set of problems that I encountered in my own practice as an illustrator working with members of a local community, in partial fulfilment of a property developer's so-called Section 106 agreement.[1] The development in question was a new hospital building for a small town in England. My commission was to produce permanent artwork for the interior spaces and to 'involve the local community' in its creation. As I worked on this commission, I gradually became aware of the contradictions of my situation: private global capital was financing a development that I was then supposed to embellish with what felt like token gestures of communal cooperation. While the developers' interactions with me were always courteous and professional, I was left with the impression that their interest in my project was minimal. Indeed, the superficiality with which conceptually complex terminology such as 'community' was used in this commission frustrated me. My resulting project attempted to critique this unreflective use of the term while at the same time fulfilling the brief – it was a slightly contorted operation that proved only partially successful. I wrote about this experience in some detail (see my article in the *Journal of Illustration*, Vormittag 2015) but continued to feel that the questions raised through this project deserved a more substantive inquiry. The results of this, dear reader, are now in your hands.

Illustrators are increasingly employed by real estate investors to fulfil their Section 106 requirements: a debate in *Varoom* (the erstwhile magazine of the Association of Illustrators) rehearsed the pros and cons of this development.[2] Going beyond the specifics of Section 106, I became animated by the ambition

[1] In the UK, Section 106 agreements are legally binding obligations imposed by local government on property developers. These obligations require the developers to mitigate the potentially negative impacts of a development proposal. They may be asked to contribute to local infrastructure, affordable housing, education and/or other initiatives that are seen to be beneficial to the local community, such as public art projects. The details of the policy can be found on the UK government's website under https://www.gov.uk/guidance/planning-obligations (accessed 3 April 2023).

[2] Emily Jost (an artist, designer and activist) and Ian Whadcock (Senior Lecturer in Illustration with Animation at Manchester School of Art) debate the merits and pitfalls of illustrators working with developers. Jost argues that developer-led 'artwashing' is a highly contentious practice that ultimately harms the communities the illustrator is asked to work with. Ian Whadcock maintains that positive outcomes can be achieved by illustrators building bridges and educating commissioners (Jost & Whadcock 2018: 58–63).

to develop a more theoretically grounded understanding of what is at stake when illustrators work in a participatory way with a community. I started to wonder how illustration might bring to light the concerns and challenges of community more generally. This line of inquiry contains several different questions: How does illustration draw out a specific set of concerns and challenges from a community? How does it represent these to the community itself as well as other publics? And, coming from a different angle, how can illustration help us think through notions of community and conditions of sociality more generally?

Traditionally, illustration is thought of as a commercial activity, whereby a professional illustrator visually enhances a text or an idea with a crafted image. Over the last few decades, however, illustration has encountered various challenges as a commercial practice, and there are an increasing number of initiatives and attempts to develop alternative ways of practising. The recently published *Illustration Research Methods* charts and discusses a plethora of innovative illustration practice models that cluster around a number of shared 'operational principles', such as communication, responsiveness and empathy (Fauchon & Gannon 2021: 16).

Illustration is also now establishing itself as an academic discipline. Notably, an editorial in the *Journal of Illustration* suggests we are witnessing a 'Theoretical Turn' in our discipline (Grove 2018: 179–190); the growing numbers of PhD students in the field, as well as the existence of the Bloomsbury Research in Illustration series to which this book belongs, alongside the work of other illustration academics support this assertion. It has been inspiring to witness the trend towards diversification and theorization in our field while working on this research. Still, there is very little published work on illustration as a method for engaging with and reflecting on experiences of community – this is a lacuna that I hope to address in the pages that follow.

Sketching definitions

My introduction opened with the characterization of illustration as 'collective, negotiated enterprise' and as 'collectively generated material culture' (Bogart 2018). This is not the way illustration is typically defined. More common definitions focus to a greater extent on how illustration is often produced in response to a commission or a text. Doyle et al. (2018), to take one example, describe illustration as '[an] artwork […] in service of an idea [that] seeks to communicate *something particular*, usually to a specific audience' (xvii, emphasis in original). Although I find this description to be applicable to much illustration in circulation today, it is not particularly useful for my purposes. Certainly, it expresses the intentions and hopes an illustrator has for the images they produce, but it leaves aside the larger social field in which these illustrations appear and operate. It also assumes a working model where an illustrator undertakes to create a piece with a particular intent and outcome in mind. While this is undoubtedly the way many illustrators work, illustration can also be an exploratory process of discovery that involves a certain level of uncertainty: see, for example, Rachel Emily Taylor's evocation of illustration as an intangible process (Taylor 2024: 25), Stephanie Black's discussion of illustration as an inductive, constructivist form of research (Black 2014) or Mireille Fauchon's proposition that illustrative work can take the form of a compilation of investigative practices (Fauchon 2024: 53).

Many writers are compelled to perform an etymological pirouette towards the Latin 'lux' (light) at the root of 'illustration' – and thus cast our discipline as one that 'shines a light', professedly illuminating a pre-existing text.[3] Seen this way, illustration is simply an auxiliary, a way to understand something else. While this might be historically and procedurally accurate for much illustration, these types of descriptions, perhaps unwittingly, give illustration the role of a secondary, perhaps somewhat submissive, partner in a binary relationship.[4]

Self-directed work – which is also called authorial practice, i.e. projects that are pursued without commission – has been receiving greater prominence and encouragement over the last ten to fifteen years. For example, renowned graphic designer and writer Adrian Shaughnessy observed in 2011 that 'it is routine to see illustrators who have produced self-directed works: books, comics, saleable goods such as clothes, posters and assorted objects' (2011: 195) – this practice continues today. It is often through these self-initiated projects that illustrators can articulate a distinct approach to their work and also develop their style, which in turn can lead to greater commercial interest. The increased visibility of this work is probably a result of the continued commercial stresses of practitioners (unfortunately, there are not enough well-paid commissioned projects for everyone), an educational

[3] An interesting counterpoint to the pervasive metaphoric mobilization of light as 'understanding' is presented by artist and academic Barbara Bolt. Finding herself blinded by the intense sunshine of the Australian desert, she questions the supposed straightforward relationship between light and knowledge: 'Light does not always shed light on the matter. Under the harsh glare of the Australian sun, light fractured form rather than revealed it' (Bolt 2007: 32). An even more detailed and – dare I say 'illuminating' – discussion of this can be found in Chapter 4 of her monograph *Art Beyond Representation* (2004: 121–148).

[4] It is, of course, legitimate to emphasize illustration's relationship to text – many illustrations respond to and sit alongside pieces of writing. Submissiveness, however, is not a prerequisite for this partnership to function. Quite the contrary – there are a huge number of possible relationships an image might have to its textual partner: illustrator and academic Steve Braund, for example, proposes that illustration can act as an expansion, counterpoint or redirection of text (2011). Braund's former colleague, illustrator and academic Catrin Morgan, takes this further, demonstrating that illustrations can also actively undermine or destabilize a piece of writing (2014a: 19). Morgan's book *Phantom Settlements* (2011) and the work of prominent art-director, writer and illustrator Leanne Shapton (see for instance her publication *Guestbook* 2019) are intriguing examples of the creative potential arising from the multitude of potentially complex relationships between crafted, found and reappropriated images and texts (on Shapton, see Vormittag 2021).

model that encourages more experimental and entrepreneurial projects and the option (or one might say pressure) to showcase this type of work on social media platforms. Shaughnessy comments that '[i]n these times of dwindling budgets, clip art and the decline in editorial commissions, the authorial instinct is no longer a choice for illustrators – it is a necessity' (2011: 195). With the additional strain that AI is putting on the industry today, it is likely that illustrators will face even greater pressure to showcase their varied talents through authorial and self-initiated projects in pursuit of paid commissions.

So-called authorial practice is, of course, incredibly broad and varied, ranging from quietly reflective work to the more colourful entrepreneurial projects on display at many illustration and graphic arts fairs. It is wonderfully enriching to see the emergence of more varied approaches and initiatives that go beyond the constraints of commercial commissioning. However, the celebration of authorial illustration projects spawns its own set of questions. Does applauding this kind of work tacitly embrace and encourage unsustainable labour practices? Journalist Liv Siddall writing for the online publication *It's Nice That* described practitioners offering their work for sale at Pick Me Up, a London-based graphic arts fair that ran from 2010 to 2017, as people 'who are hoping wildly that they might be able to make a living out of doing what they're doing' (Siddall 2015). She was actually writing in defence of Pick Me Up, which had received criticism, but inadvertently highlighted the 'cruel optimism'[5] demanded of many illustrators in this economically precarious scenario.[6] Of course, you could argue that illustrators have always worked freelance, and that precarious and individualized working models are an inevitable part of an illustrator's working life. But it stands to reason that a rhetoric that emphasizes the entrepreneurial aspect of self-initiated work and celebrates self-reliance as an idealized mode of existence exacerbates an already fraught model.

Another outcome of the promotion of so-called authorial practice is an increased emphasis on the figure of the author. It might be valuable for illustrators

[5] This resonant term was coined by cultural theorist Lauren Berlant in a book by the same title (2011) to describe the persistent attachment to irredeemable promises of the good life in the post-war period in the United States and Europe.

[6] Sociologist Angela McRobbie has been drawing attention to the flipsides of celebrating and encouraging individualized entrepreneurship in the creative industries since the early 2000s (2001, 2011). She describes young practitioners who work across different media, systems and platforms, obliged and aspiring to be multi-skilled, hopeful and endlessly optimistic. This creates a situation where failure, financial and otherwise, is privatized and experienced as a personal shortcoming, rather than a structural inevitability. McRobbie writes about young people working in fashion, but it stands to reason that her analysis equally applies to other creative industries. The (graphic) designer and writer Silvio Lorusso makes a similar set of arguments in his book *Entreprecariat* (2019), albeit in a more trenchant and sarcastic tone. Taking a wider perspective that looks beyond the creative industries, historian Erik Baker's recent book *Make Your Own Job* (2025) offers a broader critique and historical analysis of entrepreneurialism and its manifestation in individuals creating work for themselves.

to pause for a moment and take in the rich tradition of rejecting authorship as the central interpretive principle of literary works. Could something be gained by considering this critical tradition? Among the best-known proponents are Roland Barthes, who proclaimed the 'Death of the Author' ([1967] 1977), and Michel Foucault, who questioned 'What is an author?' ([1969] 1977). A decade earlier, Theodore Adorno also highlighted the limitations of author-centric criticism by suggesting that, if you subscribe to this model, '[i]nterpretation [...] becomes nothing but removing an outer shell to find what the author wanted to say' ([1958] 1991: 4). More recently, poet Kenneth Goldsmith (2011) and literary scholar Marjorie Perloff (2010) once again sidelined the figure of the author in favour of celebrating other forms of textual creation and interpretation. While the details of these writers' critiques differ, all of them reject the placement of the figure of the author at the core of textual interpretation. Instead, they propose readings that lend a greater emphasis to linguistics, the reader, and modes of circulation, evaluation, appropriation and control.

Or perhaps illustrators can learn from one of their sister disciplines? Graphic design notably grappled with the question of authorship during the 1990s, at a time when the notion of self-initiated practice was being increasingly discussed in the discipline. In his well-known 1996 essay 'The designer as author', Michael Rock highlights the irony of the fact that designers developed a desire to be authors at a moment when literary theory had already moved away from the position. Authorship, he reminds us, relies on the anachronistic and ultimately limiting idea of the heroic, creative genius.[7] Applied to graphic design, it reinforces the 'designer-as-hero' model, rather than engaging with the more radical idea of the decentred text, or the collaborative nature of the vast majority of design work. Could we, he asks, imagine a time when we stop engaging with the question of who made a piece of work, asking instead what it does and how it does it (Rock [1996] 2013)?

These questions, already radical for graphic design, sound even more so in the context of illustration. What would an illustration practice that is not built on the notion of an individual, expressive personal voice look like? How could we build a discourse on illustration that does not focus on the illustrator who made the piece? Illustrator and academic Jaleen Grove offers a refreshing perspective on these matters. She speculates that the striving for unique self-expression among some illustrators is at least partially fuelled by Romantic assumptions about the supposed purity of capital-A Art, which stands in contrast to the presumed

[7] Graphic designer and writer Ellen Lupton raises similar concerns in her piece 'Designer as Producer' (1998). Drawing on Walter Benjamin's 1934 essay 'The Author as Producer', she proposes that graphic designers 'seize control of the means of production' and 'share that control with the reading public' (1998: 162). The continuation of this debate regarding expanded and more emancipated roles for graphic designers can be seen in Steven McCarthy's book *The Designer as ... : Author, Producer, Activist, Entrepreneur, Curator, and Collaborator* (2013).

vulgarity of commercial work (Grove 2011: 292). As an alternative to this unproductive binary, she cites the position of William Morris and the Arts and Crafts movement, which celebrated the dignity of art in service.

Reading Grove's appeal to recall Morris's celebration of the 'use-value of art in communal enterprises' (Grove 2011: 292) was an inspiring moment for me. Besides drawing attention to the dignity of art in service, Grove also usefully reminded me how to proceed when trapped in a scenario that seemingly offers just two equally troublesome options: the solution is not to begrudgingly set up camp on middle ground, but to pole-vault yourself into entirely new terrain. After all, emphasizing individualized authorship and self-expression is not the *only* alternative to the constraints of commercially commissioned practice. I always felt that, as an illustrator, I wanted to be out in the world, I wanted to be *in service*; I just didn't particularly want to be in service of shampoo[8] and the forces that seek to promote increased consumption of products. But there are many other forms of enterprise beyond commercial operations that an illustrator can ally themselves to. The illustration projects I discuss here all take up a variety of causes and ideas and closely collaborate with a range of groups and movements.

So, how might I articulate an understanding of illustration that combines Morris's idea of 'art in service' with a participatory, polyvocal practice model, in the hope that this can serve as a provisional definition of illustration for the duration of this book? The most resonant terminology that presented itself to me centred on the notion of illustration as a process of relational image-making. In projects I have undertaken with community groups, as well as in similar work by other practitioners, one or more facilitators provide a framework for groups of people to jointly visually articulate a shared world. In these projects, illustrations emerge by way of an encounter and endure afterwards as a record and trace of the relationship. This record or trace is then ready and able to engage potential future audiences through its communicative qualities. Early on while I was working through these ideas, I stuck a note over my desk that says 'Illustration as a trace of a relationship' in the top half of the paper, double underlined, with an arrow below pointing upwards and the words 'I LIKE THIS' in block capitals underneath. I have relocated since then, but the note has moved with me and remains above my (new) desk as I type this.

In the work I discuss in this book, illustrations are crafted predominantly by hand – whether that be in the form of drawings, maps, embroidery, animated films

[8] I practised commercially as an illustrator for many years, as part of a creative collective called Container. We worked on a wide variety of different commissions, but it remained challenging for us to generate a stable income. Editorial work barely paid; the lucrative commissions were in advertising. Our best-paid assignment was a promotional campaign for a shampoo brand. We were ecstatic to get this job, but the actual work was unsatisfying and the relationship with the client was strained. Generally speaking, I often felt somewhat out of place during meetings in advertising agencies.

or small sculptures. As such, they conform to the generally held idea of illustration as crafted image.[9] However, I tend to use the verb 'inscribe' rather than 'illustrate' to characterize how participants contribute to the projects I discuss. I concede that 'inscribe' more readily conjures the idea of pen on paper, rather than the full range of methods used in the work I consider: drawing, stitching, rubbing, arranging, sculpting, photographing, collaging and attaching. However, I like this word because it evokes the idea of making a mark, while at the same time writing yourself *into* something (*in*scribe) – an act of enrolment of sorts. It also conjures the idea of the mark being made on a relatively stable support, and therefore having at least a certain degree of permanence. An inscription is not ephemeral; it cannot easily be swept away. Indeed, it is fixed in material form for others to see at a later point in time.

The materiality that is suggested by the notion of inscription positions the kind of image-making I consider here as an activity that is both discursive as well as material. The discursive dimension of the work is the collection of the marks, signs and meanings that participants bring to these projects. The material dimension varies among the projects I discuss: paper plays a prominent role in my work, but in other examples people gather around cloth or clay, among other materials. I do not pursue an analysis of illustrations as semiotic artefacts (this has been already done by others[10]), nor do I devote myself to an interpretation of illustration that aligns with ideas championed by advocates of 'new materialism', emphasizing the vibrancy and vitality of matter[11] (though this would be an intriguing avenue to

[9] Illustration tends to get defined as a crafted image (see, for example, Doyle et al. 2018: xvii); however, the fact that an illustration is assumed to come into existence through the creation of a *new* image, rather than through a reconfiguration of a set of relationships surrounding an *existing* visual artefact, is so widely accepted that it barely receives mention. In contrast to this illustrator and academic Catrin Morgan argues that the crafted nature of images is not a necessary precondition for something to be considered an illustration (Morgan 2014b). She makes the convincing case that the nature of illustration stems from its relational character, not its mode of production.

[10] The application of semiotic theory to images has been pursued by many theorists. Examples include the multiple editions of *Reading Images: The Grammar of Visual Design* (1996, 2006, 2020) by linguists Gunther Kress and Theo van Leeuwen, or, more specifically related to illustration, *Visible Signs: An Introduction to Semiotics in the Visual Arts* (2003, 2010, 2018, 2022) by graphic designer and academic David Crow, which contains a detailed semiotic analysis of many illustrations. By mapping semiotic theory onto designed images and other visual matter, illustrations, dismantled into their various visual components, are connected to a network of signs and symbols, a catalogue of visual conventions and codes. However, prominent art historian W. J. T. Mitchell claims that semiotics presents something of a dead end for the interpretation of visual material, arguing that 'no "neutral" or "scientific" vocabulary [such as semiotics] can transcend or master the field of representation' (1994: 417). I tend to agree, and in addition to these limitations, I also remain unsure of how, for practitioners especially, this semiotic approach might prove useful.

[11] New materialism is a theoretical approach that emphasizes the agency of matter in shaping our social, cultural and political phenomena. It constitutes a shift away from anthropocentrism and proposes perspectives that foreground relational and dynamic processes that tend to involve multiple human and non-human actors. See, for example, Jane Bennett's *Vibrant Matter* (2010) or Karen Barad's *Meeting the Universe Halfway* (2007).

explore for our discipline!). Instead, I shall attempt to think these social, semiotic and material realms as one – the relational materiality of illustrative inscriptions.

While reflecting on the outputs that result from the projects I discuss here, the idea of the 'document' offered itself to me. It took me a while to zero in on this word. Philosopher Maurizio Ferraris characterizes documents as inscriptions of an act, a form of attestation that has permanence over time (2013: 267). Reading this, I came to see my illustrative outputs as types of documents that register and attest to the social processes that led to their creation. Thinking in these terms helped me clarify what to do with the work. After all, a document begs to be filed, not left stranded on my cluttered desk. By considering my outputs as documents, I was able to conceive of a more interesting afterlife for them: they needed to be submitted to archives or housed in another place that can offer continued public access and care.

So, rather than making any general claims about the field of illustration as a whole, this book focuses on various forms of participatory illustration and conceptualizes this type of work as a form of co-produced, visual document. I found this language – words such as 'relationality', 'inscription', 'document' – helpful in opening up new ways to think through the overlapping social, semiotic and material dimensions of the work. I hasten to add that this terminology was generally not shared by other practitioners in conversations with me – rather, the choice of words is my contrivance, assembled for the particular set of concerns I was trying to work through. This language is a vehicle for travel, a thought experiment. If we think of these projects with these terms, where might this take us?

What is community?

By this point, I have already used words such as 'community', 'collective' and 'social' multiple times. Indeed, the existence of community – both of particular communities (e.g. 'the Latin American community') as well as 'community' itself as a social formation – is often taken for granted. For example, my aforementioned commission to produce artwork for a new hospital building included the prompt to 'engage with the local community', with the community's existence and nature going completely unquestioned. But what does it actually mean to think of our existence in terms of multiplicity, rather than singularity? In contemporary parlance, the word 'community' is often used to evoke a warm feeling of mutual solidarity and social cohesion, positioned in contrast to the harsh individualism of neoliberal capitalism. However, if we zoom out to larger motifs of recent European history,[12] the devastating and murderous consequences of a unified and therefore

[12] Clearly an exclusionary identitarian politics and its catastrophic escalation into ethno-nationalist violence is not exclusively the dominion of Europeans. However, some of the key thinkers I draw on in my reassessment of the notion of community and the public sphere are specifically writing in the shadow of the Holocaust and the collapse of communism into totalitarian Stalinism in the Soviet Union.

exclusionary 'we' becomes all too apparent. How might it be possible to work with ideas of 'community' in a way that acknowledges these difficulties?

Twentieth-century European philosophers such as Martin Heidegger, Hannah Arendt and Jean-Luc Nancy remind us that the very idea of community cannot be taken for granted. Their work presents us with a detailed and systematic examination of ideas regarding sociality, multiplicity and the political. I draw on their in-depth analyses in the development of my thinking on illustration and community. In particular, Nancy's careful conceptualization of the nature of community combines with my reflections on illustration practice to reveal collaborative illustration as a site for ontological disclosure. By way of this intertwinement of theory and practice, illustration presents itself as the space where we can evaluate and examine our experiences and enactments of community.

The projects I discuss in this book demonstrate how illustration has the power to reconfigure the social fields in which it appears. Illustration has the capacity to act like a magnet, gathering up individuals, modifying their relationships with one another and shifting the way they understand themselves and their environment. My invocation of the 'magnetic' power of illustration is not related to any mystical sense of animistic images, magic effigies used in rituals or ghostly apparitions – far from it. The gravitational pull I refer to results from individuals gathering and involving themselves in the creation of an illustrative document. By drawing the lines, they are drawn in and drawn together.[13]

Of course, these processes are neither predictable nor smooth. Just as paper can wrinkle and cloth can tear, so these projects frequently falter. The publics they assemble are patchy and their pull is variable, leaving swathes of the social fabric unmoved. And yet, despite this patchiness, I believe illustration has a meaningful contribution to make to thinking about the challenges of coexistence, and the contemporary discourse on community more generally.

How does it do this? How do the illustrative projects I consider in this book help us reconsider what it means to be in community? Hannah Arendt describes how a public gathering of people offers us a 'space of appearance' ([1958] 1998: 199) – in other words, a kind of arena for collective sense-making that mediates and binds us together. This overlaps with qualities in the work I am considering here. Through participating in the creation of these illustrative documents, privately held knowledge, experiences and imaginaries are translated into material inscriptions that are visible to all. This does not result in a distilled, agreed synthesis of what people had imagined prior to participating in the project, but an altogether new picture that arises through the interlocking articulations of many. The documents delineate plural, shared worlds that emerge through the process of

[13] Forgive me, dear reader, for succumbing to the 'magnetic power' of language here! Of course, not all illustration uses drawing – in this book I discuss many examples of illustration that go beyond drawing. However, this turn of phrase was too seductive to withstand.

the participants' interactions. And while it is clear that this practice of collective, generative world-making can unfold in all sorts of creative forms of interaction, I believe that the illustrative projects I discuss in this book offer us a particularly fertile ground for capturing and reflecting on these processes.

What this book seeks to do

I am attempting two theoretical moves in this book. Firstly, I develop the idea that illustration offers us a productive space to reflect on the challenges of coexistence. As I indicated above, I believe that participatory illustration projects can act as a site for ontological disclosure. What I mean by this is that they can be understood as a space where fundamental aspects of our being can be disclosed. Collaborative illustrated documents can reveal how we co-constitute each other in collective acts of sense-making.

Thinking about how this unfolds in various illustrative projects during the research for this book brought some unexpected realizations. For example, after immersing myself in this research for some time, I noticed how some of the formal challenges of participatory illustration projects actually mirror the philosophical and political problems of community. When bringing groups of individuals together to work on an illustration, we are confronted with the question of how to practically and formally manage these individuals so that they actually produce a legible illustrative document. Meanwhile, philosophical questions around ideas of community often ask how we can congregate in ways that allow for the singular perspective to make sense and carry weight in a larger, plural configuration. To phrase this question slightly differently: When we gather in social formations, how can we make sure everybody has a voice, without all of us talking over one another? How can the singular utterance be brought into meaningful relation to a polyvocal whole? Within the illustration projects I discuss, I repeatedly circle back to these questions of the singular and the plural. Nancy's nuanced philosophical work on community, including his seminal work *Being Singular Plural* (2000), provides a resonant set of ideas that help me navigate this difficult terrain.

The other claim that is woven through several chapters of this book is that illustration can act as a performative form of knowledge production. Rather than conceiving of illustration as mimetic or representational, I argue that illustration, in the process of its creation, can produce the reality it refers to. This dawned on me when working with a group of people on a project called *Walking the Elephant*. I was trying to generate an illustration of a 'collectively held urban imaginary', a collectively held mental image of a place that a group of people might have. However, when attempting to pursue this goal, I realized that collective imaginaries – should they even exist – are difficult to access and even more difficult to visualize. How was I to reliably know what goes on in people's minds?

Is it actually likely that multiple people are imagining the same kind of thing? Are imaginaries even visual? It gradually became clear to me that there were more productive ways for illustration to draw out collective worlds. Rather than attempting to represent something that existed prior to the meeting or the project, participatory illustration could be used as a process of collective sense-making, where 'sense' emerges as part of the encounter. In short, I realized that illustration can 'perform' or create novel worlds by gathering groups of people and supplying them with a framework for articulating something new together.

In making these two theoretical moves, I reflect on some of the projects I have worked on with community groups over the years. In my own work, I have collaborated with a number of individuals and groups, inviting participants to contribute to a series of illustrative documents: *Walking the Elephant* was conducted with the local community in and around the now defunct Elephant and Castle Shopping Centre; *Write Women into History* emerged from my interactions with a writing group of older feminists; and *Cracks in the Pavement* is the result of a walking and collaborative mapping project during the COVID-19 lockdown in the UK. Despite the individual projects' many variations, they also overlap significantly: all three focus on a particular geographic place in London at a distinct moment in time and resulted in the production of one or more illustrative documents that capture shared matters of concern in relation to the place and time in question.

Alongside this, I draw on the knowledge and experience of others, having spoken to a number of other illustrators and practitioners (who describe their professional identity in various related terms) about their work. My own projects have unfolded in London, but I wanted to expand my scope in this book and was therefore delighted to connect with inspiring colleagues in India and Argentina. I also found examples closer to home – some in London, others in different parts of the UK. In addition, I discovered – and touch on – other projects (from various parts of the world), without having had direct or in-depth engagement with the people who brought them into being.

With this collection of co-produced illustration work in mind, I enter into a succession of theoretical spaces, including translation studies, phenomenology, ethnography and European philosophy, each one a world into itself. Venturing into these disciplines has been a daunting endeavour at times. Indeed, trying to find your way around an unknown epistemological terrain, with its unfamiliar histories, inscrutable quandaries, seemingly sacrosanct monuments, erudite leaders and eccentric outsiders, is extremely disorienting.[14] But one must start

[14] The philosopher and literary theorist Kenneth Burke likens this experience to arriving at a party that is already in full swing. He writes: 'You come late. When you arrive, others have long preceded you, and they are engaged in a heated discussion, a discussion too heated for them to pause and tell you exactly what it is about. [...] You listen for a while, until you decide you have caught the tenor of the argument; then you put in your oar' (Burke 1941: 110).

somewhere. While researching, I found myself spending many hours going down rabbit holes that did not yield anything productive or useful; just when I was ready to give up, however, I would catch a glimpse of something, follow the metaphorical rabbit around some bends and find myself hurled onto an unfamiliar plane with a fresh outlook, where things suddenly started to make sense in a new way. Taking illustration into these spaces enabled me to recognize and draw out knowledge and insights that I was not able to perceive clearly before. I might have had a hunch – this is what led me down the rabbit hole in the first place – but it was only within these theoretical spaces that I began to recognize and articulate what might have been there all the time but had been hard for me to discern. If you hold up a picture to a new kind of mirror, you are often surprised by what you see in the reflection.

As I moved through these various contemplative spaces, I tried to be practical. It is important to have *some* degree of understanding of the theoretical landscape one finds oneself in, but I was aware of my status as a visitor.[15] A while ago, someone asked me if I was a Heideggerian, and I stuttered, laughed and answered that no, of course I was not. Yes, I found reading *Being and Time* unexpectedly fun,[16] but probably only because I knew I was free to leave whenever I wanted to. I am an illustrator and my awareness that I am simply visiting other realms of knowledge means that I do not have to carry the weight of the entire cannon. In the spaces I explored, I endeavoured to orient myself to some degree, but I did not seek to take up residence. I tuned in to the language, the concerns, the politics and the mood, but once I had what I needed, I said my goodbyes, promised to return again sometime soon, and made my way to the exit.

All of this might make it sound like there was a clear sequence of work, with me first doing the illustration work, then reflecting on it through theory. In reality, the process was a lot messier. I worked on my own projects alongside lots of reading and writing, and conversations with other practitioners also took place at various times. It turns out that both practice and theory make demands of each other. I have found it productive to combine the language and the methods used in the humanities – textual analysis, critical reflection, conceptual elucidation – with the 'doing' that is characteristic of creative practice. These two methodological paradigms form a productively unstable and dynamic relationship, where theory has the ability to generate new forms of practice and in turn practice complicates and potentially advances theory.

One might argue that I would have arrived at similar insights only by considering other people's practice, rather than working on my own projects. However, placing myself in the midst of social, discursive and material relations in

[15] My home is illustration. I am indebted to Mireille Fauchon for reminding me of the importance of a disciplinary home (see Fauchon 2024: 46).

[16] I did certainly not read the whole book – I just dipped in and out, repeatedly.

my own work pressed my face against questions with a force that studying other people's work would never have. The sheer intensity of being 'out in the world', practising illustration as a form of 'art in service' for a number of groups and causes, created situations where I was repeatedly confronted with the limitations of my preparations – both theoretically (i.e. the kinds of questions I was asking through my practice) and practically speaking (there is never enough of one thing, always too much of another thing, it never runs smoothly). The social, discursive and material realities of a project are always more complicated and interesting than anticipated. The resulting work, as well as the thoughts and questions it generates, are never quite the ones you anticipated. It is precisely this disparity between a project's expected results and the actual findings that, despite being occasionally disorienting, creates a productive force moving the research forward.

Talking to other practitioners complicated matters further still. I spoke to a range of illustrators[17] about some of their work. Unsurprisingly, this group of projects did not result in a neat collection that lines up in an orderly manner along a few shared methods or principles. And while this is unsurprising in retrospect, I must admit that, during conversations with these practitioners, I often found myself secretly hoping for my counterpart to voice a particular idea or explain a certain method that would more closely align with my own way of thinking and working. I was probably seeking some form of validation, some kind of proof that my way of doing things was indeed 'correct'. Inevitably, I found myself being told something that was slightly different from my own approach. And a hard-won insight can quickly be destabilized when you speak to somebody with a different outlook and an alternative way of doing things.

Upon reflection, I realized that these differences, on another level, confirm a long-held suspicion: that in writing this book, I do not need to announce a fixed set of methods for illustrators who work with community. There are clearly many ways to do this, and apart from some basic ethical principles, I believe that practitioners ought to figure out what best suits them and the people they are working with.[18] Perhaps some readers might be inspired to adapt an idea discussed here for a project they are working on – I would be delighted if my writing were to provide anyone with something so directly useful. Chapters 2–4 are perhaps the most practical part of this book, in that I describe and list many of the actual

[17] Some of the people I spoke to would probably describe their practice with slightly different vocabulary. But their work corresponded closely enough with my understanding of illustration to warrant being included in the discussion here.

[18] As I was writing this, I took a break and found myself reading an article in *The Guardian*. The piece was about the variable effectiveness of therapeutic interventions for prison inmates. A quote jumped out at me: 'Programmes work when they're run by the people who develop them' (Williams quoting Shepherd 2024). I believe the same to be true of participatory illustration projects. They work best if they are run by the people who develop them.

methods that illustrators use in their participatory projects. But the main purpose of this book is a different one.

I also note that, while the work I discuss is participatory and contains many different people's contributions, this book is written by a single author, and so any criticism you might harbour should be directed towards me, rather than the other practitioners whose work I champion. They are entirely innocent.

Do we really need all this theory?

It is fair to assume that, for readers who have progressed this far in the text, the overall validity of books such as this one (and indeed the other titles in this series) is beyond question. While you might disagree with my line of argumentation, despair at my choice of reference points and dislike the timbre of my writing, you probably do not take issue with the overall project of illustration research. But we should be mindful that this enmeshment of practice and theory in our discipline is still relatively new. Over the past decades, many writers and academics have commented on the relative paucity of theoretically grounded writing on illustration. In 2000, designer and educator Teal Triggs noted that, while graphic design had recently transformed into a more rigorously theorized subject, research on illustration was still in its critical infancy (Triggs 2000: 48). Ten years later, design writer Rick Poynor decried the continuing lack of a critical framework that would serve as a measure of illustration's qualities (Poynor 2010: 30). Still, in 2018, Michele Bogart lamented the lack of interest in illustration as a subject worthy of scholarly attention (Bogart 2018).

More recently, however, several new platforms and initiatives have started to galvanize scholarly illustration practice models and discourses, prompting illustrator and academic Jaleen Grove to declare the aforementioned 'Theoretical Turn' in illustration (Grove 2018). Since 2014, the *Journal of Illustration* has provided a space for the in-depth examination of emerging ideas in and around our discipline. New publications, such as the *History of Illustration* (Doyle, Grove & Sherman 2018) and *Illustration Research Methods* (Fauchon & Gannon 2021), alongside the monographs published in the Bloomsbury Research in Illustration series are making an impact. The Annual International Illustration Research Symposium and an array of more localized events and initiatives are also creating fertile places of exchange and motivation. And comics studies and drawing research are increasingly generating a rich vein of scholarship, a lot of which is also relevant to illustration. Surveying this efflorescent landscape, a colleague was sufficiently moved to exclaim that we find ourselves in a 'golden age' of illustration research.

Nevertheless, it is worth noting that not everyone is convinced of the value of this development. There are plenty of people who believe that illustrators can learn all they need to know through practice and that bringing theoretical reflection into the discipline is an elitist exercise that threatens to exclude those who are not interested in scholarly debate (see Grove 2018 for an excellent exposition of the various standpoints in this discussion). Certainly, this mode of interweaving theory and practice does not suit everyone, and neither should it – clearly, there is a superabundance of valid approaches to being an illustrator. However, artist and academic Barbara Bolt reminds us that, while art on its own can indeed be a mode of revealing and generating new insight, it is through theoretical reflection and writing that this knowledge is set in motion. The writing that flows from practice can articulate the nature and the authority of knowledge claims, and can thereby extend them beyond the particularity of a specific example (Bolt 2007: 33–4). And, indeed, there is an increasing number of research-active illustrators who are using theory to advance their practice. But even among those who *do* believe that a more theoretically rigorous milieu is likely to have a revitalizing effect on the discipline as a whole, the question of *how* practice and theory might be brought together and *what kind of theory* might be useful for such an enterprise is an ongoing debate (see Leishman 2018 for a detailed breakdown of these conversations).

Over time, through reading broadly and dipping into many different books and disciplines, I became mindful of the kinds of theoretical attitudes that I found conducive to thinking with and through illustration practice. At some point, I realized that writing that is broadly critical and deconstructive may delight with its piercing insight but at the same time impede the development of practice. For example, one piece that I read early on in my research was feminist Iris Marion Young's astutely argued article 'The Ideal of Community and the Politics of Difference' (1990). Young proposes that, when constructing terms in an oppositional binary (e.g. individual versus community), with each term defined by its negative relation to the other, the simple reversal of their evaluation (i.e. valuing 'community' more than 'individual') does not hold much critical force. When examined more closely, both concepts rely on the same basic principle: the ideal of a unified whole. Using 'community' in this way, Young argues, can actually lay the groundwork for ethnocentric identitarian politics.

While I agreed with Young's argument, I did not find this article particularly helpful for bringing forth new insights or knowledge in conjunction with my own illustration practice, or any of the other illustrative projects I was studying. This form of critical analysis serves as a useful reminder to be wary of seemingly universal or neutral terms, but its deconstructive approach, sometimes referred to as 'ideological unmasking' or the 'hermeneutics of suspicion' (see, for example, Ricoeur 1977: 32–6), made it hard for me to know how to proceed in practice. Indeed, this style of thinking can be seductive, in that it aims to expose hidden truths or agendas. Engaging with it has often left me feeling somewhat superior (I had, after all, been led to see things that, in the implicit logic of this type of critique, are otherwise concealed from view) – but it has also left me feeling a little depressed. I often found it challenging to identify a meaningful way of moving forward among the rubble left behind by this kind of sharp-witted audit.[19]

In the context of design writing, I came across an almost diametrically opposing perspective. Instead of critique, I encountered an eager yearning for practical solutions. One of the ways that this manifests itself is through a move to demystify design processes, articulate their principles and produce clearly articulated frameworks for practice. Design academic Nigel Cross's influential article 'Designerly Ways of Knowing' (1982), one of the key texts of the so-called design methods movement, initiated this tradition that seeks to convey the practical methods and intellectual processes particular to design. This drive eventually morphed into increasingly generalized methods such as 'design thinking' and 'human-centred design'. While there is certainly value in verbalizing and thereby clarifying design processes that otherwise might appear nebulous or intimidating, I remain somewhat wary of the prescriptive and solutionist universalism that often takes hold in this genre of writing. Notably, colleagues who engaged with earlier versions of this book questioned my aversion to toolkits and my occasionally recalcitrant refusal to offer a more explicit framing of my own findings' transferable applications. I concede that practical principles have emerged in my research that might indeed be useful for other practitioners (as discussed principally in Chapters 2–4), but I maintain that illustration research of the kind that I am pursuing primarily offers a different kind of reward.

What might this reward be? There is, of course, a whole host of modes (and moods) of theoretical writing, and each one of them offers its own kinds of benefits and attractions. Faced with an endless library catalogue and a notebook full of (sometimes) contradictory recommendations, it can be difficult to know how to start. I found myself laughing out loud when I came across sociologist Laurel Richardson's confession that she has 'yawned her way through numerous supposedly exemplary [...] studies', sheepishly admitting that she found many books in her field simply boring (Richardson 1994: 516–17). Yes, some books are quite dull. I mention this to make the point that when hunting around for the 'right' kind of theoretical angle, it is probably worthwhile remembering why one is doing so in the first place. I am generally not driven by suspicion or scepticism towards the illustration projects I contemplate (although this is not at all to say that any of us are beyond criticism), nor do I want to follow or prescribe a particular

[19] US-American academic Rita Felski has written on the pervasiveness and persistence of this mode of theoretical work in literary studies and beyond. In her entertaining book *The End of Critique* (2015), she speaks of this style of interpretation as driven by a spirit of disenchantment and detachment and invites us to consider imaginative alternatives. Similarly, in his article 'Why Has Critique Run out of Steam?' (2004), Bruno Latour argues that the problem we face today is no longer the public's excessive trust in ideological statements masquerading as facts which need to be debunked, but the reverse: an excessive suspicion of the scientific consensus, which is interpreted as ideology. He writes that the mode of suspicious scrutiny, once supposedly the dominion of well-read intellectuals, has become the 'potent euphoric drug' of conspiracists (2004: 239).

way of working, nor do I want to become so bogged down by my reading and writing that I find myself entombed in stifling, lifeless prose. I seek out theory with the aim of extending ideas embedded in practice, of opening up new vistas on what we are doing, of creating reflective spaces that enable us to recognize, contemplate and augment the knowledge that is contained in our work. In short, what I am looking for are theoretical attitudes that, in combination with practice, offer an animating encounter, a form of expansive vitality. If a book bores me, it goes back on the shelf.

I found approaches that grapple with thinking things anew, drawing on language's generative and productive quality, most helpful, perhaps simply because they resemble what the practitioner does. For example, in the philosophical work of Heidegger and Nancy, language does not represent or reflect reality, but cautiously attempts to sketch out the possibility of thinking things afresh. Words are handled reflexively and self-consciously. Writing thus conceived of as constructive, rather than deconstructive, mirrors the possibility of illustration as a way to conjure new worlds.

I also noted the value of theoretical approaches that display an attitude of care and affirmation towards the topic under discussion, especially during a period where our discipline is working to establish itself as a serious and credible arena for cultural discourse. Bruno Latour suggests that a productive role for the figure of the critic might be to 'offer participants arenas in which to gather' (2004: 246). Could we devise a tool, he asks, 'whose import is not to debunk, but to protect and care?' (2004: 232). To my delight, colleagues who are currently contributing to emerging discourses in illustration seem to be motivated by precisely this desire to gather ideas and practices, and to protect and care for them in a discipline that has historically been characterized by transitoriness. In this book, I too hope to contribute to the growing literature in our field that is proposing new constellations of inquiry, practice and thought.

My experience of transposing this material that previously existed in a vague associative cloud in my mind into writing turned out to be a strenuous process of creative discovery. The same insight that shifted my thinking on the possibilities of illustration – namely, that it can operate as an emergent process of situated sense-making rather than simply a device to record a pre-existing reality – proved to also hold true for the practice of writing. The ideas put forward in this book were not conceived of independently in my mind and then neatly rendered in crystalline paragraphs (I wish!). They emerged relationally and materially – from my experiences of working on projects, conversations I was having with other practitioners, lines I was reading in books, and words and syntax that offered themselves to me during the countless hours at various desks and libraries.

Language, like illustration, is always already enmeshed and implicated in the worlds we are hoping to understand and describe.[20]

For me, the most rewarding insights are gained by intertwining the processes and outputs of illustration projects with reflective, generative and interpretive writing. In doing so, I have attempted to harness the generative and productive qualities of words to think illustration anew and forge new paths for our discipline.

Chapter overview

Chapter 1 sets up the stakes of this inquiry and explains why I am taking the route I am. I introduce three projects in detail: Mitch Miller's so-called dialectograms, Sidney Mann's *Bordando Tierra del Fuego* and my own project *Cracks in the Pavement*. These projects overlap in various aspects: they are collectively produced illustrative works that refer to a space or territory held in common.

Chapters 2–5 follow more or less the temporal sequence of working on participatory illustration projects: each chapter roughly corresponds to a successive stage in this type of work. First comes the design of the overall project and decisions on the role of participants; then, one must endeavour to overcome challenges related to inviting participants to engage with creative tools and processes; next, we zero in on the role of the community illustrator as facilitator, interpreter and assembler of the participants' contributions, as well as the reflexive sensibility and expertise required to carry this out; and lastly, we reflect on the finished work. Of course, the diversity of the work I am covering means that not all four sections are equally relevant for all projects under discussion.

In these chapters I examine participatory illustration projects in greater detail and position them in relation to relevant literature from other disciplines. My main emphasis remains on the three examples I introduced in Chapter 1, but I expand this collection to open up broader avenues for exploration. This expansion results in a more varied ensemble of projects with a greater number of methods and outcomes, but they nevertheless overlap in the way they invite a number of individuals to come together and co-produce illustrative documents that relate to a joint concern or perspective.

Overall, Chapters 2–5 offer a series of theoretical, contemplative spaces that allow me to reflect on the issues that emerge when illustrators work with communities.

[20] This quote by Mikhail Bakhtin sums up this sentiment beautifully: '[L]anguage [...] lies on the borderline between oneself and others. The word in language is half someone else's. Language is not a neutral medium that passes freely and easily into the private property of the speaker's intentions. It is populated - overpopulated - with the intentions of others' ([1934–35] 1981: 293–4). It is a joyful experience to let oneself be hurled around in this forcefield of intentions and add one's own to the push and pull of language.

As Chapter 1, Illustration, Community and the Political, makes clear, I found that the literature that is directly concerned with illustration and visual images more generally does not offer a suitable, theoretically grounded context for positioning and reflecting on the participatory illustration work I am discussing here. The literature in the following chapters is therefore drawn from a broad range of other disciplines. Each chapter uses a different area of literature, corresponding to the questions raised by that stage of the projects.

In Chapter 2, Working with Others, I draw on writing that discusses participatory art and design practices. Throughout the twentieth century, a range of artists and designers pursued various strategies of inclusion, participation and consultation as a politicized working practice. I review these with reference to the (occasionally challenging) practicalities of involving participants, and how managing these practicalities plays out conceptually in the creation of an artwork. Using my own experience alongside insights from other practitioners I spoke to, I set out a series of principles to encourage the inclusion of participants in projects. For example, the use of responsive 'climbing frame' structures, gives participants a series of steps or rungs to clamber up so that they may gradually discover new abilities and a different outlook through taking part.

Following on from this, Chapter 3, 'But I Can't Draw!' is concerned with questions of drawing, skill and expertise. Many of the projects I discuss in this book invite participants to draw on or annotate shared documents. In other cases, people are prompted to use other creative processes, such as sewing, sculpting, or animation. I question, therefore, how anxieties about skill, talent and ability that many people experience play themselves out in these scenarios. I discuss these questions with reference to literature on drawing, such as by anthropologist Tim Ingold and artist and writer John Berger. I also describe the practical steps that I and other practitioners have taken to overcome the occasional resistance we encounter, and how the use of established visual formats such as 'the map' and 'the portrait' can help to provide a sense of stability during this phase.

In Chapter 4, Drawing Things Together, I discuss the various roles that illustration practitioners take on in participatory projects. During workshops, we tend to be facilitators – but what about afterwards? Participants' contributions may come in a variety of formats, including as representational drawings, sketches, written and spoken language, among other formats. In the process of drawing this heterogeneous material together, we therefore act as editors, translators, interpreters and guides, assembling, sometimes altering and reconstituting the material. Making aesthetic and formal choices during this phase can be fraught (it has certainly been for me). Ideas and concepts borrowed from critical translation studies have been illuminating here, as have studies from postcolonial and feminist scholarship. I also consider discussions that emerged in ethnographic and anthropological literature in the 1980s and that remain relevant today.

Chapter 5, World-Making, focuses on the results of participatory illustration projects. The title of this book refers to 'collective world-making'. How and why might we think of the outputs of these kinds of projects as a form of 'world-making'? Philosopher Edmund Husserl, a key figure in the development of phenomenology, advanced the concept of *Lebenswelt* (life-world) to describe a person's everyday experience. I trace how this concept is taken up and adapted by other thinkers. Notably, Nancy, for whom sense-making and 'worldhood' are central themes, relates this concept to images, which he views as an 'announcement of the existence of a world' (Janus 2016: 3). I consider these ideas in relation to a number of illustration projects. Overall, I argue that worlds are made, not found. By coming together and working creatively, we have the ability, on whatever scale, to make something new.

The main theoretical argument of this book is laid out in detail in Chapter 6, Tracing Expressions of Community. Building on the philosophy that I started to introduce in Chapter 5, I deepen the discussion around illustration and community, exploring how participatory illustration projects have the capacity to assemble community and constitute the political. I bring conceptions of community that are theoretically grounded in the political into relation with the possibilities of illustration practice. Drawing on the work of Heidegger, Arendt and Nancy, I argue that collaborative illustration has the capacity to assemble, enact and record community. I also explain what I mean when I characterize collaborative illustration as a site of ontological disclosure, as well as a performative, generative act of world-forming.

Chapter 7, Afterlives, follows the temporal unfolding of projects and considers what happens after a project comes to an end. I ask how illustrative documents can function beyond their initial role as focal points for an enactment of community and describe how, in my own work, I have decided to submit project outputs to publicly managed and accessible repositories. For audiences and publics beyond the participating group, outputs can be experienced meaningfully through their status as documents, or material inscriptions that attest to the enactments of community that took place in their creation, while also speaking to the particular concern at hand. I contend that collaborative illustration projects can connect us through shared concerns over periods of time (including well into the future), provide a 'space of appearance' for marginalized groups and contribute to the continuity of a shared and plural public realm.

Finally, the Conclusion revisits the questions I have set out here and considers, more broadly, the potential value of illustration practice and illustration research. It closes with an optimistic perspective on the potential of illustration as a cultural activity that can make meaningful contributions to many spheres – but I maintain that, in order to do so, we must be able to articulate the nature and the value of our contributions through scholarship and theory. This book attempts to offer one such articulation.

1 ILLUSTRATION, COMMUNITY AND THE POLITICAL

In Río Grande, the biggest city in Argentina's southern-most province, a group of women meet regularly to collectively embroider a map of the island they live on, Tierra del Fuego. In Glasgow, Scotland, illustrator and researcher Mitch Miller assembles people around large architectural floor plans of locations to which they are all connected and asks them to share their stories of these spaces. During the COVID-19 lockdowns in London, my project *Cracks in the Pavement* encouraged local residents to record their solitary walks on shared, emergent maps of the neighbourhood that were passed from one walker to the next. Unlike most illustrative works that are produced by an individual illustrator, these projects actually depend on the active contributions of many. They draw on the collective knowledge of a group of contributors to depict a territory held in common.

As outlined in the Introduction, I believe that such collaborative illustration projects give us the opportunity to reflect on the nature of community. By exploring this type of work through the dual lenses of illustration practice and political philosophy, I hope to reveal its capacity to record and reflect on the relations that occur in our everyday experiences – the connections we form to one another and to the places we inhabit. This is important for several reasons – and not just in the realm of illustration research.

Firstly, in our frenetic modern world, focusing people's attention on the everyday is not always easy, but the projects I am contemplating here have found creative ways to do so. I believe there is great value to be found in zooming in on the everyday relations, concerns and attachments that are crystallized in these projects. But the works I discuss here do not just help us reflect on everyday attachments; they also direct us towards wider lines of inquiry. Indeed, while these projects might appear to be small in scale and reach and while they certainly do not communicate in the registers that are usually assumed to command widespread attention or political action, I would argue that they lead us to bigger sociopolitical questions. These include: How can we act on our desire for attachment and belonging – in other

FIGURE 1.1 Sidney Mann and 'las chicas del mapa', *Bordando Tierra del Fuego* (2017–2024), a workshop session in the Niní Bernardello Art Museum in Río Grande, Argentina. Members of the group can be seen working towards an embroidered map of their province.

FIGURE 1.2 Sidney Mann and 'las chicas del mapa', *Bordando Tierra del Fuego* (2017–2024), workshop session.

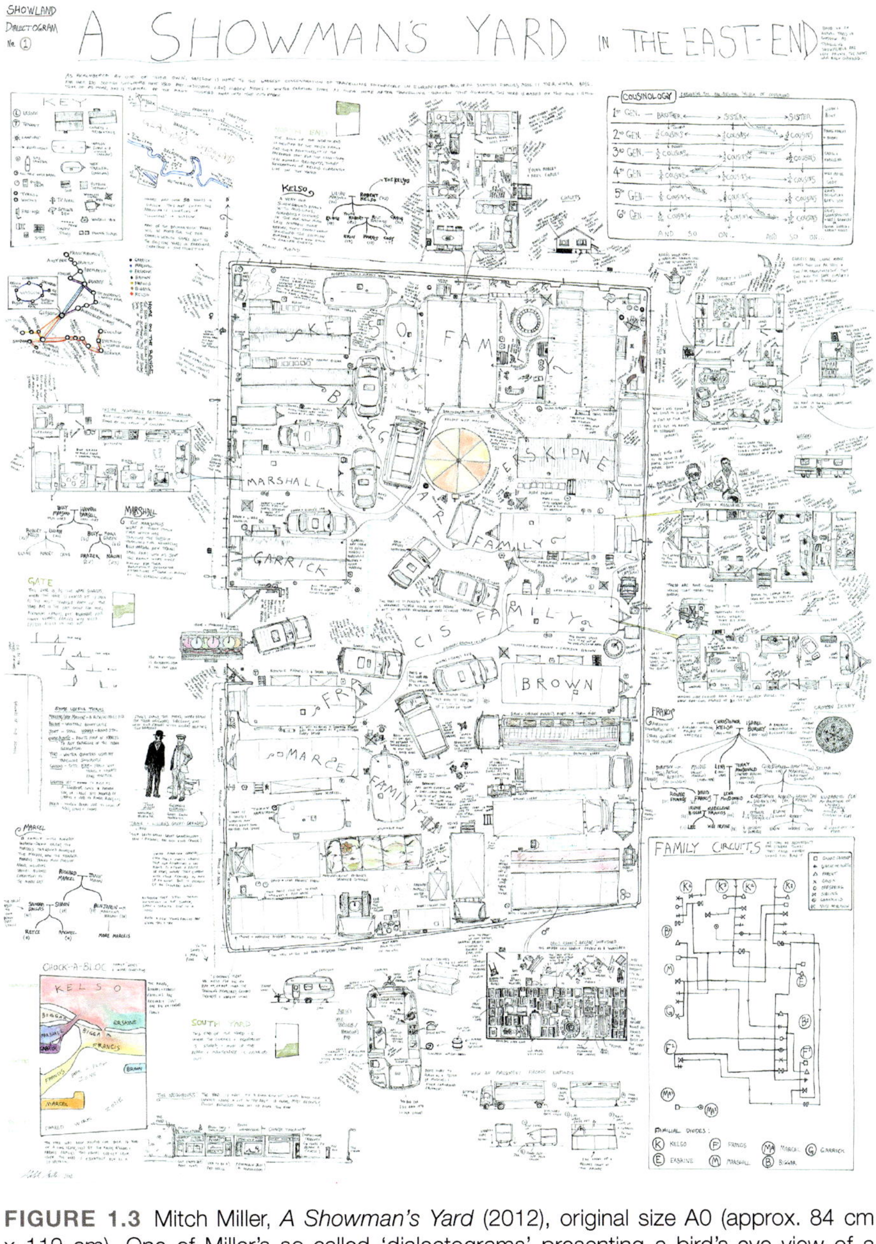

FIGURE 1.3 Mitch Miller, *A Showman's Yard* (2012), original size A0 (approx. 84 cm x 119 cm). One of Miller's so-called 'dialectograms' presenting a bird's-eye view of a location with its dense networks of social relations. *A Showman's Yard* depicts a travellers' community site in the East End of Glasgow.

FIGURE 1.4 Luise Vormittag, *Cracks in the Pavement* (2020–2021). These five A4-sized leaflets fold out to a large, lightly drawn map that participants used to record their consecutive walks in their local neighbourhood of East London during the COVID-19 pandemic.

words, our desire to be in community – without reverting to exclusionary and potentially ethnonationalist narratives? How can we reside in a common world, while the accelerating ruptures brought on by climate change make the ground we stand on increasingly unstable?

In this chapter, by introducing the three projects mentioned above in greater depth, I explain how and why this kind of illustrative work interests me. Moreover, I go on to argue that we should consider this work as a form of *political* illustration, not so much because of its overt content or subject matter (although that is, of course, important too), but because it is the result of groups of people coming together, rather than the creation of a singular, individual illustrator. In this way, it presents a unique opportunity for us to contemplate bigger questions on the nature of our coexistence.

Political illustration/political images

I am well aware that the work I discuss in this book is not the kind of illustration that is usually deemed 'political'. When one hears the phrase 'political illustration', a long, established lineage of illustrators creating images that draw attention to

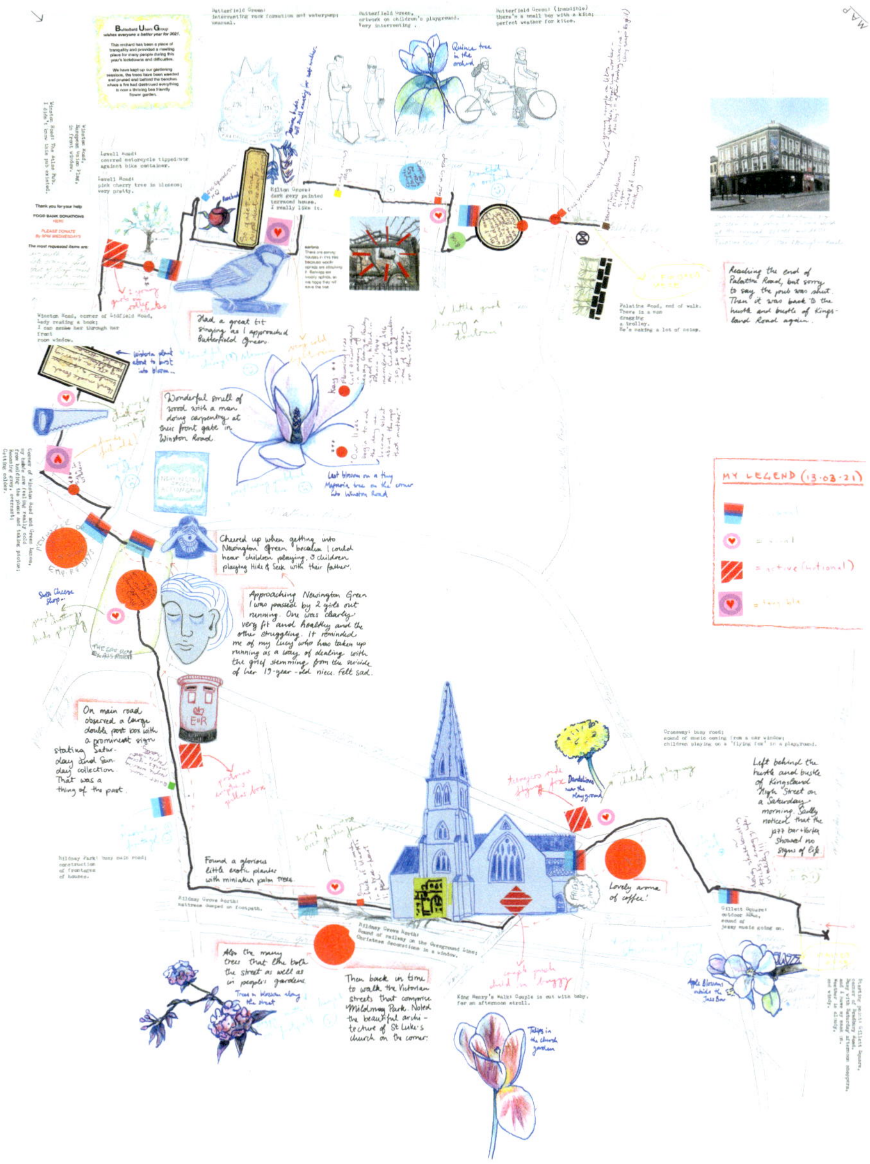

FIGURE 1.5 Luise Vormittag, *Cracks in the Pavement* (2020–2021), Map 5: Butterfield Green – Newington Green. With contributions from Jeanne Farr, Ena Fry, Jeremy Sharp and Gabriel.

and comment on specific political and social issues generally springs to mind. Illustrators working in this tradition tend to communicate their opinions through the images they produce and thereby position themselves as authors (and authorities) on the subject. While there are, of course, innumerable ways in which this might unfold, I will very briefly sketch out two commonly used rhetorical strategies employed by illustrators, thereby making it clear how my focus in this book differs.

One method is to use satire to comment humorously on political events of the moment. Satirical illustration has a rich and variegated history, but the political caricature that became popular in Britain in the eighteenth century serves as a particularly good case in point.[1] During this time, illustrations by James Gillray, George Cruikshank and George Townshend, among others, that ridiculed high society, politicians and royalty were distributed to a large audience via cheap prints. This strategy of humorous and mocking visual commentary remains popular in news publishing today. As I write, practitioners such as Martin Rowson and Steve Bell in the UK and Edel Rodriguez and Barry Blitt in the US continue this tradition with their barbed, satirical illustrations that comment on current political events. In addition, the rise of social media has created a further platform for the production and distribution of illustrations that ridicule those in power; see, for example, Cold War Steve's photomontage work.[2]

The second commonly used rhetorical strategy consists of illustrators depicting a pressing concern in a sombre, emotionally impactful or shocking manner in an attempt to mould opinion and ultimately provoke action in the viewer. The main aim here is to use illustration to reveal or draw greater attention to a political or

[1] Art historian David Kunzle's work on popular graphic arts provides a detailed account of this. For a chronicle of (political) cartooning, see *The History of the Comic Strip II: The Nineteenth Century* (originally published in 1973, reprinted 1990), or the more recent *Rebirth of the English Comic Strip: A Kaleidoscope, 1847–1870* (2021). Graphic arts historian Robert Lovejoy provides a more condensed summary in one of the chapters of the *History of Illustration* (see Lovejoy in Grove, Doyle & Sherman 2018: 170–83).

[2] There are, of course, other forms of illustrated satire that circulate on social media, such as image-text composites that are creatively reformatted by multiple users, and that therefore do not depend on the talents of an individual illustrator. I realize that any example I mention here will most likely feel pathetically out of date by the time this is being read, but I will risk the charge of obsolescence in order to give a fuller picture of what I mean. The 'How it started/How it's going' meme, for instance, humorously juxtaposes two images to express the unfavourable development of a project. The 'Distracted boyfriend' and the 'For the better, right?' memes work by using the same single image or sequence of images in combination with a humorous caption to comment on current affairs. This type of work does not tend to be commented on in discussions on illustration, presumably because the creative intervention is the repeated recaptioning of an exhausted stock image, rather than the creation of a new image. Illustrator and academic Catrin Morgan, however, proposes that we think of these nodal or nomadic images that are continually reposted and creatively reused as an 'illustrative strategy' (Morgan 2016: 26). In light of this, one could probably argue that social media has democratized satirical political illustration and expanded it beyond the authorial practice model. All of this, while fascinating, is beyond the remit of this book.

social injustice in the hope of mobilizing public opinion (and on some occasions behaviour) to change things for the better. See for example Sue Coe's (illustration) and Holly Metz's (text) publication *How to Commit Suicide in South Africa* (1983) or the illustrations created by Dutch illustrator Bodil Jane and others for UNICEF's air pollution campaign (Pritchard 2016). Often, as in the example of Sue Coe, illustrators producing this kind of work are motivated by strong personal convictions and take it upon themselves to produce and distribute this work. However, this type of work can also be generated through commission, as in the case of the UNICEF project.

Of course, I support illustrators using their practice to publicly express their political convictions. But despite the witty, thought-provoking, revelatory and impactful nature of this kind of work, my focus in this book is different. When I set out on this research path, I was curious about the possibilities of practice models that might be considered political as a whole, rather than as a consequence of an illustrator's choice of subject matter. In other words, I was interested in forms of practice that call into question the overall method of image creation and distribution in reference to political thought, rather than an individual illustrator's use of their practice for political ends.

I should note that, in addition to the strategies commonly adopted by illustrators in their work to promote and publicize a specific political cause, images can also be politicized through subsequent acts of interpretation. The critical reappraisal of existing images that were not necessarily intended to be perceived as political in the first place became particularly prominent in various academic fields broadly associated with the humanities, such as British cultural studies in the 1960s. In turn, this influenced the new field of visual studies that established itself in Anglo-American universities in the early 1990s.[3] A common approach within these critical traditions is to take a seemingly innocuous image and, through contextual analysis, expose and thereby attempt to dismantle the political and ideological biases that underpin it. For example, critical scholarship on the abundance of images depicting a picturesque, English rustic idyll reveals this to be a distinct pictorial trope that emerged around 1800. Art historian Ann Bermingham offers a thoughtful interpretation of this phenomenon in her book *Landscape and Ideology* (1986). She argues that these pictorial renditions of bucolic bliss should be considered in the context of both the agrarian and industrial revolutions as well

[3] In 1994 art historian W. J. T. Mitchell coined the phrase 'Pictorial Turn' – incidentally referenced by Grove when advancing the idea of the 'Theoretical Turn' in illustration (2018) – to highlight how the humanities have become increasingly interested in studying visual representation. The emergence of the field of visual studies in the 1990s is evidence of this development. Visual studies initially aimed to supplement art history with an interest in other types of images that had previously been ignored by scholarship, predominantly by drawing on methods from British cultural studies and poststructural theory. The field has since diversified; see James Elkins (2013: 3–15) for a detailed discussion of its development.

as a steady increase in British global, imperial power. According to Bermingham, the idea of the 'green and pleasant land' evoked by William Blake in his 1804 poem *Jerusalem* and rendered in idealized images of rural England by John Constable or Samuel Palmer was partly born out of a desire to counteract the turmoil of the period's recently industrialized urban centres. Artists responded to a renewed interest in representations of home as the imperial heartland, which in these images was portrayed as idyllic, unspoilt, supposedly stable and ahistorical.

In the Introduction, I commented on the 'hermeneutics of suspicion' – a style of theoretical work exemplified by Bermingham's book. This mode of critical analysis seeks to reveal or uncover an ideological substructure, which is, according to the logic of this analysis, hidden underneath a superficial display of innocence. I found Bermingham's book and others written in a similar vein both informative and captivating, and I certainly spent some enlightening hours letting myself be absorbed by this material in various libraries. But when I stepped back outside, I was never quite sure what to *do* with it. The work of demystification is certainly important and has a vital role to play in culture, society and politics. But as an illustrator – that is to say, someone invested in the *production* of images, not their dismantling – I felt unsure of how to work with this theoretical tradition.[4]

With all of this in mind, I began to ask myself whether there were other ways to think of the political. While I appreciated (and continue to appreciate) the rousing rhetorical power of illustrators setting out their position in their work, as well as the importance of interpretive practices that are aimed at ideological unmasking, neither of these modes of expression appealed to me. However, recognizing these modes of practice and thought as *particular modes* or styles was in itself revelatory. The aesthetic-affective dimension of this admittedly wide range of work that I am lumping together is often characterized by a combative and confrontational edge, much like the toing and froing in the everyday arena of political and social power relations. Despite the many considerable qualities and achievements of this kind of work, I was keen to find a different mode, a different register in which to think and act. One might say I was curious about the possibilities of a different atmosphere. So, while I celebrate the vitality and importance of confrontation, contestation and exposé, I will now provisionally bracket these traditions of practice and thought and see if this act of wilful elision might open up other possibilities for thinking about illustration and the political.

[4] Both W. J. T. Mitchell and James Elkins, two prominent academics in the field of visual studies, reflect on the paradox of a discipline that at times is rather hostile to its own subject. Mitchell in particular laments how tiresome these forms of critique can sometimes become. He writes: '[there is] something radically unsatisfactory about them. Perhaps the most obvious problem is that the critical exposure and demolition of the nefarious power of images is both easy and ineffectual' (2005: 33). See Mitchell (2005: 28–56) and Elkins (2013: 31–60) for more detailed analysis of this issue.

Alternative manoeuvres

But what might these other possibilities be? I mentioned my desire to identify practice models that might be considered political because of their overall structure and operation, rather than due to the declarative content of images or subsequent interpretive endeavours. Are there particular ways of working collectively that might be considered political?

The work of William Morris suggested itself as a historical example. It is well known that Morris was involved in socialist politics during his lifetime. However, instead of reading up on details of his political activism, I took note of how he realized aspects of his political vision in the organization of his publishing house Kelmscott Press (1891–1898). Here, his idea of medieval, craft-based communities living and working together and producing art and design for the elevation of everyday life was (at least partially) realized. Kelmscott Press produced books where layout, typography, border design, illustration and print technology worked in harmony to create a unified whole. While Morris apparently did not consider illustrations to be essential to book design (Ashbrook & Syme 2018: 236), many of the books he published did include them – they were often produced by his friend and collaborator, the painter Edward Burne-Jones. In accordance with Morris's principles of non-hierarchical collaboration, the illustrator had to create work that harmonized both with the typographic design and the affordances of the print technology, collaborating closely with the engraver to ensure an outcome where individual elements worked together.

There are, of course, more recent examples of creative collectives which incorporate illustration into their shared overall outputs, although the extent to which political consciousness played an active role in their formation varies. Presumably groups such as Push Pin Studios (founded in New York in the 1950s) or Peepshow (founded in London in 2000) were mainly motivated to join forces for increased commercial clout, shared business infrastructure and general camaraderie. In contrast to Kelmscott Press, many of these graphic arts collectives function as umbrella associations for a host of related but individual practices.

However, sometimes these groups *do* produce visual outputs that have been worked on by more than one member and are credited to the collective rather than an individual. For example, the French group Grapus, which emerged as part of the Parisian student movement of May 1968, always attributed their activist graphic posters simply to 'Grapus' (McQuiston 1995: 56). Similarly, the Dutch group Wild Plakken, active in Amsterdam over a similar period, did not credit individual members for their politically motivated visual poster designs (Bruinsma 2018: 214). Other examples of illustration collectives working on images collaboratively include the partnership Vault49 (which has now morphed into a brand experience and packaging design agency), UK–US collaborating illustrators Craig & Karl and my own partnership Container, which was active from 2003–2012. The UK-based illustration collective Nous Vous, which produces collaborative illustrations alongside works by individual members, has playfully foregrounded the tensions that can arise when a number of illustrators attempt to work on a piece collectively. During a residency at the House of Illustration (today the Quentin Blake Centre for Illustration) in London in 2016–2017, Nous Vous built an entertainingly low-tech drawing machine that allowed for three pairs of hands to simultaneously control a single pen, brush or sponge. The result was a portfolio of delightfully awkward illustrations that were the result of continuous, careful negotiation.[5]

Besides these kinds of professional collectives, various participatory practice models – where a professional works with a group of *non-professional* contributors

FIGURE 1.6 Nous Vous, *A Big Ship* (2017), one of the collaborative drawings the group produced using their drawing machine.

[5] During a presentation in 2024, Nicolas Burrows, one of Nous Vous's members, explained that, while it can be understood as concerned with collaboration, the group's primary interest in this project was loss of control. The convoluted drawing machine was intended as an obstacle to interrupt the burdensome notion of romantic, subjective expressiveness that has been associated with the artist's hand since the nineteenth century (Burrows 2024). See also the next footnote!

– have been developed in other areas of creative practice, such as fine art, architecture, product and service design. However, they have remained rare in illustration. This is understandable. After all, it is not immediately obvious *how* illustrators might include others in their working process in a meaningful way. The celebration of individual authorship and personal expression in our discipline is hard to set aside.[6] Illustration students often tell me about their ambition to develop a personal style, a recognizable way of working that emphasizes their individual, unique take on the world. I have a lot of sympathy for this ambition, as a consistent, personal style often leads to more commercial illustration commissions, presumably as this guarantees a predictable outcome for the commissioner. And besides the demands of commercial practice, I suspect another rationale may lurk in the background that goes some way to explain this desire for a form of expression that is both consistent and unmistakably one's own (at least ostensibly[7]). A coherent and recognizable style hints at the ideal of a self with similar qualities: a subject that is a unique, discrete and autonomous unit, transparent and unified unto him- or herself. Just as unreflective conceptions of the idea of community can slide towards a desire for a unified, coherent and exclusionary 'we', perhaps the desire for a unified and self-sufficient subject can lead to the refutation of (internal) heterogeneity and difference?[8]

So, what might it actually look like to develop a participatory practice model in illustration that allows for the inclusion of others? What way of working would embrace the differences that others bring? It is not immediately clear how one

[6] It is fascinating to consider the historical origin of the contemporary illustrator's persona, which emphasizes individuality and subjective expression. In their brilliant book *Objectivity* (2007), science historians Lorraine Daston and Peter Galison describe how ideas about the role of artists and scientists became polarized during the mid-nineteenth century: 'Artists were exhorted to express, even flaunt, their subjectivity, at the same time that scientists were admonished to restrain theirs. In order to qualify as art, paintings were required to show the visible trace of the artist's "personality"[...]' (2007: 37). So, while scientists tried to develop working procedures that sought to avoid human interference in the production of knowledge, artists were required to foreground their individual subjecthood. One might argue that we still operate under the shadow of these ideas today.

[7] Of course, there are trends that pull practitioners in similar directions. For example, the style of flat, bold, colourful, vector-based illustrations, sometimes called 'Corporate Memphis', manages to be quirky and bland at the same time. See Anne Quito's analysis in her article 'Why Editorial Illustrations Look So Similar These Days' (Quito 2019).

[8] Through conversations with cartoonist and academic John Miers, I learned that, in contrast to illustration, comics studies contain a greater degree of self-reflexive stylistic experimentation, where other people's visual languages are adopted as a form of citation or pastiche. Miers himself uses this strategy to great effect in his autobiographical comic *Conflict or Compromise* (2021), in which he alternates between other people's styles to express different facets of his own story. He explained how placing incidents from his own life into the nihilistic universe of Mark Beyer's *Amy & Jordan* strips, for example, highlights the sense of dislocation he was trying to convey when recounting his experience of receiving a devastating medical diagnosis (2021: 25). Incidentally, his comic also contains multiple and contradictory versions of his self, so it appears that for him, embracing a multiplicity of visual styles and languages goes hand in hand with the idea of a multiplicious self.

goes about creating a polyvocal illustration practice that not only supports and champions this multiplicity but is also able to find a suitable formal configuration for it. In other words – how might an illustration practice *look* that meaningfully includes a plurality of voices, while also finding a form that acts as a vehicle for this work to attract audiences? In this book, I have set myself the task of focusing on illustrative work that does just that; work that not only strives to gather together individuals in an attempt at collective sense-making but also has the capacity to relay this sense to other audiences and publics.

This process has seen me conduct interviews with practitioners who have similar concerns and working methods – it has been a delight to engage with them. Everyone I have spoken to has worked on illustrative projects with groups of participants in response to a place, its inhabitants and histories, and they are all making hugely inspirational contributions to the field of participatory illustration practice. (I should note that not all of them explicitly identified as illustrators, but I am taking the liberty of claiming their work as illustration.) Participants included: Glaswegian illustrator Mitch Miller, whose so-called 'dialectograms' draw on ethnographic methods to create polyvocal, collaborative illustrations, and Argentinian textile artist Sidney Mann, who has been working with a group of embroiderers to jointly create a large, illustrated map of the territory they inhabit. I also spoke to practitioners such as Rebecca Davies, whose energetic and joyful work combines illustration, performance, speculative thinking and a heterogeneous chorus of community voices, and Nina Sabnani, whose collaborative illustration and animation projects see her working with communities in Rajasthan and Gujarat in India. I will draw on these and other projects at various points in this book, picking up and interlacing thematic threads at different points in my discussion.

Perhaps equally as important as the direct insights I took from these conversations was the sense of companionship I gained from spending time with these inspiring practitioners. Our long, sometimes meandering conversations confirmed to me that the questions I was asking did indeed have value, and I was also heartened to find that there was a network of people driven by similar ambitions and grappling with similar challenges to me.

Three projects

Over the following pages I will now sketch out three projects in a little more detail: Mitch Miller's dialectograms – he coined this expression to describe the innovative genre of illustration he developed around 2010 in Glasgow; Sidney Mann's *Bordando Tierra del Fuego* (2017–2024), a collective embroidery project from southern Argentina; and my own project *Cracks in the Pavement* (2021), which I carried out in London during the various lockdowns and public health restrictions of the COVID-19 pandemic. I have undertaken, heard of and thought about a multiplicity of projects while working on this book, but I found that these three formed a particularly resonant constellation. All three of them bring together groups of people who share a geographical terrain (i.e. a site, a neighbourhood, a region) and are invited to jointly articulate a novel understanding of this common ground. Participants reflect on their ways of inhabiting a place and then visualize their own understanding of the site in relation to everybody else's. Later in this book, in Chapter 6, I will argue that these emergent landscapes, the composite topographies produced by such projects can be understood as a trace of collective world-making. But I am getting ahead of myself. For now, let me introduce the work.

Dialectograms

I still remember the first time I learned about Miller's work. In the autumn of 2012, I was nervously preparing to present at a conference (for the first or second time), and to my bewilderment, I noticed that there was another speaker, Miller, with a strikingly similar title to mine in the programme: 'Illustration as a collaborative, socially engaged practice'. I emailed Miller to point out the overlap and we joked about this unlikely coincidence. When we finally met and I heard him speak about his hugely ambitious project *DRAW DUKE STREET* (see Miller 2013), I was immediately impressed. At the time, I had just completed two projects of my own (with my then collective Container) in a big East London hospital, where we had spoken to patients about various, mainly positive aspects of their lives and (with their consent) used these accounts as the basis for an illustrated publication and installation. Reflecting on that work, I had started to sketch out some initial thoughts on the possibilities of a participatory illustration practice, exploring how illustrators may initiate dialogic encounters with others in order to generate material for their practice (see Vormittag 2014). At the time, I had not yet found my way into the various theoretical spaces that I will outline in greater detail in the next chapters, such as translation studies, phenomenology, ethnography and European philosophy, which ended up being enormously enriching arenas for my research – I was still predominantly occupied with participatory practice models in art and design. But when I first learned about Miller's dialectograms, they opened my eyes to a much richer way of thinking about and working with illustration and community.

Before embarking on his PhD research, during which he articulated and finetuned the genre of the dialectogram, Miller studied history, politics and social research methods. He also previously worked as an ethnographic researcher for an organization supporting nomadic communities in Scotland. These influences and experiences have clearly fed into his work. The dialectogram blends ethnographic research methods with architectural and comic book drawing conventions to create dense, large-scale illustrations of marginalized urban sites. The locations Miller chooses for this work tend to be characterized by precarity, such as a Showground Travellers caravan site in the East End of Glasgow (*A Showman's Yard*, 2012), the Red Road Flats – a series of high-rise apartment blocks in the north of Glasgow earmarked for demolition (*The Concierge Station*, 2009–2010; *The Nivens from S(i)even*, 2011; *The Brig Bar*, 2011; *The Mecca Bingo and Social Club*, 2011; *Red Road Flats – An Overview*, 2015) and an unconventional health centre (*The Piershill Community Flat*, 2013).

In Miller's multiphase process, a self-selecting group of participants repeatedly negotiates the nature of a shared site with him and with each other. They share views, stories and experiences relating to the location – and Miller uses these collectively and personally held narratives to gradually populate an empty framework in the form of a roughly drawn architectural blueprint. Notably, what is included and how things are represented is repeatedly debated during a series of meetings, where participants gather around the gradually emerging illustration – the result is part-comic strip, part-ethnographic writing, part-diagram.

In Miller's dialectograms, participants' contributions are linguistic in nature and oriented towards either the past and/or the present: they share oral narratives of personal memories and individual as well as communal histories, and Miller then uses his skills as an illustrator to add them to the piece. In this way, his work visualizes otherwise invisible social relations, perceptions and habitual

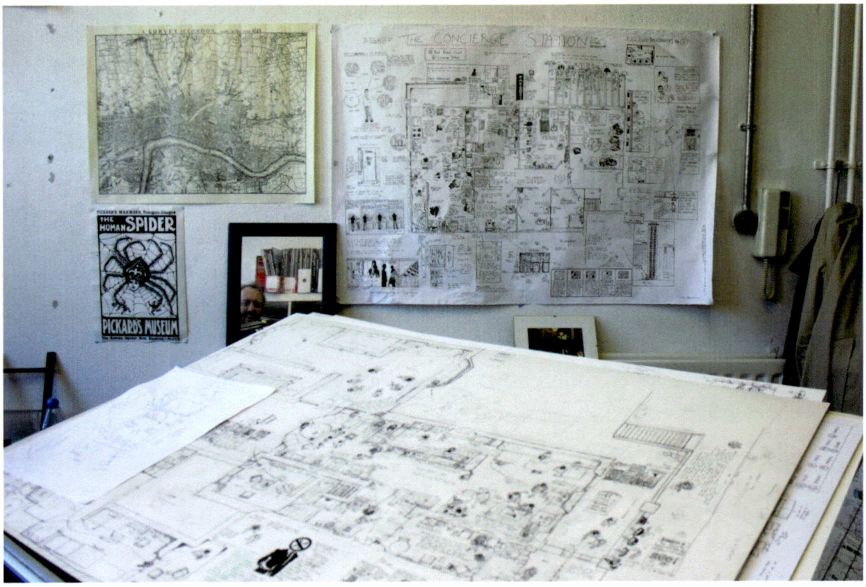

FIGURE 1.7 In Mitch Miller's studio in Glasgow (2016).

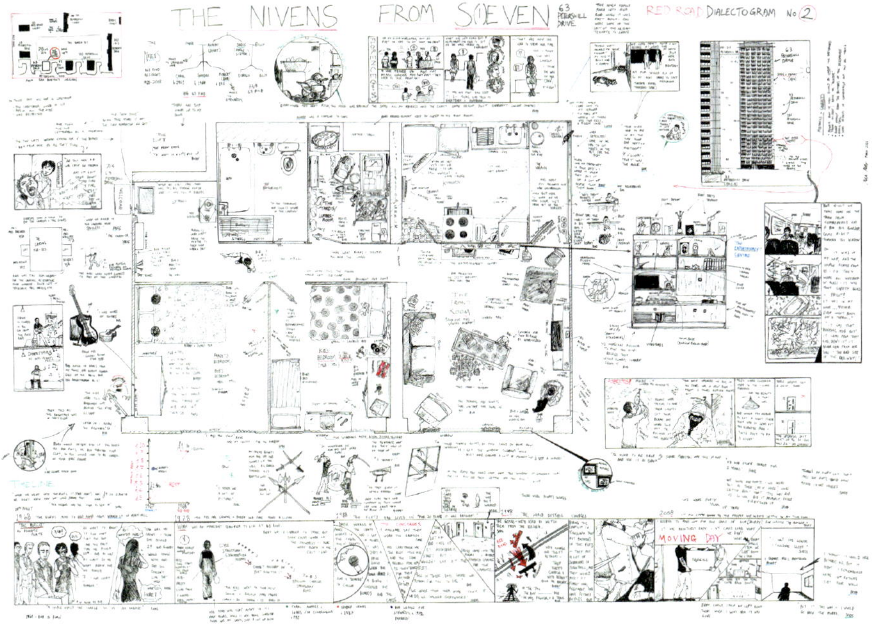

FIGURE 1.8 Mitch Miller, *The Nivens from S(i)even* (2011). From Miller's series of dialectograms capturing aspects of the Red Road Flats, a series of high-rise tower blocks in the north of Glasgow, not long before they were demolished.

uses of a place, resulting in a graphic palimpsest of spatially grounded stories. His dialectograms confront us with the richness and complexity of these places, thereby challenging the myth of terra nullius that is often employed when these marginalized sites are earmarked for redevelopment. 'I suppose I do this as a satire on a lot of the images I was seeing: you know, glossy, architectural renderings, the way architecture has of creating space', Miller told me when I visited his studio in 2016. 'We know there are actually loads of things happening, but [they] pretend there's a white space they're drawing onto, rather than a very complex ecosystem in its own right.'

And while Miller builds on architectural drawing conventions to produce a dialectogram, 'it's a drawing of social architecture, rather than architecture', 'a method for depicting space, place and social networks' (Miller 2016). In other words, Miller has found a way to make otherwise intangible connections visible, foregrounding the multiplicity of perspectives and drawing out their relational and geographical configurations. He does this while encouraging collective sense-making in peripheral places that are often teetering on the brink of erasure.

Bordando Tierra del Fuego

Unlike Miller, whose work I have known and appreciated for over a decade, Sidney Mann, a textile artist and art educator from Argentina, is a recent contact. I came across her work online, during an evening spent down an internet rabbit hole, when I was keen to widen my knowledge and networks. Upon finding a set of photos showing groups of women sitting together embroidering a map, I was intrigued and decided to get in touch. A week later, I had managed to arrange a video call with Mann, the project coordinator and facilitator of *Bordando Tierra del Fuego* (Embroidering Tierra del Fuego).

Tierra del Fuego is the southern-most province in Argentina, incorporating approximately half of the island of the same name (the other half belongs to Chile), alongside some other, smaller islands (including the Islas Malvinas) and a segment of Antarctica. As Mann explained to me, the population of this region today tends to be transient: tax incentives have made this province attractive to businesses, leading to the development of home appliance and electronics manufacturing, but this means that many people move to Tierra del Fuego for a few years to take advantage of the economic benefits, before leaving again.

The idea of working on a collective, embroidered map of the region first arose during an embroidery workshop Mann hosted in 2017. The workshop participants were chatting about their feelings of belonging to the area, and in response Mann printed the outline of a map of Tierra del Fuego onto fabric and cut it into sections. She gave each workshop participant a square to take home and embroider. This proved only partly successful: not everyone found the motivation to do this work at home and various squares got lost. But after some time passed, including the interruption of the COVID-19 pandemic, some of the original embroiderers made contact and expressed their desire to finish the map. The project was restarted in 2021. A number of participants from the original group rejoined, and new group members were also recruited via an open call. When I spoke to Mann in late 2023, there was a core group of about sixteen embroiderers, but a total of around thirty people had contributed to the project overall.

In contrast to the original project's set-up, Mann organized the second iteration around the principle of working together in a group setting. Over the following few years, the group met regularly to embroider – initially in people's homes, then in a space that had been made available to them by a museum, and afterwards in public places, such as cafés. Mann spoke to me about the convivial and amicable atmosphere that was cultivated over time. One of the women commented that 'on a social level, among the people who participated, it was very meaningful. Having a space to gather, to share, to embroider and to tell stories was truly enriching' (quoted by Mann 2025a).

Initially, each embroiderer was assigned to one specific square, but over time this became more fluid. For one thing, more regions were added to the map. Individual members took on certain areas, such as Antarctica, as a personal challenge, while others became collective projects, with multiple people working on the same section. In addition, the embroiderers began to include some of their personal histories in their work, as well as looking up and learning new information about the regions they had never visited.

The project was completed in 2024 and subsequently exhibited in the Virginia Choquintel Museum in Río Grande, the capital of Tierra del Fuego. (It later also toured to other cities in Argentina.) Looking at the photos of the exhibition opening, I saw a group of women crowded around a large wall-hanging with assembled patchworks of maps showing various areas and territories of the province of Tierra del Fuego. Mann had already told me that this project was worked on exclusively by women. She explained:

> [e]ven though I've always made the call for new members to join entirely open, it has only been women who wanted to take part. There is not a single stitch [in this project] that has been made by a man. We are embroidering over an existing map that almost definitely has been made by men. Perhaps this project is a way of showing how women inhabit a land, women's relationship to territory (2023)?

In this vein, could the project be understood as a specifically feminist way of making connections? Mann spoke to me at length about how the work created bonds (or threads?) of relating and belonging, both among the group members

FIGURE 1.9 Sidney Mann and 'las chicas del mapa', *Bordando Tierra del Fuego* (2017–2024). The finished map on display at the Virginia Choquintel Museum, Río Grande, Argentina, July 2024.

FIGURE 1.10 Sidney Mann and 'las chicas del mapa', *Bordando Tierra del Fuego* (2017–2024). Assembling the pieces of the map.

as well as to their shared territory more broadly. In addition to the feminist reading offered by Mann, I found myself thinking about the brutal obliteration of indigenous cultures in the region during the nineteenth and early twentieth centuries, which replaced ways of life that were deeply connected to the land, its flora and fauna with a lifestyle characterized by transience. Of course, this destructive history is not unique to Tierra del Fuego. Colonialism, modernity and a ruthless global regime of natural resource extraction have made many of us see the land we live on as a mere backdrop for human enterprise and a resource for our myopic anthropocentric ambitions. I suspect that many people who come to Tierra del Fuego to take advantage of the tax incentives are likely to feel detached from the landscapes around them. But through *Bordando Tierra del Fuego*, a small group of women aspired to find something of a foothold. They attempted to ground themselves in the land they inhabit, to come down to earth.

Cracks in the Pavement

My own piece *Cracks in the Pavement* (2020–2021) also represented an attempt at geographical reorientation and reattachment during the period of COVID-19 related lockdowns. I conceived of this project specifically in this context, at a time when most of our relationships and interactions were migrating into a seemingly weightless and disembodied online space. In contrast to this sudden near-total virtualization of our life-worlds, I wanted to create a project that was focused on embodiment and materiality.

When the public health regulations in the UK were at their most severe, one of the few admissible reasons to leave the house was to go for a walk, preferably alone. In response to this, I decided to design a project that enabled people to walk 'together' along the same routes in my East London neighbourhood, but at different times. Participants would annotate their thoughts, ideas and observations on a shared A1-sized sheet of paper, which would be passed from one walker to the next.

I enlisted a number of people who agreed to 'lead' a walk. I knew many of the walkers I recruited through various connections, but I also approached some people I did not know personally – for example, a prominent local tour guide. And soon others began to hear about the project on social media and contacted me to volunteer. The first walkers set out in December 2020. Before starting the walk, they sent me an approximate description of their intended route. I then sketched out a rough pencil map on an A1 sheet of paper, which they would annotate during and after the walk. After a few weeks, I had five maps in circulation. Once the route had been laid down, subsequent walkers, one by one, more or less followed in the footsteps of those who went before them, adding to and expanding upon their predecessors' notes, drawings and observations. In this way, each map grew in complexity with each contributor. I asked each contributor to nominate the next participant, thereby creating a chain of socially connected walkers. This worked most of the time. When it did not, I would step in and nominate others to pick up the baton.

Before their walk, participants received a ziplocked envelope containing the large physical paper map they would be engaging with. I designed each map to fold down to the size of a leaflet; it contained instructions and suggestions on the reverse, alongside illustrative collage-style vignettes and some reflective writing on the challenges of lockdown. The pack also included a selection of materials like stickers, tape, pens and paper. I cycled around East London to deliver them to pre-arranged dropping off points – usually people's front doors – where walkers received the pack in a COVID-secure way.

Each participant went on the walk by themselves (or on some occasions with members of their household), marking up and annotating their route, thoughts, discoveries and observations. Sometimes the annotations happened during the walk itself, sometimes afterwards at home. If walkers were reluctant to draw and mark up the map themselves, they sent me photos, notes or audio files and I would annotate the map on their behalf. Walkers returned the map and materials to me in the ziplocked envelope. I subsequently produced an interim scan of the map, uploaded it to a specially designed website, restocked the materials and delivered the map to the next walker.

As restrictions were gradually lifted during spring and summer 2021, the project petered out. While each map was designed to accommodate up to six walkers, they ended up with four to five layers each. Upon deciding to end the project, I produced thank-you packs for all of the participants, containing prints of the maps and a leaflet that described and reflected upon the process. Then, in the following year, I got in touch with a local archive (Hackney Archives) that was collecting creative projects which had emerged in response to the pandemic – they were therefore keen make the maps part of their collection. In September 2022, once all COVID-19-related public health restrictions had been lifted, Hackney Archives and I organized a show-and-tell event on the project, which was attended by about half of the original participants. It was a wonderful opportunity for many of us to meet face to face for the first time and look at the five different maps in detail.

Now that the COVID-19 pandemic is largely behind us, it is easy to forget quite how disorienting that period was. For many of us, it was hard to know how to make sense of life during lockdown. Looking at the maps, I can see that many walkers sought to do so simply by using their senses, by being open to the world as it presented itself to them: 'Absolutely freezing' (Map 2), 'Chip shop smells of chips – for obvious reasons' (Map 4) and 'Had a great tit [bird] singing as I approached Butterfield Green' (Map 5).

When I was planning this project at the height of the pandemic, I was not particularly thinking of cold hands, musical birds or the smell of chip shops. The question that had propelled this project was whether and how it might be possible to be alone, but still somehow acting together, or towards one another, across intervals of time. *Cracks in the Pavement* does this by highlighting individual sensory impressions of a space that is experienced separately but remains shared. The resulting maps speak of relations and attachments: I read them as a record of the bonds we formed – and strengthened – to our shared neighbourhoods and each other during these peculiar, solitary months.

Taking these three projects together, what can we see? At the beginning of this chapter, I announced my conviction that these kinds of participatory illustration projects can be understood as a form of political illustration. But does the work I have highlighted really support such a claim? Critics may argue that, while these projects have their charms, they are limited in their reach, involving only a small number of participants and a modest level of public exposure. Furthermore, the explicit content of the work could be described as almost entirely innocuous.

FIGURE 1.11 Luise Vormittag, *Cracks in the Pavement* (2020–2021). A pack delivered to the doorstep of a participant during the COVID-19 pandemic.

Who cares if a handful of women sit together and sew, why should we pay attention to drawings of a block of flats in Glasgow, and what is the value in some battered old pieces of paper documenting shared walking routes in London? I must admit that I have often worried about these objections myself while working on my projects and drafting this book. It cannot be denied that this work lacks the fiery, combative edge that tends to characterize the kind of work usually described as 'political'.

However, while these projects might appear unassuming to some, I believe that they present a unique opportunity for us to think about what it might mean to be in community. This term – community – is frequently used in everyday parlance without much thought. But as the climate emergency worsens, gradually rendering swathes of land uninhabitable, the question of how we might develop and express a shared attachment to an increasingly crowded terrain as well as to each other is more urgent than ever. We must ask ourselves: In the face of widespread pollution and erosion, exhausted soils and destroyed habitats, how might we find our collective footing? How can we bond with one another and connect meaningfully with the terrains we inhabit, without falling back on discriminatory, nationalist narratives?

FIGURE 1.12 Luise Vormittag, *Cracks in the Pavement* (2020–2021). The four stages of Map 2: Chatsworth Road, as participants gradually populated the map with their inscriptions. With contributions from Jørn Tomter, Steph von Reiswitz & Lucia (7), Eleanor Bembridge and Linda Culverwell.

In the projects I discuss in this book, participants reveal themselves not as isolated individuals, but as relational, plural subjects who strive to make sense of their geographical, historical and interpersonal connections. The illustrative documents generated by these projects demonstrate that it is possible to delineate heterogeneous, shared worlds – indeed, composite topographies emerge through the process of participants' interactions. Of course, it would be unreasonable to claim that this work holds any kind of solution to the world's many grave problems (it does not). Nonetheless, it *does* offer us a material exposition (an illustration?) of what a lively and dynamic relationship between people and place can look like. In these projects, illustration demonstrates that it is capable of being a site for ontological disclosure: it offers us a space where we can experience and see who we are. It gives us an opportunity to enact, record and reflect on our collectivity. Ultimately, what is at stake in this work is how we make sense of our place in the world, alongside others.

Being in relation, being in common

So, why is it that I am calling this work 'political'? Is the process of reflecting on our experiences and enactments of community itself political? French philosopher Jean-Luc Nancy has most influenced my thinking on this matter. Widely regarded as one of the most important contemporary contributors to the questions of community and coexistence, Nancy's philosophical work on these areas was developed in the shadow of totalitarianism and its genocidally destructive manifestations in twentieth-century Europe. Surveying the wreckage, Nancy was compelled to reject the notion of community as being a naturally occurring group based on hereditary features, where community becomes an 'organic communion with its own essence' (Nancy 1991: 9). Instead, he re-examined anew the relationality of the social body at the most fundamental, ontological level.

In Nancy's view, rigorous questions concerning the essence of social relations are by their very nature political. Together with his colleague and friend, philosopher Philippe Lacoue-Labarthe, he proposes that philosophy, rather than political science or political theory, is needed to establish new ground from which to think future possibilities of human association (Lacoue-Labarthe & Nancy 1997: 109). This is necessary because, before reflecting on questions of statehood or power, one needs to think about assumptions surrounding the nature of the human subject and the kinds of human relations that follow from that, which in turn underpin these political formations (Lacoue-Labarthe & Nancy 1997: 117). Nancy and Lacoue-Labarthe were concerned that the notion of 'the political' was being treated as self-evident, despite lacking this essential grounding. Their joint essays are by no means conventional works of political theory, where philosophical argumentation is generally offered as a precursor or justification for political prescriptions. Instead, they present detailed philosophical reflections on historical conceptions of 'the human' and how these ideas have underpinned notions of political community. They argue that the way in which we perceive the relationality of society must be the basis for all other forms of political theory.

I found Nancy's focus on fundamental questions of coexistence extremely resonant. In his philosophical work on community and the political, he sets aside questions of power and ideology in favour of a detailed examination of the inherent qualities of being with others, being in community. Similarly, in this book, I do not want to focus my attention on the various existing traditions of political illustration practice. Instead, the work I consider here is (primarily) political in the Nancean sense, in that it offers us opportunities for reflecting on ways of being in community.

However, there is another side to this. My research is not pursued in the abstract, but through staging and interpreting collaborative illustration projects associated with particular people, places, histories and concerns. Therefore, it necessarily spills over into what is more conventionally understood as the political – the everyday wrestling for power and influence in the public sphere. And while the projects I discuss are perhaps less combative than other kinds of political illustration, they nevertheless *do* take up a number of causes and campaigns. Many of the projects I discussed with fellow practitioners sought to amplify the voices of groups that are frequently overlooked in the public sphere – for example, young single mothers (Billy Ash Sakula), older people at risk of isolation in London (Grace Holliday) and communities repeatedly displaced in India (Nina Sabnani). Moreover, two of my own projects have been directly involved with political causes in the conventional sense of the word: the callous eviction of well-established migrant traders from a neighbourhood they had helped build up in South London in *Walking the Elephant* and the continuous struggle for women's rights in *Write Women into History*. Similarly, as previously mentioned, Mitch Miller's dialectograms tend to foreground the perspectives of marginalized communities and vilified places, such as a Traveller community or high-rise flats housing council tenants and asylum seekers. And while my project *Cracks in the Pavement* is not engaged in such clearly established causes, this project too can be seen as political in its gentle encouragement for hyper-local larking about, in opposition to contemporary society's default imperatives of individualistic striving, efficiency and economic growth. Similarly, Sidney Mann's *Bordando Tierra del Fuego* is less obviously taking up a specific cause but also presents a quiet rebuke to the Argentine government's industrial tax incentives in the region.

In short, unlike theoretical writing that sometimes adopts abstract language to establish an argument, these illustration projects are action-oriented in their engagement with people, events, places, and histories. That means that the work operates on two registers simultaneously. The projects are political in the more conventional understanding of the word, as well as in the Nancean sense – exploring fundamental ontological questions about our being in common and the manner in which society is produced. As a result, the knowledge that flows from this work also falls into two categories. On the one hand, these projects refer to and help us learn about specific and particular matters or issues. At the same time, through the theoretical considerations presented in this book, we can use each project as a site for considering more general questions on the nature of being and acting together.

Correspondingly, the beneficiaries of this work also fall into two camps: all the practitioners I spoke to do their best to serve the group they are working with, to produce outputs that reflect the group's needs and interests – this strongly echoes my own intentions for my projects. At the same time, through the writing of this book, I am also striving to provide my fellow illustrators and academics with new thinking about the affordances of our discipline, sketching out new terrains for what I believe illustration can do.

Inclusion and empowerment

Through my conversations with other practitioners, it became clear to me that a shared set of values animated our work. It was rare for these to be explicitly named, but they can probably be best described as the principles of inclusion, diversity, creativity and empowerment. For example, illustrator Grace Holliday, while talking to me about her work with older adults (*Wending Our Way Along the River as Time Goes By*, 2023), described the group she worked with as 'a very diverse group, culturally [...] a really fantastic group' (Holliday 2023). She went on to explain how she always referred to participants as 'artists', undoubtedly an inclusive and empowering term. Similarly, London-based illustrator Alaa Alsaraji, reflecting on a range of workshops she has facilitated with various groups, spoke about how she responds to participants who arrive to a session with very low self-esteem: 'I see my work as a reintroduction to visual creativity, which can be really powerful. [...] I try to give people a different way to connect to the arts' (Alsaraji 2023). Again, this attitude is clearly underpinned by a commitment to include and empower people who are otherwise discouraged from participating in forms of creative expression.

Representation and diversity matter, and the majority of projects I discuss make a serious and thoughtful effort to correct systemic forces that have prevented many voices from being afforded due prominence in society. Still, while it is vital to broaden the scope of whose contributions are noticed and celebrated in the public realm, we must remain mindful that inclusion cannot be an end in itself; too easily can it be employed as a superficial tactic that deceptively signals change, while actually maintaining the status quo. As it happens, it was a version of this very scenario that prompted this research in the first place. In the Introduction,

I described working on a commission for a property developer that required me to engage with the local community on themes relating to their heritage in order to produce a permanent artwork for a new healthcare facility. At the same time, the construction itself was financed by global investors who were set to make a profit by leasing the facility to the national healthcare provider. Including a range of local voices in the artwork resulted in a benevolent display, but this inclusion did nothing to challenge ruthless concentrations of global corporate power.

The values of inclusion, creativity and empowerment can also feel misplaced or misused when illustrators and other creative practitioners are tasked with providing a level of societal repair that is substantially beyond what can reasonably be expected of us. For example, Billy Ash Sakula, a London-based illustrator, animator and arts facilitator, spoke of their frustration at having to fill the gaps in a threadbare social welfare system in numerous community arts projects they worked on (Ash Sakula 2023).

Nevertheless, many people's experiences are still marked by social structures that generate and perpetuate their exclusion, and thus the demand for them to receive increased presence and recognition remains valid and vital – as are art projects that seek to support these aims. Over the years, this argument has been

FIGURE 1.13 Grace Holliday introducing a session with a group of artist-participants at The Peel Institute for a project commissioned by the Quentin Blake Centre for Illustration (2023). Photograph by Valentina Zunino.

FIGURE 1.14 Artist-participants of Grace Holliday's project at The Peel (2023). Photograph by Valentina Zunino.

made by many; see, for example, *Mapping the Terrain* (1994), a book edited by the prominent, socially engaged artist Suzanne Lacy, in which numerous contributors celebrate work that combines inclusive activism and aesthetics. A more recent example presents itself in *A Restless Art* (2019), a book by British community artist François Matarasso. Drawing on the British community arts movements from the 1960s to the 1980s, and connecting this to the Universal Declaration of Human Rights adopted by the UN in 1948, Matarasso reminds us that everyone ought to have the opportunity to participate in the cultural life of their community and asserts that community art has a unique potential as an emancipatory and democratic force.

I greatly admire Lacy's work and completely agree with Matarasso regarding the importance of greater inclusivity in the arts, but I feel little would be gained by me simply transposing their claims to illustration practice and repeating them. I wholeheartedly embrace the values of inclusion and empowerment and trust my readers to take this as a given as I use the pages that follow to delve into additional issues and concerns. In the remainder of the book, I will continue to draw out the themes I have started developing in this chapter: how participatory illustration projects offer us ways to reflect on relating, both to one another and to the places we inhabit. I continue to argue that these projects thereby constitute a form of political illustration, not necessarily because of the explicit content of the work (although they do that too!), but because they offer us an arena in which to reflect on possibilities of human association more generally.

2 WORKING WITH OTHERS

Despite the fact that illustration is traditionally conceived of as a solitary activity, working with others has become an important part of many illustrators' practice. In Chapter 1 I briefly mentioned several well-known illustration collectives – both historical and contemporary – and described how members of these groups work together to galvanize creative reach and output by combining their skill sets and artistic visions. However, for the purposes of this book I am interested in illustrators working with groups of *non*-illustrators, who join projects because of a shared interest or concern, rather than in a professional capacity. To work together effectively in such contexts, they need to find ways to bridge gaps and create space for all parties to provide input – which is what I will explore in this chapter.

While the number of illustrators who work in this way is relatively modest, there is a rich and diverse lineage of artists and designers (primarily in the fields of architecture, environmental planning, and product and service design) who have grappled with the idea of participation as a politicized working process. These practitioners have generally been driven by a progressive impulse towards greater inclusiveness and democratization in their work. For example, during the 1960s and 1970s, so-called 'New Genre' public art in the US and the community arts movement in the UK saw artists working with and championing marginalized community groups: through these projects, artists sought to depict people affirmatively and campaign for their interests. Around the same time, architects and designers also broached questions of democratizing working processes so as to better involve future users, often from marginalized backgrounds, in design processes, thereby giving these users the opportunity to shape their own tools, services and environments. Building on this, in this section I examine the key characteristics and tensions of these art and design movements and discuss how participatory illustration projects offer a different take on the dilemmas that can arise in this type of work.

Critical assessment of politicized participatory art is often celebratory, with much of the discussion focusing on social impact. For example, Lacy's book

Mapping the Terrain (1995), draws on the previous thirty years of artistic practice in the United States and enthusiastically endorses artists who practise at the nexus of activism and aesthetics. Impressive pieces such as Judith Baca's *The Great Wall of Los Angeles* (1978), Lacy's own *The Crystal Quilt* (1985-1987) and Sheila Levrant de Bretteville's *Biddy Mason – Time and Place* (1989) are described and discussed as powerful examples of artistic projects in which the effective communication of a community's concerns and social impact more generally is a central motivation.

More recently, Matarasso charted and promoted similar practices in *A Restless Art: How Participation Won and Why It Matters* (2019) with a stronger emphasis on artists in the UK and Europe. He advocates for working with flat, non-hierarchical structures that necessitate continuous negotiation among all parties, rather than a predetermined set of aims, objectives, standards and processes. He sees this working method as an exemplar of a more progressive, democratic and inclusive practice model. Conceptually, this approach is aligned with urbanist Sherry Arnstein's famous 'Ladder of Citizen Participation' (1969), a metric that can be used to assess the relative success of participatory consultation models in urban planning. The ladder's rungs range from 'manipulation' (lowest rung) via 'consultation' and 'partnership' to 'citizen control' (highest rung) – this highest rung is the most desirable in this model.

The architecture and design literature of the 1960s and 1970s also laudatorily endorses these ideas and approaches. For example, architect Giancarlo De Carlo's influential essay 'Architecture's Public' (1970) presents a critique of the modern architect's distance from society and its needs, concluding that 'architecture is too important to be left to architects' (De Carlo [1970] 2005: 13). De Carlo calls for the abolishment of barriers between the multiple stakeholders involved in architectural projects in favour of a collective participation process that works with, rather than for, future users. A fantastic example of this attitude is provided by architect Walter Segal's project in Lewisham, London (1978), which used self-builders on the local housing list: under the guidance of Segal and funded by the council, people were supported to come together and build their own homes (see Blundell Jones 2005: 130–2).

Similar ideas have also been advanced in engineering and industrial design. Nigel Cross's book *Design Participation* (1972) contains many contributions that speak to a desire to eradicate hierarchies that place the designer at a remove from future users. Practitioners describe what they perceive as the unnecessary secrecy and mystique surrounding professionalized design and explain how one might create a transparent process that allows for a more equal exchange between designers and end-users. Certainly, there is a pragmatic motive – alongside a political one – at play here: after all, it is sensible for a designer to draw on the situated knowledge of future users to design a better product, service or townscape. But politically speaking, these developments stem from and further the emancipatory impulses seen in the movements discussed above – the desire to foreground otherwise marginalized communities in creative processes and ensure they have an opportunity to contribute to their own environments.

Unfortunately, these initially progressive impulses in architecture and design soon became institutionalized. Architect and academic Jeremy Till, among others, laments that participatory components quickly became part of the bureaucratic process they initially intended to disrupt (Till 2005, 2006). Indeed, now that mainstream architectural practice has incorporated participation as an often-unsatisfying step in the process, a vocal set of architect-academics has begun to critique this situation with publications such as *The Violence of Participation* (2007) and *The Nightmare of Participation* (2011) (the first edited by and the second mostly written by Markus Miessen).[1] Critics speak of hollowed-out participatory mechanisms acting as a legitimizing tool for dubious urban developments and call for a renewed recognition of the conflictual and disruptive possibilities of participatory practice.

My own experience of interacting with these very bureaucratic processes in architecture through an illustration commission I completed in 2014 (which I have already touched on in the preceding chapters) corroborates Till's analysis. Working under the commissioners' designated project title *Our Heritage* (I later retitled it *Rumour Legend Tradition Fact*), I was asked to produce permanent artwork for a new so-called community hospital and to work with local residents in its realization. After I learned that the construction of the hospital was being financed using private, foreign investment and that the facility would then be rented back to the National Health Service for profit, I felt increasingly uncomfortable with my role. I wondered if I had been hired, at least in part, to smooth over the obvious discrepancy between the global corporate structures of the project and the proclaimed narrative of a community hospital. This kind of scenario was pointedly described by architectural critic Eyal Weizman as an agency 'outsourc[ing] its ethical self-consciousness' (Weizman in Miessen 2011: 10) to an external body, in this case me – a troublesome situation to find oneself in as an illustrator.

Participatory art practice also has its critics. Art historian Claire Bishop conducted a rigorous analysis of this type of work in her humorously titled book *Artificial Hells* (2012). She sets out a plethora of sharply observed insights, problems and contradictions, paying forensic attention to the often unspoken assumptions, values and worldviews that are implicit in this type of work. Other art critics have also published sceptical analyses on this topic, including Hal Foster's essay 'The Artist as Ethnographer' (1996) and Miwon Kwon's book *One Place After Another* (2002).

[1] See also contributions to *Architecture and Participation* (2005), edited by Peter Blundell Jones, Doina Petrescu and Till.

Engaging with all this material was incredibly valuable for me, as it helped me gain a thorough understanding of these movements and their focus on inclusion, democratization and the promotion of marginalized voices. It struck me that a common aspiration of this large and diverse group of practitioners and thinkers is to (at least contribute to) eradicating the power structures that are inscribed in the art world and design processes. And, of course, I applaud and share this progressive impulse towards greater inclusivity and the demystification of creative practice.

However, I also found it instructive to notice the tensions between these projects' generally laudable political aims and their practical realization. Reading the detailed and sometimes stinging critiques that trail these movements – the book titles alone, such as *Artificial Hells* (Bishop 2012) and *The Nightmare of Participation* (Miessen 2011), are evocative – left me wondering whether illustrators, on *some* occasions at least, might actually be better placed than artists or designers when it comes to generating participatory scenarios for creative work that are less fraught than the ones frequently described in this body of literature. Illustration is generally light-footed (typically materials are cheap and the work can be completed relatively quickly), has a comparatively problem-free relationship with aesthetics (visual appeal is generally appreciated among illustrators, in contrast to fine art's uneasy relationship to visual pleasure) and its practitioners are often communicative, responsive and empathetic. This means, in short, that illustration practice should be able to address many of the points of criticism raised by Bishop and others. What follows over the next few pages is a more detailed elaboration of this point. I use three of Bishop's sharply articulated observations to draw out the potential of illustrators to do things differently.

Climbing frames

Firstly, Bishop highlights how gestures of *authorial renunciation* tend to be a key characteristic in these movements (2012: 22). Ideas of originality, authenticity and identity, formerly attributed to the artist, are now ascribed to a participating community, their expressive powers, culture and legacy. Kwon (2002) points out similar developments in the realm of site-specific public art: previously, large-scale public sculptures by famous artists rarely had any relationship to the site. However, more recent public art often foregrounds local heritage and community participation. Meaning is now considered to be found in the location and the people living there. Under this new paradigm, the task of the artist is transformed: instead of producing work that reflects their personal and aesthetic concerns, the artist must now endeavour to reveal something about the participating community and their environment.

Arguably, Matarasso's championing of community art that democratizes all decisions in the creative process furthers this move towards authorial renunciation, as does Arnstein's ladder, which stipulates that participatory design (she is writing about urban design) should aim for 'full citizen control'. Bishop observes how many of these kinds of projects aim to devise the most ethical and democratic process possible to the detriment of other artistic concerns, because, as she pointedly phrases it, 'all forms of authorship are equated with authority and indicted as totalising' (2012: 25). To put it another way, while these approaches undoubtedly grow out of the best possible intentions, the impulse to rid oneself of an undesirable leadership role by rejecting all forms of authorship or expertise can result in unstructured groups with little direction and no agreed-upon decision-making protocols.[2] The limited effectiveness – and occasionally downright injustice – of these kinds of groups was insightfully described by feminist Jo Freeman in her 1972 essay 'The Tyranny of Structurelessness'. Drawing on her experiences in the women's liberation movement, Freeman argues that unstructured groups, far from being fair and equitable, often result in an informal and unacknowledged, but still binding, structure. Decision-making takes place through meandering discussions, but these privilege those who have the most time and are the most articulate. In other words, decisions are still made by a select few – in this case by those who demonstrate the greatest oratorical stamina and persuasive delivery.

As previously mentioned, attempts at authorial renunciation in disciplines like fine art, where single practitioners are customarily credited with the creation of large and complex works, stand in contrast to illustrators' (and graphic designers') bids for increased authorial recognition: these are, after all, disciplines in which practitioners often feel overlooked, and where the desire for so-called authorial practice can be (erroneously, in my view!) seen as the only alternative to commercial work, imbued as it is with the hope of greater prestige and recognition. Essentially, both approaches lack nuance: the privileged practitioners guiltily seeking to rid themselves of their authority and expertise, and the anxious clamouring for recognition by those who feel undervalued.

In the projects I have undertaken thus far, there has been no 'full citizen control', nor was this something I desired to emulate. This is also reflected in the terminology I use to describe the people I work with in my projects. I call them 'participants' rather than 'collaborators', as that most closely reflects their type of involvement. (However, it must be said that, while they 'participate' in my

[2] Of course, democratic inclusivity does not necessarily result in unstructured groups. A notable example of a working process that is both inclusive and incredibly well-structured is Loraine Leeson and Peter Dunn's Dockland Community Poster Project that they worked on during the 1980s in London. The two artists collaborated with graphic designers, activists and multiple community groups in a well-organized structure that allowed everyone to work to their strengths and skills, with channels for feedback and a steering group with decision-making powers (see Leeson 2019). The impressive results speak for themselves.

projects, they 'collaborate' with each other while doing so.) A similar orientation also holds true for Mitch Miller in his dialectograms and Sidney Mann in *Bordando Tierra del Fuego*. In order to include others, we design responsive project frameworks that participants can use as 'climbing frames', clambering up and finding themselves in novel configurations, perhaps with newly found abilities and a different outlook. The metaphor of the climbing frame is apt: it allows people to pull themselves up, using their (climbing) skills and individual strengths to elevate themselves. They can decide where and how to position themselves within the frame, they can rely on it as a sturdy and supportive structure, and they can cooperate with each other or regard each other from new perspectives as they climb. In short, it gives participants a new view of their territory, their companions and themselves.[3]

Perhaps the somewhat unreflective mobilization of the spectre of the author is at least partly to blame for the various contortions artists and illustrators find themselves in? We find ourselves in a false binary: On the one hand the emphasis on illustrators' authorship, in 'authorial illustration', and on the other hand gestures of authorial renunciation, as for example in Matarasso's celebration of community art. Does it not serve us better to modify the notion of authorship, as exemplified in the work of Miller, Mann and my own projects? Rather than authorship being exclusively associated with the expressive and original realization of an artist's vision and identity, authorship can also manifest itself in other forms, such as in the responsive construction of frameworks that offer both direction and creative opportunities for others.

In *Illustration Research Methods*, Fauchon and Gannon list several principles of illustration practice, including qualities such as communicativeness, responsiveness and empathy (2021: 16). Imbued with these characteristics, I believe illustrators are particularly well suited to construct responsive climbing frames that offer guidance, support and vision. These structures are not necessarily ready-built at the start of a project, but they can emerge or be modified during the project in response to participants' contributions.

I previously worked on a project with a writing group of older feminists in East London, called Hackney HOWLers, which provides a good example of this. The format of the anticipated outcome – a booklet – was set by the organization that funded and initiated the project. I was recruited by the funders as an 'artist' who would guide the group of fourteen women to create visuals that would sit alongside their writing and help them produce the booklet itself. After attending a few meetings of the writing group as a (mostly silent) listener,

[3] Delightfully, this analysis holds true for actual climbing frames on playgrounds too. Psychologists Withagen and Caljouw, who study movement and interaction on playgrounds, describe how swings and slides dictate children's movements, while the open climbing structures by radical playground designer Aldo von Eyck offer many more creative possibilities for play (2017).

FIGURE 2.1 Front and back cover of *Write Women into History* (2021). Cover artwork by Ayesha Khawla Usmani, BJ, Carol Smith, Catriona Courtier, Celia Burgess-Macey, Gail Chester, Gilli Salvat, Helen Bishop, JS, J. Copperman, Jennie Lazenby, Stephanie Henthorne, Sue O'Sullivan, Wendy Knight / assembled by Luise Vormittag.

I proposed that we produce illustrated cover artwork for the publication. It was I who set the theme of the illustration (protest march) and the method by which this would be produced (participants were to draw each other's portraits and design slogans for placards, and I would do the rest). None of these decisions were negotiated, but they were not arbitrary either. I made these propositions after spending considerable time listening to the group's conversations, gaging their interests, skills and predispositions. Within my proposal, there was plenty of room for the participants to contribute something of their own, and to surprise themselves and each other with their contributions. If we had adopted a more democratic decision-making process, there would have been no illustrated book cover at all. Many adults are extremely fearful of the drawing process, so it is likely the women would not have agreed to contribute to an illustration if this had been presented as a topic for debate. In fact, one woman told me later that 'if [she]'d known that she would have to do art, [she] would have never joined the group' (2022). Some of the other group members also told me quite emphatically that they 'can't draw'. But the way the project was designed (I discuss this in greater detail in the next chapter) enabled them to co-illustrate a cover, which they ended up being extremely proud of. Indeed, when I presented the finished cover artwork, the group was delighted at how it had all come together, and the women were pleased to recognize their individual contributions within the overall design.

It is no coincidence that the formal device I used to unify all the cover artwork contributions was a graphic framework. The grid design gives each character a place to be and then binds them all together successfully. In fact, I initially attempted to design a more amorphous crowd shape, but this proved visually incoherent and made the differences in how each figure was rendered jarringly apparent. But with the support of the grid structure, the diversity of the visual material emerged as a strength, rather than an obstacle to a coherent image: the grid is a powerful tool for bringing multiple contributions together, while also respecting their individual flair and style.

Mann also used this device in *Bordando Tierra del Fuego*: she cut the map into squares (with a small number of bigger, differently shaped sections for distinct territories like Antarctica), members of the group embroidered the individual

FIGURE 2.2 Sidney Mann and 'las chicas del mapa', *Bordando Tierra del Fuego* (2017–2024), detail.

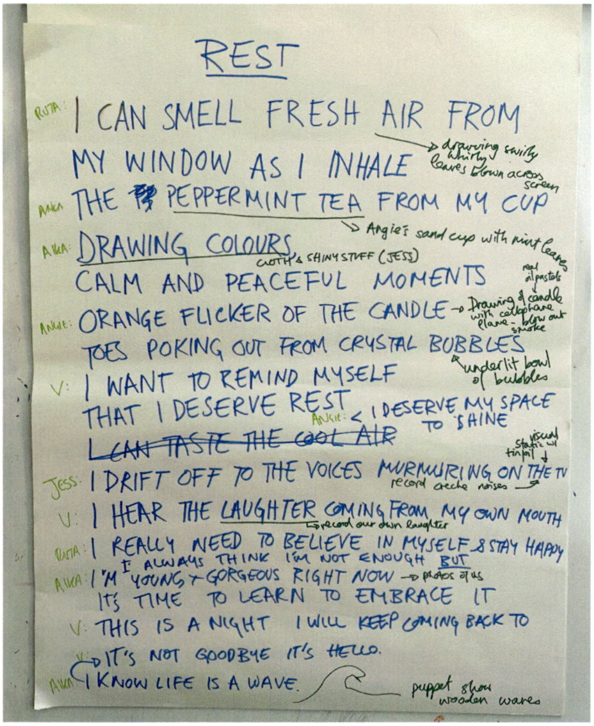

FIGURE 2.3 Working on the poem for the animation *Rest* (2023) with Billy Ash Sakula, Cecilia Knapp and young parents supported by All Change (Inspire! and Mums the Word). Commissioned by the Quentin Blake Centre for Illustration.

pieces and then she assembled them. Similarly, Miller's dialectograms are also underpinned by a graphic framework in the form of the empty architectural floorplan, which is gradually filled (again, by Miller himself) with a rich array of participants' stories.

Nonetheless, a supportive framework for a participatory illustration project does not necessarily have to come in the form of an actual grid design. Illustrator and animator Billy Ash Sakula, for example, employed a different method when working with a group of young mothers on an animated film called *Rest* (2023). In an impressive move, Ash Sakula, in collaboration with poet Cecilia Knapp, guided the group members to create their own structuring device for the film in the form of a spoken word poem. To do this, Knapp asked group members to complete the sentence 'When I rest I feel … '. The responses were then amalgamated into one collective poem, which in turn became the basis (or framework) for the animated film. Each participant was given a sentence to work with (not necessarily the one they had written and spoken themselves) and asked to produce a short, animated

FIGURE 2.4 Working on the animation *Rest* (2023) with Billy Ash Sakula, Cecilia Knapp and young parents supported by All Change (Inspire! and Mums the Word). Commissioned by the Quentin Blake Centre for Illustration.

FIGURE 2.5 Stills from the animation *Rest* (2023) created by young parents supported by All Change (Inspire! and Mums the Word) with Billy Ash Sakula and Cecilia Knapp. Commissioned by the Quentin Blake Centre for Illustration.

sequence to accompany the words. Ash Sakula then assembled all the different elements into a short film.

Another example of a supportive framework that does not mirror a literal grid can be seen in my project *Cracks in the Pavement* (2021). Here, multiple frames and protocols provided a structure for project participants: they walked within the confines of the map they were given, and their subsequent visual contributions were framed within the existing graphic elements of the pack and the website. Perhaps more importantly, the project protocol, which contributed significantly to the way the work acquired its meaning, was designed by me. The 'rules' of the project enabled multiple participants to 'walk together across intervals of time' (as stated by the accompanying explanation), giving each participant a window of time during which they were invited to go on the walk and annotate the shared map. Thus, the unit of time that each participant had to complete their contribution could also be seen as a form of gridded structure, since it was marked by delivery and collection arrangements and embedded in an overall logic of social relay and accumulation.

Synthesis of divergent needs

In addition to the questions around authorship discussed above, Bishop draws out another point regarding the *evaluation* of much participatory art in her critique: she argues that the ameliorative and therapeutic inclination that is often at the heart of this kind of work can result in simplistic, consensual collaboration – which comes at the cost of other artistic values that have been central to Western art practice throughout the twentieth and twenty-first centuries: disruption, uncomfortable exposure of inconvenient realities, artistic finesse or contextual and affective complexity. Bishop highlights how both artists and critics often emphasize ethical criteria and social usefulness in their analyses, rather than focusing on aesthetic qualities, which are sweepingly equated with cultural hierarchy (2012: 190).

One of Bishop's related arguments revolves around the unquestioned presumption in much of this work that the participating community group will benefit from the exchange. The exact nature of this payoff, however, is rarely articulated. Often, it is assumed that community members will be sufficiently rewarded by the act of participation itself – perhaps, as fellow art historian Kwon wryly suggests, by seeing themselves affirmatively represented in the work or 'by experiencing the joys of supposedly unalienated artistic labour' (Kwon 2002: 95–7). These concerns were previously stated even more forcefully by Foster in his influential essay 'The Artist as Ethnographer' (Foster 1996). He decries how collaborating communities can unwittingly be cast as 'anthropological exhibits' in an act of sociological condescension. The resulting work, which purports to be a collaboration, morphs into an artist's self-presentation, where the artist, resplendent with 'fresh' cultural imports from an exoticized other, turns out to be the only beneficiary of the partnership (1996: 196–8).[4] Foster's scenario may sound extreme, but the reward for the participating community is clearly a key ethical consideration in this type of work.

Taking up the baton for illustrators, I would argue that ameliorative inclinations (and working towards a range of quite different evaluative criteria) are not as alien to us as they might be to cultural critics steeped in the avant-garde's *raison d'être* – perpetual disruption and provocation. Indeed, as previously discussed, illustrators are accustomed to serving others and catering to extrinsic needs through their work, while *simultaneously* maintaining an artistic vision of their own. While I agree that some projects which lean heavily on affirmative and therapeutic gestures *can* end up lacking vitality and vim, the illustrators I discuss here demonstrate that accommodating non-professional participants and working with them in a

FIGURE 2.6 Meghiben Rupa Meriya (Kala Raksha Trust) *Map of the Village* (2006). One of the embroidered textile panels that was used by Nina Sabnani as a basis for the animation *Tanko bole chhe/The Stitches Speak* (2009).

[4] This conundrum in artistic practice was accurately foreshadowed by the influential political theorist Carole Pateman, who points out that not all systems of participatory democracy necessarily benefit the participating individual (1970): in some models, participation acts as a palliative to ensure the preservation of the overall system, at the cost of developmental opportunities for a significant part of the population.

way that takes their needs, interests and abilities into account does not necessarily result in unambitious project plans or in formally underwhelming outputs – quite the opposite! Bishop laments that ethical evaluative criteria are held in higher regard than aesthetic ones, but this seems to be more of a problem for the critic, whose task is to evaluate, than for the illustrator, who is used to incorporating a whole variety of criteria into their work. Illustrators are accustomed to evaluating a project both in terms of effectiveness ('How well does this piece of work achieve its stated aims?') and aesthetics ('How elegantly does it do this?').

It is precisely this ability to integrate the needs of others into our own creative practice that puts us illustrators in a strong position to address this particular point from Bishop. After all, illustrators, many of whom are trained to respond to commercial commissions, work well when combining a client's needs with their own creative vision and flair. We are generally adept at responding to briefs, and thus particularly well placed to design projects that are focused on the needs of a community group, while also maintaining our own artistic direction.

The collaboration between Indian illustrator-animator Nina Sabnani and the Kala Raksha Trust in Kutch, western India, serves as a good example of this. The Kala Raksha Trust is an organization dedicated to the preservation and celebration of traditional textile arts in the region. When they approached Sabnani about transforming some large-scale, narrative textile panels into an animation, Sabnani was initially unsure about the necessity of doing so. After all, the textile pieces already existed and contained the story the trust wanted to tell. But after some consideration, she realized that she would be able to amplify the reach and impact of the pieces by working on a film, together with the artists and makers at the trust. Sabnani subsequently spent time at Kala Raksha, recording innumerable conversations, scanning the textile panels, coming to a nuanced understanding of the trust's work and more generally learning about people's lives and experiences. She then worked in her studio to assemble and animate the material, alongside travelling to Kutch several times for review and discussion sessions. The resulting eight-minute film, *Tanko bole chhe*/*The Stitches Speak* (2009), takes the form of an animated documentary and was screened to critical acclaim at film festivals around the world.

Multiple different needs and ambitions were successfully brought together in Sabnani's project. The Kala Raksha Trust's objective to increase the reach and impact of their work was certainly met, and simultaneously the film's two main protagonists, the elderly textile artists Megiben Rupa Meriya and Raniben Ratilal Bhanani, were offered an arena to reflect on and record their personal histories of struggle, advancement and success: they speak about displacement and migration, developing as craftspeople and artists, and overcoming some caste-related restrictions in their new environments. As a result of this film, Meriya and Bhanani received greater recognition, a rise in status and a surge in commissions. At the same time, Sabnani herself was also able to use the film-making process to progress

FIGURE 2.7 Stills from the animation *Tanko bole chhe/The Stitches Speak*, Nina Sabnani (2009).

her skills in animating cloth (a creative process she had started developing in a previous piece) and more generally extend her participatory animation method as a form of ethnographic practice.

Similar to Sabnani, I also tend to design projects through a process of negotiation, during which I discuss with the relevant organization how their aims might intersect with my own ambitions and abilities. For example, when I first met with the charity Latin Elephant to discuss a potential collaboration – which eventually became *Walking the Elephant* (2021) – I specifically asked them what kind of output would be of value to them and what were their concerns at this moment in time. In response, they explained they wanted to produce something that could highlight the importance of small businesses in the local community, which would be helpful for their campaign against the sale of the shopping centre where many of them were located. The project then developed from the overlap between their and my aims, rather than being determined by one side, as for example would more likely be the case in a traditional client commission, or the other, as for example an artist who surprises an unsuspecting community with their ready-made idea.[5]

As such, Bishop's points of critique can be effectively addressed by drawing on qualities typically associated with illustration. A personalized creative illustration

[5] A good example of this latter case is Swiss artist Thomas Hirschhorn's monument series: *Spinoza Monument* (1999), *Deleuze Monument* (2000), *Bataille Monument* (2002) and *Gramsci Monument* (2013), where he staged festivals celebrating these three philosophers in socio-economically deprived urban areas.

practice can integrate an empathetic appreciation of others' needs and concerns. An 'ameliorative inclination' does not have to lead to lacklustre results.

Communicative outputs as shared goal

The final point from Bishop that I would like to mention here is how the demands of participation and subsequent spectatorship often appear to be mutually exclusive. Bishop describes how the experience of the participating group in many art projects tends to be valued above the formal resolution of a project and its exhibition or presentation to a secondary audience. As a particularly resonant example, she describes the experience of spectators of the Chicago-based exhibition 'Culture in Action' (1991), which encompassed eight geographically and socially situated projects in different parts of the city. Viewers had to either negotiate their own journeys to disparate neighbourhoods or join a weekly bus tour, only to find themselves stuck in traffic, straining to spot the work or awkwardly trying to engage with artwork that mainly consisted of a set of finely tuned social relationships (Bishop 2012: 203–5). The accompanying catalogue, which could have presented an opportunity to synthesize the disparate elements of the show, also failed to create a more resolved viewing experience, with underwhelming photographs embedded in a bewildering layout alongside other confusing editorial decisions (2012: 206).

However, once again, I would like to sketch out how illustration can operate differently in this kind of scenario. Writing specifically about catering to secondary audiences, illustration scholar Stephanie Black suggests that illustrators, who generally are much more focused on communicating with a public, are more likely to take audience needs into consideration in their work and present a carefully crafted output that generously opens itself up to the viewer. This is the case even if the piece's primary function is to document a prior event (2012: 56–7).

I would like to take this idea one step further. In participatory *design*, where practitioners are often working with future users to generate a service, tool or environment, the participatory phase is generally understood as an important research and development stage. By contrast, for many participatory *art* projects the interaction with others constitutes the piece itself. Building on this, I believe that, in the case of illustration projects, engagement with others can take on a hybrid status, where the encounters are neither purely pragmatic, in that they purely aim to generate knowledge or insights for a predetermined future design goal, nor framed as the 'work itself'. Indeed, the goal of many participatory illustration projects is to orientate all parties towards a formally resolved output that articulates the group's shared concerns and also bridges the schism between the needs of the participating group and that of subsequent audiences. In fact, these moves build on each other: the group members' primary task is to produce a collective output that will effectively communicate their concerns to other audiences – but attending to this task also helps bind them as a group. Miller presents this very argument in his PhD thesis: he asserts that the production of a formally resolved output can be an important focus of the participatory process itself, rather than simply a secondary documentation of it (2015: Booklet 4, 4–5).

Billy Ash Sakula adds another interesting facet to this idea. When reflecting on working with a community group on a project that required no specific result, Ash Sakula commented: 'We were told [by the commissioners] that this phase doesn't need an outcome. But having such an open-ended brief has made me feel that no-one really cares what we do. Generally, people want to make something specific because it gives you direction' (2023).

Overall, I believe that working towards a collective output, for example the completion of one of Miller's dialectograms or the production of the finished map in *Bordando Tierra del Fuego*, can serve as a focal point that galvanizes action. With the supportive framework of a well-designed project structure, project participants can generate a formally resolved output that benefits the community in question as well as communicating with secondary audiences. Miller's dialectograms tend to be exhibited close to where they were made. Mann's finished map toured museums across Argentina and offered an occasion for celebration for the group.

My own projects also generally culminate with an output that both documents and communicates the work that has been accomplished together. In *Write Women into History*, the prospect of achieving a formally resolved, printed output gave the final group meetings a strong focus and sense of forward momentum. Then, once the booklet had been printed, it functioned both as an item to give back to the participating community (every member of the writing group received a free copy) and also as a communicative device for secondary audiences. In the case of *Cracks in the Pavement*, I sent each participant a thank-you pack of materials once the project was complete and was also able to insert the five original maps into the local city council's archive, alongside explanatory texts that furnish future secondary audiences with the necessary context to view the work. So, in summary, giving a dematerialized social encounter a formal resolution is not only possible but can lead to extremely satisfying results.

These three ideas – the construction of supportive climbing frames, the synthesis of others' divergent needs with personal creative vision and the establishment of communicative outputs as a shared goal – are principles which have guided my own work, and which I have also seen in many other similar projects. The first principle – the construction of supportive climbing frames – is not particular to illustration practice. Indeed, it is a metaphor that is more generally applicable to pedagogical practice, and my adoption of it grows partly out of my years of experience designing workshops and curricula. However, the other two principles are more closely related to illustration as a discipline. Fauchon and Gannon notably

FIGURE 2.8 Gail Chester and Barbara Susman from the Hackney HOWLers Writing Group selling copies of *Write Women into History* at an event at Stoke Newington Library, London (2024).

FIGURE 2.9 Luise Vormittag, *Cracks in the Pavement* (2020–2021), contents of thank you packs. The A4-size leaflet contains a description of and reflections on the project, alongside a full colour insert with small reproductions of all the maps in the series. Each participant also received an A1 full-colour print of the map they contributed to.

describe how illustrators tend to produce work that 'actively seeks to engage and be understood', use 'methods [that] are responsive and adaptable, [...] tailored to the task at hand, the environment, people and situations the illustrator is engaged with' and also work empathetically, 'engaging through emotion', in the realization of our projects (2021: 16). As illustrators, we are used to integrating many different demands into our work, all while maintaining our creative outlook and direction. But before this little summary solidifies into a definitive checklist, let us briefly pause and consider a cautionary tale.

Lest my methods fossilize: Staying with the particular

While it is helpful to reflect on and highlight some operational principles that might be useful for others to consider, as I do in the preceding paragraphs, I want to quickly intervene before this guidance fossilizes into an overall method or toolbox. It is certainly tempting to slide into a pedagogical mode, eagerly sharing guidelines and growing increasingly convinced of their validity. But this lurch towards a certain kind of universalism has always made me uncomfortable – and there are reasons to be cautious. In participatory art, problems tend to arise from artists struggling to consolidate a variety of seemingly opposing demands – social usefulness *and* aesthetic value; clear communication *and* nuanced complexity; creatively orchestrated encounters for the participating group *and* coherent experiences for subsequent audiences – but participatory design suffered from another kind of affliction: it became formulaic.

One of participatory design's issues centres on questions of exactly *how* to involve future users in the design process. They might well have a detailed understanding of which tools, services or environments might best resonate with their needs and desires, but they generally do not have any design expertise. The design community has tried to address this by demystifying the design process, making it more open and transparent and therefore more accessible to non-designers. For example, design researcher and academic Nigel Cross has written extensively on clarifying cognitive approaches and modes of behaviour particular to design. Over time, this evolved into an articulation of broader and more generalized processes, such as 'design thinking' and 'human-centred design'. Today, the global design and innovation firm IDEO, founded in the early 1990s in California, is one of the most prominent examples of a company working in this tradition, driven by the progressive impulse towards greater social inclusion, and the involvement of otherwise marginalized voices in the design process.

While IDEO undoubtedly manages many successful projects, there are some obvious limitations. In a video explaining their approach (see Design Kit, www.

designkit.org), IDEO proposes that innovative solutions to complex problems can easily be achieved by following a few simple steps. The clip in question is accompanied by cheerily upbeat music – a strumming acoustic guitar accompanied by a whistled tune – which ostensibly aims to conjure a breezy atmosphere of effortless competence. IDEO's publications, including the *HCD Toolkit* (2009) (HCD stands for 'human-centred design') and *The Field Guide to Human Centred Design* (2015), embody a similar universalist design approach. While I recognize that these structures can support the inclusion of people into a process that otherwise might appear nebulous and intimidating, I fear that, in some cases, the universalist solutionism embedded in these guides threatens to paper over the specificities and nuances of highly complex situations.

Design academic Lucy Kimbell discusses the limitations of these formulaic toolkit approaches in her carefully researched and meticulously argued articles, 'Rethinking Design Thinking: Part 1 and 2' (2011, 2012). She highlights the rich diversity of practices, cognitive styles and cultures that fall under the all-embracing term 'design' and questions whether any generalized pronouncements about a shared knowledge practice are actually plausible. She suggests that, rather than succumbing to the universalism inherent in this approach, it might be prudent to focus on design as a 'situated, embodied material practice' (2011: 300). She also points out how designers working with the methods promoted by IDEO can slip into interpreting future users' input in the design process using ethnographically inspired techniques, but without demonstrating any of the self-reflexivity that is now routine in that discipline.[6] In contrast to ethnographers, she argues, human-centred designers are not trained to question the political, social or cultural biases they bring to a project. I will take up this line of thought again in Chapter 4.

During an early phase of my research, someone suggested that I could produce a toolkit for illustrators working with community. While this might be a laudable ambition, I decided that this was not the kind of work I was interested in pursuing. Instead, I decided to use illustration practice – my own and that of others – as a site to reconsider, record and reflect on the nature of community itself. I reiterate, then, that this book is not a set of 'how to' instructions for illustrators hoping to work in participatory ways with community. Instead, I wish to transpose Kimbell's idea of design as a 'situated, embodied material practice' (2011: 300) to illustration. I am interested in participatory illustration projects not as a formulaic sequence of actions and tasks, but as a responsive practice that emerges in relation to the environments and situations it emerges in. This positions illustration practice as a form of listening, an empirical encounter with the world, where something might be observed or discovered. To be sure, this form of this listening is different to what you might find in other, more traditionally empirical practices, or at least

[6] Art critic Hal Foster makes a similar point regarding artists working in the ethnographic tradition without observing any of the accompanying ethical principles (Foster 1996: 196–7).

it has been for me: rather than trying to observe things with as little involvement as possible, I have actively intervened in and, taking matters one step further, even orchestrated situations. According to this model, illustrators do not seek to be invisible, instead acting as influencers (in the traditional sense of the word) and using their practices to bring about novel scenarios. I see illustration practice as a way of drawing people into new social constellations while simultaneously recording and then presenting the worlds they collectively engender in this process.

It is also worth highlighting that none of the projects I discuss are easily generalizable in terms of the methods they enact, or the steps they involve. Each of the projects named here would have produced fundamentally different results if a different illustrator had conceived of them and carried them out.

This was thrown into particularly sharp relief by the events that followed my interactions with the Hackney HOWLers writing group: after the completion of our publication, the group members decided to run a one-day training workshop for other women who were interested in setting up a writing group of their own, with the aim of replicating what had been achieved through our project. I was invited to talk about the collaborative creation of the cover artwork, as well as the overall design and production process.

But it quickly became clear that there was a fundamental contradiction in what I was being asked to do. Our project had been successful precisely because it had not followed a predetermined, replicable schema – and the publication that resulted from my engagement with the women in the group was an outcome that grew out of the confluence of a specific set of circumstances and people. As such, there was no formula I could share. This is not to say that I or the women in the writing group had extraordinary or outstanding talents that placed us above other women who were keen to start a similar project. While we are not special, we are specific and situated. The particular set of skills that I brought to this project – empathetic listening, workshop design, illustration skills, some (rusty!) knowledge of graphic design, a general tendency to be relatively organized and the capacity to ride a bike (cycling around the neighbourhood became crucial for collecting and distributing materials to group members, as the project unfolded during the COVID-19 pandemic) – interacted with other resources, such as my large collection of Letraset dry-transfer lettering and my ability to work for minimal pay on this occasion. Additionally, the fact of the pandemic itself meant that members of the group brought a particular kind of attention to the project, as there were fewer other things to do. In turn, the platform we used for meetings (Zoom) enabled focused breakout rooms that supported the portrait-drawing task for the cover design. All of this was specific to us as a particular collection of people at a particular moment in time and in a particular place.

In the end, my presentation for the one-day event took the form of a narrative account of what we did, with a few generalized suggestions about arts facilitation – but I felt awkward delivering this to an audience of women, who were expecting to learn how to do it for themselves. If I had been given more time, I could potentially have shared the principles I have elaborated in this section, including how an illustrator-facilitator can provide metaphorical climbing frames, can synthesize divergent needs while maintaining an overall creative vision, and can establish the creation of a communicative output as a shared goal. However, beyond these principles, this kind of work remains improvisatory, responsive and emergent.

Thus, despite the principles I have drawn out in this chapter, many questions remain about how participatory illustration projects play themselves out. In the next chapter, I turn to questions of skill and expertise.

3 'BUT I CAN'T DRAW!'

Thanks to the previous chapter, we have some principles for participatory illustration projects in place. But the question of *how* exactly to incorporate participants' contributions remains thorny. While they may bring vital knowledge and experience, often in the form of insights about the issue or concern at hand, many project participants do not bring design or illustration expertise. This creates challenges as to *how* to visually encode and materialize their contributions. What processes can illustrators draw on to record their insights, thoughts and observations?

Participants in the projects I have undertaken and studied while working on this book have been involved in a number of different creative activities in the projects, including but not limited to sewing, animating, sculpting and writing. However, the core activity I will discuss in this section is the act of drawing or – to phrase this more broadly – creating a range of marks and inscriptions on paper. This seemingly simple task often prompts an anxious response. As previously mentioned, when I was first introduced as an 'arts facilitator', one of the women in the Hackney HOWLers group told me quite emphatically that she (and many of the other women) could *not* draw. Similarly, in the case of *Cracks in the Pavement*, I noticed that, during our conversations prior to dropping off the packs, most walkers expressed excitement about the prospect of observing and noticing things on their walks, but they then voiced concerns about their ability to capture these observations on the map. Observing is clearly distinct from recording.

Many of the practitioners I spoke to about participatory illustration projects shared similar experiences. Grace Holliday and Alaa Alsaraji, both London-based illustrators and community arts facilitators, were particularly vocal on this topic. Holliday, for example, spoke about the intimidation of the white page, about how nervous it makes people feel (Holliday 2023). Alsaraji made the interesting point that illustration's close association with drawing and draughtsmanship[1] can put

[1] Even though 'drawing' and 'illustration' are sometimes used interchangeably, the two terms are distinct. Jaleen Grove has called illustration 'designed images' (Grove 2011: 288) – a pithy description that clarifies its difference from the exploratory and processual nature of drawing. However, drawing is often used as part of the process of producing an illustration, and conversely illustration can also be used in an exploratory manner.

people off getting involved, especially when compared to some other art forms: 'There is a huge barrier [to getting started with illustration] compared to, for example, photography, because a phone camera feels so accessible. It is much easier to make people believe that they can do [photography]. With illustration, you have to accept that it will take a while longer for some people' (Alsaraji 2023).

This anxiety, occasionally cloaked in defensiveness, presumably stems from a perceived lack of skill and the shame attached to this sense of deficiency. Anthropologist Tim Ingold reflects on how Western education tends to disregard drawing at an early stage and notes how 'those who have been educated into its values are happy to admit [...] that they "can't draw"' (2011: 177).

This defensive rejection of drawing is exacerbated by a misconception of its nature and purpose. Ingold describes how many people erroneously assume that when we draw, the mind projects an already finalized image onto the paper, which is then traced by the draughtsperson. In this fantasy, the image slides like a transfer from mind to page (2011). Practitioners know this not to be the case. Ingold proposes that 'drawing has little or nothing to do with the projection of images and everything to do with *wayfaring* – with breaking a path through a terrain and leaving a trace, at once in the imagination and the ground, in a manner very similar to what happens as one walks along in a world of earth and sky' (2011: 178, emphasis in original). Similarly, John Berger in *Berger on Drawing* (2007) emphasizes the exploratory and emergent nature of drawing. In his essay on life drawing, he writes that ' ... drawing is discovery [...] a line, an area of tone, is not really important because it records what you have seen, but because of what it will lead you on to see' (2007: 3).

However resonant these reflections on drawing's exploratory and emergent characteristics may be, it is doubtful whether they would reassure an anxious group or individual, quivering at the thought of having to pick up a pen. Discovery and exploration are predicated on an acceptance of uncertainty and potential failure. As such, giving oneself over to these processes requires a certain measure of confidence, as well as trust in the value of open-ended practice, neither of which can be conferred upon someone in a limited time frame. So, rather than pontificating on the exploratory nature of drawing, which in all likelihood would have an alienating effect on participants, I generally try to devise activities and prompts that assuage anxieties; these can be thought of as the metaphorical rungs, bars and steps of the climbing frame I described in the previous chapter. If these are well calibrated, I find that they can balance reassurance with the right amount of exploratory openness.

For example, my project *Cracks in the Pavement* contained two distinct prompts for participants. Firstly, I encouraged walkers to draw a line on the map that indicated their route (although not all of them followed this instruction).[2] While many people are intimidated by the idea of drawing per se, drawing a route seems far less daunting. Echoing Ingold's association of drawing with wayfaring, but limiting its vertiginous openness, this prompt simply asked participants to map their course on the shared piece of paper. A route is 'just' a line on a map after all – and it is almost impossible to draw a route 'badly'. Yet, despite its simplicity, this opened up a rich vein of reflection: walking bodies drew lines through space as they moved around the neighbourhood. Subsequently, the hand mirrored the path of the body on the terrain with a pen on the shared document – a transposition that required a change in scale but was a manageable task for most participants. For those who still felt reluctant to hold a pen, I offered coloured tape as an alternative way to mark their movements.

The map is a commonly used genre of visual representation and its familiarity is reassuring for participants.[3] It makes no difference that even a rudimentary engagement with ideas in contemporary geography or critical cartography quickly reveals maps as much less reliable and trustworthy objects than they are generally assumed to be.[4] And as my research is not particularly concerned with cartography and mapping, I have resorted to this graphic format in participatory projects as a stabilizing device. Beyond their perceived stability, maps also offer the possibility of producing one of the most easily achievable drawings there is – the route. My pencil outlines of familiar streets and buildings made it simple for participants to know how to position their pen on the shared document and chart their movements around the neighbourhood and each other.

The second task for participants in *Cracks in the Pavement* was to 'annotate their thoughts, ideas and observations' stemming from the walk – a prompt that allowed for plenty of freedom and variation. By using the word 'annotate' I wanted to encourage any kind of mark-making – be that drawing lines, writing notes by hand or affixing items such as stickers or cut-out pieces of paper. It was a word I chose to encompass the broadest possible range of gestures that could lead to the material surface of the map being worked on and altered. Alongside this second prompt, I offered a plethora of examples and suggestions of what people might do.

[2] The first walkers on each route received a lightly sketched map as a base layer for their contributions to the project. Subsequent walkers added to the annotations prior walkers had marked up on this layer. Since the instructions invited them to follow in the footsteps of those who had gone before them, they often walked the same route, but some walkers nevertheless added their own route lines to the paper – either because they wanted to, or because they slightly deviated from the route that had been set out by the previous participant(s).

[3] In my project *Write Women into History*, I made use of another familiar genre of visual representation, namely the portrait. Of course, portraits are more difficult to render than routes on a map. But when I split the group into pairs and asked them to draw each other's portraits, the use of this visual convention meant that there was at least a clear understanding of the task at hand. I mitigated against censorious self-doubt by suggesting a few restrictions, such as 'Draw with your non-dominant hand!'

[4] See, for example, Harley (1989) on the map as a manifestation of power, or else Kitchin and Dodge (2007) on the transitory and fleeting nature of maps.

Still, despite the relative straightforwardness of these prompts, questions abounded in their actual implementation. These included: Do I take the map with me on the walk and draw while I am out? The map is large (A1 size), and the weather is bad, so I am concerned about damaging it. If I were to take it, what surfaces would I work on? I might not be comfortable getting down to pavement level. Will I remember the correct route if I don't take the map? If I decide to draw at home, do I even have a table big enough? How will I remember what I've seen? How do I attach things to the map that I've collected, seen or thought about?

I did not give any guidance on these practical issues. Despite the potentially destabilizing openness of this second task, participants were already too involved in the project at this stage to allow worries about drawing to prevent their participation. They were also able to respond to these prompts in private and in their own time, rather than in a pressurized setting. As it turned out, almost every walker used a different set of methods to complete to this task. Some drew directly on the map while they were still on the walk, some drew on separate pieces of paper or sketchbooks and attached these to the map later, some simply took notes and photos while on the walk and then worked on the map at home. Others wrote on the map, inscribing their thoughts by hand, or added markers with stickers, introducing various numbered systems, codes and legends. Others sent me digital material – such as photos, audio notes and typed-up thoughts – and asked me to

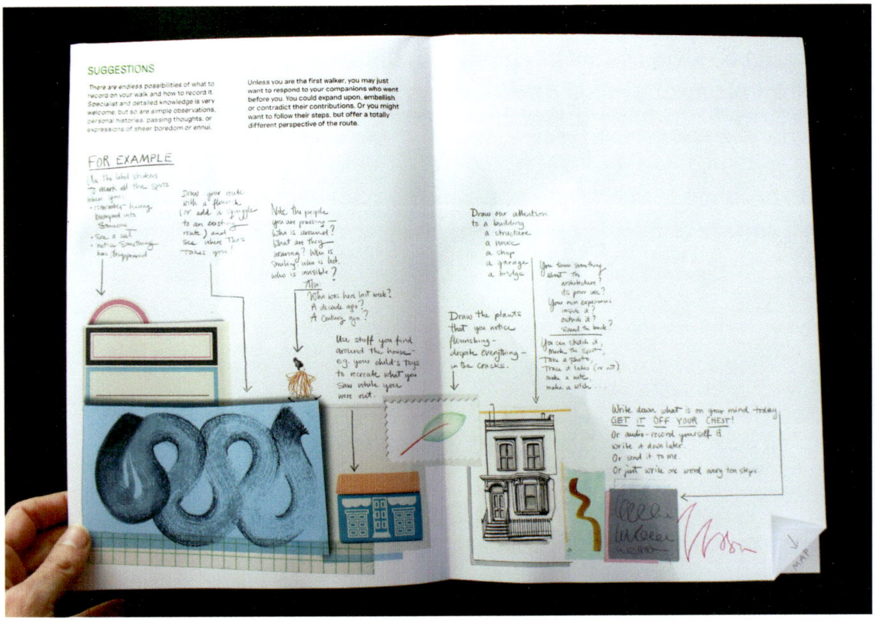

FIGURE 3.1 Luise Vormittag, *Cracks in the Pavement* (2020–2021), some suggestions to help participants select a focus for their walk and methods for recording it.

add them to the map: I had offered this option to participants who did not want to or were unable to add to the map themselves (one walker, for example, had very poor eyesight). In the cases where I was asked to act as a scribe, each walker had their own system of relaying the information to me, both in terms of the format in which it was sent and their instructions regarding its placement on the map. Thus, the resulting inscriptions, marks and drawings of this project can be thought of as an undulating flow of visual and textual languages, signs and symbols, overlapping and colliding with each other.

An alternative approach with more rigorous instructions and predetermined graphic systems would clearly have led to a distinct result. For example, the well-known US-American urban planner Kevin Lynch chose a radically different method in his attempt to make spatial perception visible. In *The Image of the City* (1960), Lynch introduces the notion of a spatially grounded mental image that individual residents use to orient themselves in urban environments. In an effort to extract this mental image from people's heads, he conducted interviews with residents which were transcribed and then encoded in simplified graphics. The process of translating residents' spatial perceptions was achieved through an act of radical reductionism and streamlining: interviewees' accounts were parsed into five predetermined categories and their corresponding graphic representations

FIGURE 3.2 Luise Vormittag, *Cracks in the Pavement* (2020–2021). A participant records their architectural knowledge on Map 3: Arnold Circus to Cat & Mutton Bridge.

(paths, edges, districts, nodes and landmarks). Lynch's method is reminiscent of a positivist social science approach, drawing on surveys and statistical data – and it is particularly useful for producing generalizable knowledge based on a larger unit of population.[5]

By contrast, my methods do not aim at generalizations. Where Lynch translated perceptual complexity into a small number of simple graphic categories, *Cracks in the Pavement* left the actual process of translation wide open – I instructed participants to 'Draw, scribble, write, stick, collage in whichever way suits you.' I was not trying to extract knowledge about a whole population, but about particular, individual, situated experiences at a specific moment in time. By leaving open this complex process of translating spatial perception into illustrative and graphic languages and by rejecting streamlined categories and universalizing simplifications, I encouraged a different kind of sense to emerge on these maps. The routes drawn on the maps demonstrate quite literally where passages intersect, converge or run in tandem. The entangled lines and overlapping observations and annotations speak directly of our involvement with each other and of our capacity to create a shared world. Indeed, in this project, the participants' acts of drawing became spatialized, material inscriptions that put segments of their own biography, however briefly, in direct physical relation to others.

The other practitioners I spoke to generally shared my inclination towards messy specificity. Community illustrators tend to see themselves in the role of educator-facilitators, eager to encourage individual expressivity. Our projects typically revolve around activities that are aimed at fostering creativity, compared to participatory design projects that often place a greater emphasis on acquiring and capturing specific pieces of information or data, which can then be synthesized with comparative ease.[6] Naturally, a profusion of idiosyncratic, individualized contributions make subsequent processes of assembly more challenging, as I will discuss in the next chapter – but the tapestry they create is all the richer.

Like me, other practitioners draw on carefully calibrated prompts to cajole participants into picking up a pen. Alsaraji, for example, has an exercise where she asks people to draw for five minutes without lifting the pen off the paper. 'It

[5] It is interesting to note that, even though his method is designed for arriving at generalizations derived from scale, Lynch interviewed a surprisingly small number of participants to generate his graphics (see Lynch 1960: 15).

[6] Participatory design is generally more geared towards using participants' input in the service of a bigger project or for a specific purpose. Peter A. Hall and Patricio Dávila discuss a number of such projects in their book *Critical Visualization* (2023). For example, design group Iconoclasistas worked with communities engaged in the informal economy around a Buenos Aires garbage dump on a participatory mapping project titled *La República de los cirujas*. This project's specific aim was to advocate for the improvement of the communities' working conditions (2023: 26–7). Similarly, London-based group Data4Change collaborates with local civil society organizations across the globe to collect data and 'crowdsource stories' from communities on a multitude of social issues to raise awareness and push for change (2023: 108–114).

feels to people like they are learning a technique, but it also makes all drawings look quite similar, so there is less of a pressure when comparing' (Alsaraji 2023). The principle here is to set an activity with constraints that restrict the drawing so as to render comparative judgements of individual drawings irrelevant. I implemented this principle when working with the Hackney HOWLers on their portraits to minimize the risk of immobilizing self-criticism, telling them: Draw with your non-dominant hand! Draw without looking at the paper (look only at your subject)! Draw within an unknown time frame (subject may say 'stop!' at any moment)!

Going further, some illustrators have told me about (benign!) methods of tricking participants into drawing. Holliday, for example, sometimes tells participants that a particular sheet of paper is merely intended for testing their materials – and participants are generally happily to trial their pens and brushes. Once they are in the flow of things, it is not a big step to expand the 'testing' to

FIGURE 3.3 Illustrator and facilitator Alaa Alsaraji often uses continuous line drawing in her illustration workshops, where participants are not allowed to lift their pen off the paper.

FIGURE 3.4 Grace Holliday testing materials (2023).

other types of drawing. Then, as a bonus, the so-called 'tester sheet' can make a reappearance later as a component of a collage illustration (Holliday 2023). Korean illustrator Yeni Kim has shown even more shrewdness in her attempts to get around participants' reluctance to draw. She recounts how she would initially cast herself in the role of the illustrator-scribe in interview situations with subjects who were describing cultural objects and practices. But during the course of the conversation, she would intentionally start to make mistakes in her drawings, which would then prompt her interlocutors to pick up a pen in an impulse to correct the otherwise faulty record (Kim 2022: 245).

All this tricking and coaxing does of course beg the question: What is the point of persuading people to take part in activities they emphatically claim not to enjoy? How do the processes of drawing and inscribing actually enrich these projects? Could similar outcomes not be obtained through other, ostensibly more straightforward means, such as sharing knowledge, observations and experiences simply by talking about them? Why force people to draw? What is achieved through the inscriptive work of hands on paper?

I have three points in response to this. Firstly – and this is something that was highlighted to me in discussions with other practitioners – working creatively by hand has the capacity to foster a convivial atmosphere and enhance a group's cohesiveness. For example, Sidney Mann, speaking about *Bordando Tierra del Fuego*, said:

> While we embroider, we talk. Many group members work in high-pressure jobs, and it's a relief for them to switch off their phones during our sessions. The act of embroidering, the involvement of the body and the rhythm of the work helps you talk more freely. We reflect on our relationship to the land, how we inhabit it and how we want to represent it.
>
> (Mann 2023)

Alsaraji made a similar point when she spoke about using clay in one of her community projects. She had prompted participants to make one clay model of how they saw their creativity now, and another model for how they would like it to be.

> While the group was modelling, they started talking. Because they were working with their hands at the same time, they were connecting in a whole different way. [...] People allowed themselves to be seen in a way that I've never been able to achieve [through other methods] with a group. It was amazing to get people to share something that's beyond the basic [social conventions].
>
> (Alsaraji 2023)

While these observations clearly highlight how creative work that is performed in supportive group environments can foster a sense of well-being and cohesion, I hesitate to overstate this aspect of participatory projects. I am mindful of the risk that illustrators who take on community projects may inadvertently assume therapeutic roles that they are generally not equipped to fulfil. Mitch Miller voices a similar concern about his dialectograms. Even though their creation is not predicated on participants drawing anything, Miller is nevertheless concerned that this type of practice may 'lapse into feel-good gestures, [...] becoming the soft edge of neoliberal social and economic policy' (Miller 2015: Booklet 5, 14).

Artist and animator Billy Ash Sakula articulated this point particularly forcefully, and it is worth quoting them at length on this matter:

> I feel uncomfortable about community illustration being used in the space of social services. [...] I think it's a dangerous idea, that art should stand in for [the welfare system]. It can make it seem that the government doesn't have to plug those gaps. Sometimes when I'm working on a project, I find myself thinking: I'm doing work here that actually needs a trained care worker. It's unfair on me because I end up having to fill the holes left by the government, but it's also unfair on the service users, who are essentially getting artists to help them with their very real problems, which art cannot fix. You can connect through art

> and express yourself, but it has its limits! It's *not* therapy, it's *not* the financial support [that some people need].

> It's paradoxical because a lot of my work [is commissioned because of] austerity. [...] I wonder whether, if we had a well-funded welfare state, there would be a lot less community illustration about? I know none of this is my fault, but I do feel like a scab in some ways [doing this work]. It can be an ethical dilemma – there are lots of interesting commissions, but they are [sometimes] coming from commissioners I don't necessarily want to be working for.
>
> (Ash Sakula 2023)

Ash Sakula makes it very clear how the role of the community illustrator can easily be exploited, especially when their work is viewed primarily as a tool for social or emotional healing. While the restorative effects of creative work can play a positive role in these kinds of projects, overemphasizing these aspects undoubtedly carries risks of reducing participatory illustration work to a therapeutic technique, to the detriment of its many other values.

The second point I want to make about the value of drawing in participatory settings takes us back to its processual nature. Berger and Ingold both highlight the fact that drawing does not simply mirror a pre-existing reality; rather, in the process of inscription, a new reality is realized. To put it another way, the inscriptive work of the participant's hand does not serve to represent things as they are already perceived and comprehended. Instead, inscription offers an opportunity to see things afresh, make new discoveries and gain a novel understanding of the world. It is this gradual journey – moving towards new knowledge through the act of drawing – that I wish participants to experience in these participatory projects. It may be that the total processual openness of 'drawing as discovery', as Berger describes it, is too unsettling for participants who lack confidence in their creative abilities; still, these types of supported activities allow for some aspects of that experience to emerge.

This brings me to my final point. In his reflections on drawing, Ingold gradually zeros in on the practitioner themselves. He proposes that '[a]s they make things, practitioners bind their own pathways and lines of becoming into the texture of the world' (Ingold 2011: 178). I found it intriguing to think of our 'lines of becoming' and how these might be bound or woven into the 'textures of the world' through the process of drawing. On the one hand, this could be understood in terms of a straightforward change of perspective: by drawing, the practitioner gains a new understanding that is expressed and revealed in the drawing. Hence the drawing is, among other things, a record of this personal transformation – their personal 'lines of becoming'.

However, this sentence can also be interpreted on a material and corporeal level. After all, acts of drawing and inscription are intimately connected to the body and our life stories: a drawn line is a trace of a gestural hand movement, and even tape or stickers that have been applied to a surface allude to the hand that placed them there. By creating a drawing, we have left a material trace of ourselves in the world. Comics scholar Hillary Chute expresses this idea, when she notes that handwriting carries 'a trace of autobiography in the mark of its maker' (2010: 10). Indeed, all of the projects discussed here contain traces of people's gestures, miniscule pieces of their biographies and evidence of their embodied engagement with the piece. Building on Chute, one might argue that the embodied moment of creation, as experienced by the participants in these projects, leads to a deeper connection with the work than a mere verbal contribution.

Thus, if it is not too bold to say so, overcoming people's aversions to drawing and creating opportunities for all participants to visually encode their insights, thoughts and observations is well worth the effort in participatory projects. The works I have discussed here testify to this: to take just one example, the abundance of diverse annotations, illustrated vignettes and interwoven lines on the maps of *Cracks in the Pavement* reflect the heterogeneity of our spatial perceptions knitted together by our intersecting paths. Is it not a quiet revelation to see these processes of collective inscription (or entwining?) momentarily placing parts of an individual's personal history in direct, physical connection with those of others?

Many of the themes I have introduced in this chapter will be picked up in later parts of the book: I take up the idea of collective world-making, hinted at here, in Chapter 5; the ways in which these collective acts of inscription enable us to encounter one another in expressions of community will receive ample attention in Chapter 6; and Chapter 7 will offer reflections on the materiality of inscriptions and their importance as traces of past encounters. However, for now, I will focus on the next urgent question at hand: Once everybody has been persuaded to contribute to a project, what do we do with all this wonderfully heterogeneous material that is scattered in front of us?

4 DRAWING THINGS TOGETHER

Just as the acts of observing and recording present distinct challenges, so do collating and presenting. In the previous chapter, I described how the prompt to manually inscribe or draw often induces anxiety in participants. The subsequent stage of the process – translating a rich jumble of criss-crossing lines or a stack of coloured papers that contain a variety of sketches, drawings and typographic designs into something visually more accessible – has at times induced anxious feelings in me. After all, while being creative in a communal setting can be delightful in and of itself, this is ideally the starting point in a chain of connections – and the onus is on the facilitator-illustrator to catalyse the next stage of the process. The aim is to somehow (somehow?!) consolidate individuals' illustrative accounts of themselves and their concerns into a coherent form that can be interpreted by other audiences and publics, while simultaneously respecting the heterogeneity (and sometimes incongruity) of the different inputs. Faced with this task, I have wondered: What exactly is my role in drawing together these scattered contributions? How might I do this without suffocating the rich vitality of this 'undulating flow of systems, overlapping and crashing into each other'? Wherein precisely lies my expertise as an illustrator and how can I harness it in the service of the project at hand? Thus, this chapter reflects on the tasks that community illustrators perform in gathering up, collating, arranging and, on occasion, altering participants' contributions.

In his essay on the nature of illustration expertise, illustrator David Blaiklock suggests that this can be defined as the fusion of technical skill with 'vision' – a term he describes as being somewhat elusive (but also fails to clearly define himself) (2019: 185–95). In any case, 'vision' does suggest an ability to pre-imagine, plan and realize images in order to achieve a particular effect – which is a skill distinct from the exploratory 'wayfaring' practice of drawing. This notion of 'vision' as a central quality of illustration expertise resonates with me. While Blaiklock's definition might not be a sufficiently rich concept for the kind of work I am considering in this book, it does illuminate an important point: it reminds us that illustration is not simply an unmediated, direct form of expression or communication that naturally flows from participants' contributions. People taking part in projects may bring stories, knowledge and certain kinds of expertise,[1] coupled with specific cultural and social backgrounds and experiences. They may also bring creative talent. And a good illustrator-facilitator will support participants to harness their creativity and express aspects of themselves. This on its own, however, does not an illustration make. Illustration requires something else, be that technical skill or vision, as Blaiklock suggests, or any other combination of capabilities, tools and networks that will transfigure participants' contributions into a piece of visual communication.

So, what makes something a piece of visual communication? I maintain that one of the central qualities of an illustration is that it shows an inclination for movement. It should possess the agility to leave my desk, be passed on and show up elsewhere, beckoning new audiences and publics to take note. Simply giving a group of people pens and paper (or embroidery needles, or any other tools and materials) is probably not enough to produce this effect. Critical mobilization of illustrators' expertise is needed to make the jump: one might say that the work needs to be adapted and prepared for its onward journey. What this expertise involves precisely will differ from one context to another. The methods required to make scattered perspectives coherent, legible and eloquent and to find a form and an aesthetic that can sensitively accommodate a multitude cannot be neatly parsed into a straightforward guide.

In order to reflect on these aspects of the illustrator's role, I draw on multiple areas of scholarship. I turn particularly to the fields of translation studies and critical ethnography, which have both emerged from the examination of distinctive and rich creative writing practices and which both deal with transposing complex systems of signification from one cultural context to another. In other words, their ambition is to make knowledge and meaning travel. Prominent translation scholar Susan Bassnett expresses this when she refers to translation as an 'intercultural transfer' (Bassnett 1998: 132); meanwhile, ethnographers Anand Pandian and Stuart McLean describe ethnographic writing using the metaphor of a crumpled paper boat, a fragile vessel, which precariously carries stories of one place to

[1] Illustrator and arts facilitator Jhinuk Sarkar deserves special mention here for her thoughtful and sensitive approach to enabling participants to contribute their expertise. In a community illustration project with the charity Islington Mind she encouraged a group member to take a leadership role in guiding the group through the process of using cyanotype. 'The technical training was then circulating in the group, rather than coming centrally from me' (Sarkar 2023). Similarly, Sidney Mann also commented on how the teaching of technical skills became distributed in the group, as the project progressed: 'Originally, when the project began, I was the teacher, but I have tried to move out of that role. I am now embroidering alongside everybody else. We share our skills and teach each other' (Mann 2023).

another (Pandian & McLean, 2017: 1–2). In what ways might an illustrator engage with these ideas?

Furthermore, trying to think through questions of beauty and aesthetics became something of a knotty problem for me. I had a gut feeling that it was part of the illustrator's duty to make the work aesthetically appealing – perhaps it was even our *responsibility* as conscientious caretakers to equip the work with formal qualities that would increase its likelihood of finding future audiences. And yet, it was difficult to articulate this desire for aesthetic appeal without stumbling into normative, universalist ideas about beauty. And besides, who am I to say what is beautiful? I eventually found my way out of this dilemma with Donna Haraway's help. Her work may not be concerned with aesthetics, but her ingenious intellectual manoeuvring in her famous 'Situated Knowledges' essay (1988) provided me with a roadmap of just how to navigate this dilemma. Visiting other disciplines and immersing myself in talented thinkers' work once again proved invaluable as I sought to find my way through these complex questions.

Harnessing vitality

In their introduction to *Constructing Cultures: Essays in Literary Translation* (1998), Susan Bassnett and André Lefevere describe how translation studies gradually emerged as a distinct academic discipline during the 1970s and 1980s. Previously, the key evaluative concepts for translation were limited to questions of equivalence and fidelity to the original text. But as the field matured, it gradually positioned itself as an independent discipline adjacent to linguistics, comparative literature and anthropology. The subject expanded: where it had once been focused on educating and training translators, as well as formally evaluating translated texts, it became concerned with 'analysing the process through which international understanding comes into being' (Bassnett & Lefevere 1998: 7). This act of reformulating existing material in an attempt to expand its reach seems relevant to my line of inquiry. Indeed, the debates and dilemmas I encountered in translation studies chimed with some of the difficulties I experienced when assembling, consolidating and (re)drawing participants' contributions in an attempt to produce accomplished illustrated documents.

These difficulties can best be illustrated by referring to a project I worked on with a charity called Latin Elephant between 2017 and 2019 – it was called *Recorriendo Elephant* or *Walking the Elephant*.[2] Latin Elephant is an organization that represents the interests of the Latin American and other minority ethnic communities in an

[2] I discuss this project and the complications I faced at great length in my article 'Walking the Elephant: Drawing as enactment of community' (Vormittag 2024a).

area of South London called Elephant and Castle, which was undergoing a rapid and destructive process of gentrification at the time. In consultation with Latin Elephant, I decided to host a number of participatory mapping workshops in and around an iconic shopping centre which was soon to be demolished. Initially, it was my intention to process and reformulate the outcomes of these workshops into visually legible illustrated documents that would, I hoped, be of value to the charity in their efforts to campaign against the destruction of the centre: Latin Elephant argued that the continuing presence of small businesses in the area supported a thriving and diverse community. Alas, in planning this, I somewhat naïvely skipped over the details of this 'processing and reformulating' stage, not really considering what it might entail. As an experienced illustrator, I believed myself to be well practised in interpreting and visualizing textual materials. What could go wrong?

As it was, the workshops went well and resulted in four large-scale maps, covered in an abundance of drawn lines and coloured sticking tape representing people's habitual routes, alongside a multitude of post-it notes, stickers, drawings and other markings and notes in both English and Spanish. To begin with, I was thrilled. However, soon after the workshops, I found myself in a predicament. In my previous illustration commissions, I had worked almost exclusively with textual prompts. Faced with this abundant array of visual markings, however, I was at a loss, struggling to identify principles that would guide my decision-making as I adapted the materials into more accessible and communicative illustrated outputs. The energetically intersecting lines, the vibrant (but chaotic) graphic inscriptions and the fact that these were, in effect, material records of four lively afternoons completely threw me off. As a first step, I decided to transcribe the participants' notes, identify the most frequently named places and produce a poster that visually highlighted some of them. But beyond this simple analysis, I was unsure how to translate the information into a coherent illustration that did justice to the multiplicity of contributions.

Due to the fragmented nature of the project (there was no continuous group of participants, and the work also faced disruptions due to various factors), I was not able to return to the group for a meaningful conversation about a possible visual resolution. So, in the end, I settled for producing a long, concertina-like strip of illustration, which strung together, in a fictionalized route across the site, the most frequently mentioned places from the maps. The backdrop comprised architectural elements found at Elephant and Castle, such as steps, ramps, platforms and arches, with the route marked by two overlapping and then diverging lines of coloured tape. The key places, including specific cafés, bars and shops, were represented through their names, with quotes transcribed from the original maps scattered around them. While I carried through participants' quotes verbatim, the rest of this synthesizing illustration was solely created by me – a fact that concerned me, but I also found myself unable to remedy.

Another problem I encountered was how to represent humans in this illustration. Initially, I wanted to avoid drawing figures altogether: it felt crude to do so. Their bodily features and sartorial characteristics, as well as the connotations of whatever drawing style I used, were at odds with my developing ideas around community. Nonetheless, I was ultimately unable to resolve the illustration without the use of figures, as the piece looked lifeless without them. I settled on simplified characters without facial features, but I remained unsatisfied with this solution and the cartoonish (and face-less!) sensibility it brought to the work.

Still, I eventually finished the piece of work: I produced a pack of materials, consisting of the concertina leaflet with my synthesized drawing that I titled Enter/Entrar, alongside two other leaflets that contained reproductions of the original maps as well as photos of the workshops. I sent these, with an accompanying piece of writing, to all workshop participants. Meanwhile, the situation on the ground had shifted significantly. My initial ambition to provide Latin Elephant with a suite of materials to use as visual evidence in their multipronged battle against the urban redevelopment plans was, unfortunately, no longer relevant.

In any case, the seemingly opposing demands of preserving the contributions' vitality and heterogeneity (mirroring the qualities of the group made them) and producing an illustration that 'made sense' for a range of audiences and publics had crystallized as a key tension in this project. I came to experience this tension

FIGURE 4.1 Luise Vormittag, *Walking the Elephant/Recorriendo Elephant* (2017–2019) for Latin Elephant. Conversation with a participant during a workshop at the Walworth Street Festival, July 2017. Photograph by Daniel Hopkinson.

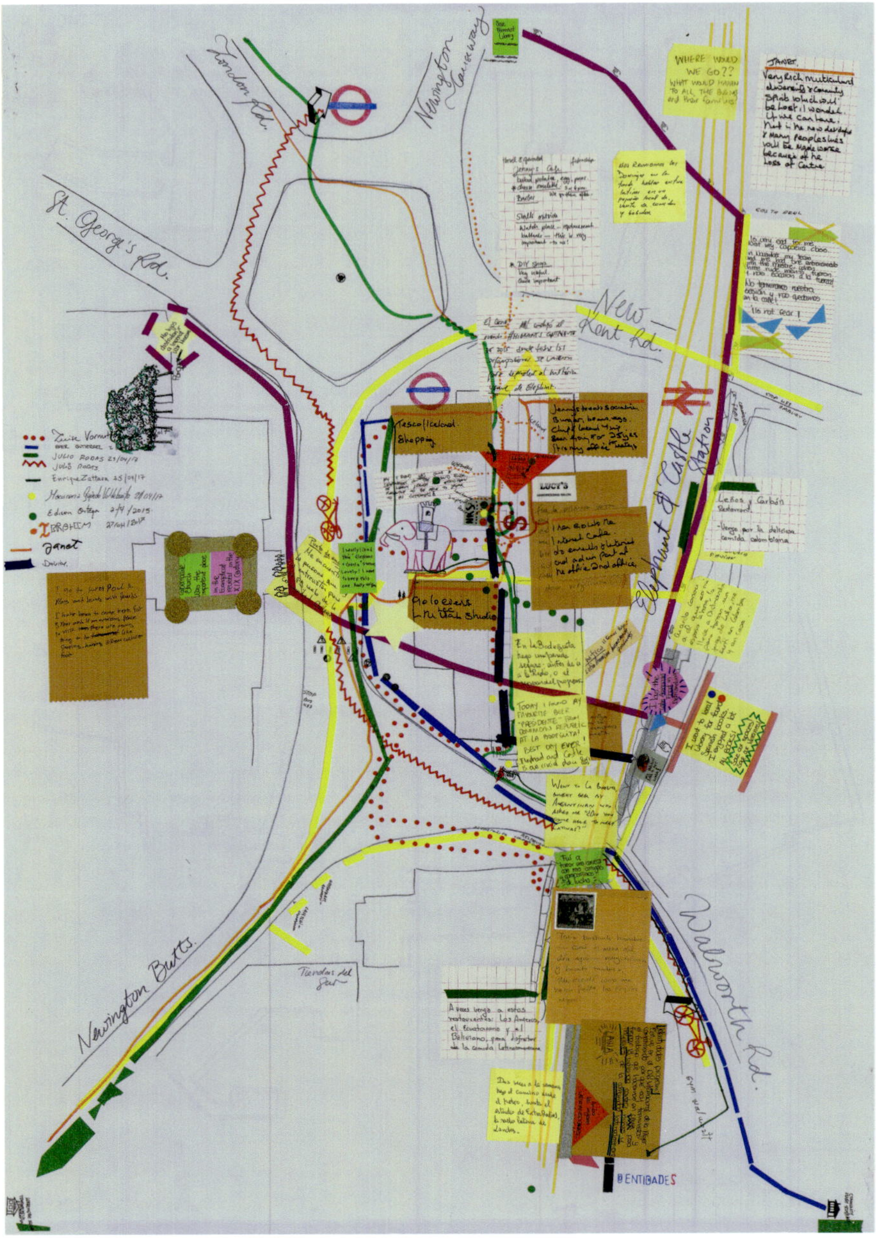

FIGURE 4.2 Luise Vormittag, *Walking the Elephant/Recorriendo Elephant* (2017–2019). Combined results of two workshops, April 2017.

FIGURE 4.3 Luise Vormittag, *Walking the Elephant/Recorriendo Elephant* (2017–2019). Concertina leaflet Enter/Entrar that shows a synthesized route through the Elephant and Castle shopping centre.

as a prolonged and somewhat torturous crisis. But, as I gradually realized, this was actually the crux of the problem in this type of project – and grappling with it was important. Later, and by this I mean *a lot* later, I realized that the key tension I was struggling with – between the desire not to homogenize participants' contributions on the one hand and the ambition to produce a communicative illustrated document on the other – mirrors the conceptual problem of being in community. I had started to understand, with a clarity that had eluded me for years, that what I was attempting (assembling a range of diverse materials in a manner that produces sense) actually spoke to the questions of how we might cultivate forms of togetherness that are coherent and meaningful, but do not swamp or erase the individual. How might we create a bond that is strong enough to sustain a collective, to hold otherwise fugitive singularities, yet also flexible enough to allow them to express themselves freely? I came to wonder, to use an acoustic metaphor, how we can be in community without all of us simply talking over one another – how we might accommodate, or better *celebrate*, individual voices while also still making sense as a whole. These are questions that ended up occupying me for a long time, and I will return to them in detail in Chapter 6.

My work for Latin Elephant ultimately resulted in a web page that now sits alongside other material collated by the charity to record the life of the shopping centre in Elephant and Castle before its demolition. In addition, I later logged the project on a map-based history website called 'Layers of London', giving it another arena where it might open itself up to new audiences and connections. And I remain in contact with Latin Elephant, who recently invited me to host another mapping

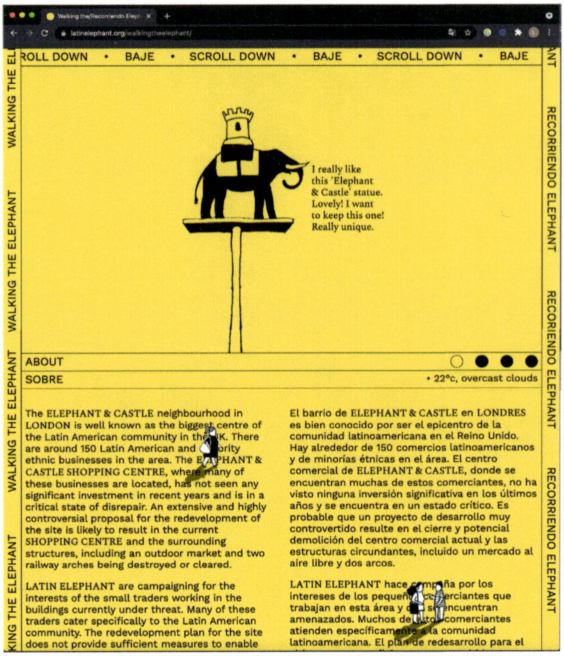

FIGURE 4.4 *Walking the Elephant* web page designed by See, Also (Lucy Maria and Mike Stevens). This web page sits as a tab on the main Latin Elephant website.

workshop at their anniversary celebration. So, yes, they were happy with the result, and I just about managed to assemble an illustrated piece that went out in the world as a small connective node, recounting one of London's many histories.

But what to make of the discomfort I felt when replacing the original workshop outputs with my own illustrative work in an attempt to synthesize and clarify them for future audiences? One strand of thinking in translation studies suggests there was no need for such qualms. Bassnett, for example, claims that translators are effectively writers, practically dissolving the concept of translation itself (1998: 25–40, 2006). In lieu, she positions translation as a textual rewriting practice, which raises doubts about outdated notions of singular authorship and originality. Quoting Barthes' famous 1977 essay *The Death of the Author*, Bassnett asserts that all texts are but a 'tissue of quotations' and that the binary of 'original' and 'translation' therefore no longer holds. She also argues against the notion that translations or 're-writings' are in any way inferior or subservient to previous versions of the text.[3]

[3] These ideas resonate with a range of other theoretical contributions, such as Walter Benjamin's claim in *The Translator's Task* ([1923] 2021) that the translation can function as the 'afterlife' of its source text in a process of transformation and renewal (91–2). Similarly, Maurice Blanchot argues that translations live out 'the solemn drift and derivation [dérive] of literary works' (Blanchot quoted in Venuti 1995: 307) and Homi Bhabha understands translations as a sign of cultural renegotiation (Bhabha quoted in Bassnett 1998: 137).

This invocation of free textuality might temporarily feel liberating. Nonetheless, the notion of flat hierarchies in textual production does not leave space for possible (one might even say *likely*) power differentials. It must also be said that there is a marked difference between the literary rewriting that Bassnett is referring to, where the source material is a formally resolved piece of professional, published work, and the visual reworking I attempted in my illustration for Enter/Entrar. In this particular case, my source material was polyvocal, jumbled and intimately bound up with the workshop participants' lives – in other words, my starting point revolved around the traces of an embodied, situated set of encounters with people to whom I felt a responsibility, rather than a disembodied text.

Another prominent translation scholar, Lawrence Venuti, puts forward a much more politically charged proposition. In his seminal book *The Translators Invisibility*, he speaks of the 'ethnocentric violence of translation' (1995: 18): he accuses translators of complicity with hierarchies of domination due to their obliteration of source cultures' particularities, particularly in the context of translations from less widely read languages into English. Rather than attempting to make translations sound fluid and smooth, he proposes that translators should 'foreignise' texts in order to highlight their linguistic and cultural differences and thereby practise creative ways of resisting the dominant values of the (mostly English) target language. Venuti also calls for greater visibility of the translator, not only in terms of greater respect and appreciation for their work, but also so that they might be held accountable for the various forms of reduction and exclusion they inflict on the writing. He stipulates that there are basically two translation methods: either the author is left in peace and the reader is moved towards them (the 'foreignising' method he favours), or else the reader is left in peace and the author moved towards them, which results in an ethnocentric reduction of foreign texts (1995: 19).

Venuti's choice of words ('ethnocentric violence of translation') might feel somewhat extreme and punitive, but I agree with the basic principle. It is our responsibility to be alert to difference when dealing with other people's creative artefacts, and we have a duty to handle them with care. In fact, Venuti's criticism touched a nerve in me, because it clarified a discomfort I harboured about *Walking the Elephant*: in an attempt to achieve greater visual fluency, I had overwritten the participants' contributions. With all this in mind, I was left wondering how it might be possible to maintain the visibility of 'foreign' contributions in a project, while still working towards a formally resolved output. I decided to redesign the 'climbing frames' for future endeavours in a way that would enable me to 'leave the authors in peace' to a greater degree and to find better ways of maintaining the integrity of their contributions, without compromising the legibility of the result.

In *Write Women into History*, I had the opportunity to put this into action. I used the original portraits rendered by the participants and drew around them, adding bodies and hands. Some women submitted more than one portrait, in which case I selected the one I felt worked best. For some of the drawings, I also thickened lines, removed smudges, added some hair (when it had been cropped or covered) or filled out areas with a block colour to add more weight to otherwise lightly drawn images. I proceeded in a similar way with the placard designs the women had made, altering them subtly and only doing so when it was necessary to bring out their strengths. The cover illustration then gained its coherence through my use of a unified colour scheme and the introduction of a grid structure that 'housed' the individual figures.

I should also stipulate that I shared draft versions with the group members and sought feedback, thereby extending their participation in the illustration beyond the initial drawing phase. Thanks to this review opportunity, the women were able to highlight and tweak certain details of the output – for example, I received requests to not alter a figure's hair too dramatically, to exchange one placard for another and to change the design of a shirt. The result is probably the most visually coherent illustration I have ever made with a group of participants. It most closely resembles a commercial commission, in that it communicates in a clear and visually impactful way. At the same time, however, it showcases the heterogeneity of the group. (See Figure 2.1, p.57.)

Alaa Alsaraji used a similar method when she worked with a group of young people on a project that became the *Redbridge Nature Guide* (2021). This piece of work invited participants to engage with photography, rather than illustration, but the principle is the same: Alsaraji devised a unifying system that could house many different and disparate contributions – the zine format. 'The zine was a great way to bring different perspectives together,' she said. 'What is good about this format is that I can bring my aesthetic skills without overriding other people's work. I can use my skills to pull it all together, but the main highlight is still the participants' work' (Alsaraji 2023).

Another way to 'leave the authors in peace' is to integrate a stable, structuring system into the project from the start. For example, Sidney Mann's *Bordando Tierra del Fuego* barely involved any intervention from Mann in the actual embroidery panels – but she provided the conceptual framework through which everyone made their contributions. Indeed, Mann initially occupied the role of the teacher, but she gradually moved out of that position, preferring to let the group members share skills and teach each other. This ultimately resulted in individual contributions that have some similarities, but which are still quite distinct from one another overall. Still, the piece has visual coherence thanks to the graphic outlines of a map of the region, which extends itself over all individual pieces. (As a reminder, Mann printed the map onto fabric, then cut it into more or less equally sized squares and distributed them among the group's participants.) Because of the cohesion of the cartographic layer, the women working on individual pieces could be 'left in peace' to do whatever they may choose. And indeed, the result

FIGURE 4.5 Alaa Alsaraji, *Redbridge Nature Guide* (2021). Alaa Alsaraji worked with a group of young people, encouraging them to take photos of and write about green spaces that were meaningful to them. Alsaraji subsequently compiled the material in a zine that was launched at an exhibition showing the work.

is a communicative piece jointly made by twenty-eight women, who, as Mann explained, 'were able to invoke a vision of Tierra del Fuego that was subjective and [individual], as well as collective and communal' (Mann 2025b).

The various projects discussed above can be neatly arranged along a sliding scale of decreasing levels of interference, with my work on Enter/Entrar in *Walking the Elephant* being the most 'interventionist' piece, the cover of *Write Women into History* occupying a middle ground, and Mann's embroidery project and Alsaraji's zines being the most hands-off examples. However, I am reluctant to hold up the level of intervention in the project participants' work as an easy measure of success (or virtue?). To suggest that the extent to which one 'leaves the author in peace' directly equates with a 'better' project is simplistic – and also not in the spirit of Venuti's argument. It may be worth remembering that, in his dialectograms, Mitch Miller takes on sole responsibility for transcribing and transferring his participants' contributions into visual form, but it would be absurd to suggest that his work is therefore inferior. Indeed, Miller contends that, in these scenarios, an illustrator 'can offer aesthetic expertise and experience, not to override or ignore the experience or expertise already [there], but in a spirit of encounter, where it can engage and correspond with it' (Miller 2015: Booklet 5, 10).

So, instead of making hasty judgements, it might be prudent for us to implement Venuti's proposal of continuous self-monitoring (1995: 308–9): he invites us to harness our expertise in a self-reflective way, with a critical awareness of the power relations and hierarchies of dominance and marginality at play. I would argue that this reflexive position is a more nuanced response to the inequalities an illustrator encounters in participatory creative projects. After all, rather than attempting to rid ourselves of our expertise in hasty gestures of authorial renunciation, would it not be better to put it to good use?

In fact, this is the steer I received from project participants. During a feedback session with the women who were part of the Hackney HOWLers writing group, I asked about the finished cover artwork for *Write Women into History*. In response, one of the group members commented:

> These are pictures of us [...] and they are *by* us. And you have [used] your skills as an artist, you know, to put them into these blocks, to put the colour, to do the bodies [...]. What I would say is, that's an example of someone using her skills as an artist to empower us all. You empowered us, [...] to be able to represent ourselves and express ourselves and create something visual, which we couldn't have done on our own. So, you know, what a triumph!
>
> (2022)

How does it look?

Of course, it is one thing to develop a way of working that is 'self-conscious and self-critical' in theory, and quite another to put this to practice. How might an illustrator trying to collate a lively (but disparate!) range of materials proceed? How might it be possible to achieve the twin targets of authenticity and impact?

When I was working with the material for *Write Women into History*, I took pragmatic and intuitive steps forward: as described above, I made selective choices according to what I felt 'worked best', subtly altering drawings to 'bring out their strengths' to produce a result that 'communicates clearly in a visually impactful way', or so I claim. But who is really to say what 'works'? My instinctual choices are undeniably influenced by my previous experience working as a commercial image maker in the creative industries in London, my Western European background and education, and – dare I say it – my aesthetic taste. I put all these skills and inclinations to use in these projects, but taste and experience alone are clearly not the only qualities required here: they need to be supplemented with an awareness that one's knowledge and background have limits, a sensitivity to the experiences of others, and a respect for the vitality and 'foreignness' of these others' contributions. Only then will be one be able to interpret, edit and perhaps gently rearticulate the contributions effectively.

Happily, a member of the Hackney HOWLers noted my efforts to consider the group's attitudes, beliefs and experiences during our work together. In a feedback session, she expressed:

> What I want to say [...], is that you were very respectful of us. I must admit, I was anxious about that issue, whether somebody who wasn't of our experience and generation would get it. I thought you were extremely sensitive to the mood and the atmosphere and the content of our book, and of us as women. I think that's a real achievement because you were not there. It could have been disastrous, if we had had to argue with you [about the illustration and the overall design]. But we didn't have to argue with you. That's a great credit to you.
>
> (2022)

Can we conclude, then, that all is well, that this project achieved my ambition to 'leave the author[s] in peace' to the best of my ability? It is, of course, truly gratifying to receive such positive feedback from the people I worked with and whose interests I endeavoured to support through this project. But after writing these paragraphs, I was left unable to shake the feeling that there is something more to say. It feels too easy to simply acknowledge my background, remind myself (and the reader) of my limitations and state the need to be continuously sensitive of others' requirements. These things are certainly important, but I can still sense other questions hovering in the ether. For one thing, I feel compelled to state that a major influence on all my aesthetic decisions was my desire to make the final piece visually attractive. I wanted the result to be of 'high quality' – and I wanted it to 'look good'.

I have put these expressions in quotation marks, as notions of quality and aesthetics in participatory creative projects are generally not discussed. Most of the practitioners I spoke to avoided this territory and, if the conversation did stray in this direction, were quick to state that they refrain from value judgements and that everybody's contribution is equally valid. This is entirely understandable. This kind of work clearly requires a tolerant and supportive attitude. Still, I could not help but remember Claire Bishop's charge that participatory practice tends to privilege ethical evaluative criteria above all else (2012: 190) – and feel that there was something worth considering in her criticism. But how to proceed? Introducing a discussion about quality or aesthetics when working with community groups who are not professional illustrators seems downright obstructive, or worse regressive and conservative. It quite rightly carries ugly overtones of an outdated, narrowly defined, exclusionary cannon. For a long time, this felt to me like an intellectual impasse.

By all means, ethical conduct – and by extension ethical evaluative criteria – is crucial in this kind of work. Illustrator-facilitators have a duty to support and encourage the people participating in the work. Then, during the consolidation phase (when working towards an outcome), we should do our best to represent a group's concerns fairly, not overshadow what they have contributed and present their work in the best possible light. I consider this to be self-evident, and therefore do not think it is necessary to make this argument at length here. However, *in addition* to this, I wondered whether it might be possible to think about notions of quality and aesthetics. Surely it must be possible to have both?

At the start of this chapter, I suggested that one facet of illustration expertise is the capacity to imbue a piece of work with a propensity to travel, to mould it in such a way that the likelihood it will be passed on increases. Thus, expert illustrators create the possibility for future audiences and publics to connect with the work. And the work's likelihood of travel is linked, among other things, to how people respond aesthetically to it. But even before a 'visually attractive' piece of work encounters a potential audience, something that 'looks good' will also make the members of community group themselves feel differently about what they have made.

I am not entirely alone in my desire to somehow bring aesthetic quality into participatory illustration practice. Alaa Alsaraji had similar thoughts:

> It's a tricky balance. You want to move away from traditional judgements – like what you get taught in school to think of as 'good' – because any kind of art is art. If you had an amazing time doing it, it really doesn't matter what it looks like in the end. But on the other hand, people still come with an expectation of wanting to create something that is okay to hold up alongside other people's work. So, you want to think a little bit about quality [too].
>
> (Alsaraji 2023)

Notably, I found my inner turmoil on this matter reflected in a particular moment in postcolonial literary studies. From its inception in the 1970s, this discipline had at least partially built its reputation on an emphatic rejection of aesthetic evaluation in favour of identity and recognition. This discourse empowered minoritized communities and authors and attempted to 'bear witness to the uneven forces of cultural representation' (Bhabha 1994: 171). In the early 2000s, however, the field underwent a so-called 'aesthetic turn'.[4] Renowned scholar Deepika Bahri provides a pithy analysis of the key stakes, highlighting how, for a long time, a fear of universalism alongside the recent long and bitter 'battle with the tyranny of the canon' would have made it seem 'provocatively conservative' to suggest a focus on aesthetics (Bahri 2003: 15). However, Bahri goes on to argue that, when reflecting on postcolonial literature, we should consider its aesthetic values, in addition to its ideological coordinates, because 'a criticism uninterested in exploring its aesthetic

[4] For a more detailed account of this discussion, see Robert J. C. Young (1998), whose piece 'Ideologies of the Postcolonial' contributed to initiating these debates. In addition, John J. Su (2011) provides an excellent summary of the various positions that ensued.

dimension will fail to glean its possible contribution to the emancipatory project' (Bahri 2003: 17). I believe the same is true for participatory illustration projects. Disregarding their potential to impart visual pleasure will only diminish their ability to have an impact.

Bahri subsequent pursues a revival of ideas associated with the Frankfurt School, enabling her to reintroduce aesthetic appreciation for literary works as a key criterion in their evaluation. This, however, is of no use to me. Bahri's project sits within literary criticism, seeking as it does to recalibrate evaluative criteria for a set of highly accomplished literary works. My objective, by comparison, is to explore questions of collective production and find a way to frame my ambition to enhance the quality of a communal project in the making. Alsaraji has a refreshingly straightforward solution for this scenario. 'How can you use your skills to push something towards the best quality it can be, without taking the pen out of their hands and drawing for them?' she asked. '[By using] the format of the zine, I know that I can do things with layout and with colours to make the work look professional, so people can be really proud of what they made' (Alsaraji 2023).

As delightfully effective and practical as that sounds, it still does not help me find a theoretical approach to think through this impasse. Grappling with this, I felt trapped in an unproductive binary. On one side was a non-judgemental and encouraging celebration of creativity in all its forms. This rejection of authoritative (one might say authoritarian) aesthetic value judgements can be described as a kind of relativism, where aesthetic ideals are seen as the product of specific norms, conventions and frameworks. These, in turn, are suspected (justifiably so!) to perpetuate exclusionary practices in a bid to maintain the status quo. The problem with this position, however, is that many people do still perceive differences in terms of visual competence. And because of these differences, some illustrations are more likely to find audiences than others. On the other side of this binary are punishing, old-fashioned and culturally conservative discourses on 'standards' and 'quality', suggesting universalist principles for what counts as 'good'. This set of values has received ample criticism for how it marginalizes and excludes cultural contributions from broad swathes of society. I could not see a way to think about aesthetic value that did not feel uncomfortably close to this idea of authoritarian universal standards, but I equally felt uncomfortable pretending there was no distinction to be made at all. How to proceed?

I found a way forward in an unexpected place. Donna Haraway's seminal 1988 essay 'Situated Knowledges' starts with her describing an equally unproductive binary that, in its structure, is strikingly similar to the one I felt trapped by. In this essay, Haraway examines how knowledge claims garner legitimacy in the sciences: on the one hand, a social constructivist argument maintains that knowledge is relative, created and maintained by networks of people, institutions and things. If we lean into this relativism, however, everything becomes contingent. And if this is the case, Haraway asks, how can we meaningfully share knowledge, how can we give an account of a shared reality? On the other hand, a totalizing objectivity maintains that there are indeed universal truths. According to this paradigm, science creates new knowledge on a disembodied, neutral plain, through a 'conquering gaze from nowhere' (1988: 581). This totalizing scenario, however, fails to account for embodied subjectivities and difference. This gave me fresh clarity on the situation I was trying to find my way through. When Haraway asks 'How do you have simultaneously an account of radical contingency and a commitment to a shared world?' (1988: 579), she seemed to be speaking to my own dilemma.

As a potential route forward, Haraway suggests that we recognize that both of these options are deficient. She proposes that objectivity does not actually need to promise totalizing transcendence; instead, it can be redefined as an objectivity that is particular, specific in its embodiment and limited in location. In other words, 'the alternative to relativism is not totalization [...], but partial, locatable, critical knowledges sustaining the possibility of webs of connections [...]' (1988: 684). Mobility of meaning does not require universality: it actually requires locatable and partial knowledge that offers an opportunity for shared conversations.

This can easily be transposed to the scenario of the illustrator working with community groups. In these circumstances, I see my role, at least partially, as foregrounding perspectives that are frequently overlooked in the arena of cultural production. I hope to use my skills to further the agendas of the groups I have committed to work with, enable them to connect with others and help them find an audience. My desire to make something 'look good' by mobilizing my skills and my aesthetic judgement does not mean I am claiming to uphold a universal standard of beauty. If my aesthetic choices are recognized as impactful and appreciated *by the group of participants*, then that must surely count as a success. If the majority of the group regards my interventions as having improved the result, it will make them feel proud of what they have achieved. It will also increase the likelihood of the final piece finding new audiences, who may connect with the aesthetic choices we have made together. Thus, I am not enforcing a transcendent idea of 'beauty'; I am creating the possibility of meaning being shared and facilitating a potential network of connections.

In the case of *Write Women into History*, there were one or two reservations among the women about the cover, but the group was very positive overall and particularly appreciated its potential to attract an audience. For example, one group member said: 'I think it's a fantastic cover. I have it on my computer, among other pictures, as I was using it in on Facebook to advertise our book launch. It really sings out. Among a whole set of pictures, it really sticks out. I feel so proud.' Another added: 'Yes, it's impressive. Everyone I've given it to has really liked the cover. I've had lots of positive feedback. I think it really stands out. If it were on a stand – I'd be drawn to it, because it's different. It draws me in. It's fun' (2022). The book has indeed done reasonably well, and, to my delight, it keeps travelling. Of course, its voyages remain local (perhaps that is the point?), but I have been

FIGURE 4.6 Celia Burgess-Macey and Gail Chester from the Hackney HOWLers Writing Group present *Write Women into History* at the Hackney History Festival at Sutton House, London (2024).

pleasantly surprised to come across the book on display in various places in my East London neighbourhood, 'singing out' and inviting new audiences to connect with it.

Representation and invention

Earlier in this chapter, I borrowed from translation studies to think about the role of the illustrator in assembling and consolidating a participatory project, reconfiguring the work in such a way that it may move from one context to another. There remains, however, a vital distinction between the task of a translator and the kind of interpretive work community illustrators perform when assembling a collective output. As previously mentioned, our source material is not a published piece of work, but the messy traces of human encounters: we start with groups of people, rather than written texts.

Against this backdrop, ethnographic scholarship offers itself as a productive point of reference. Both translation scholarship and ethnography concern themselves with writing practices, but the difference is, ironically, that the translator is engaged in much less dramatic acts of translation than the ethnographer. After all, the translator's primary source is already in the same format as the desired output: written language. By contrast, the ethnographer grapples with the fraught business of finding adequate ways to represent aspects of others' culture and lived experiences in writing. Even though this does not precisely correlate with the task performed by community illustrators at this stage of a project, I found the debates in this discipline helpful. Ethnography crystallized two key questions for me. Firstly, there is the issue of the researcher's (or, in our case, the illustrator's) subjectivity. Clearly, our presence and involvement necessitates a reflection on what *we* bring to the work: our predispositions and biases, social and material status, and skills, interests and concerns all combine to form an important part of the work – probably just as important a part as that made up by our participants' contributions. So, if we think of the work as arising from encounters between an illustrator and a group of participants, what might be the adequate means to acknowledge these encounters? Secondly, the instability of the categories of documentation and invention – or, to put it simply, fact and fiction – must be taken into account. If the researcher (again, in our case, illustrator) is so deeply implicated in the creation of the piece, how can this be squared with the idea of faithful representation? How can we think (and work) our way through this constellation of documentation, representation and invention?

In Chapter 2, I discussed how artists, designers and associated theorists wrestled with how to include a greater range of perspectives in their work from the 1960s onwards. During this time, anthropologists and ethnographers were asking probing questions of their own. For the scholars of this discipline, however, working with people from different cultural contexts was clearly not an innovative addition to their practice (as it was for many artists and designers); rather, this constitutes the core orientation of their discipline. Indeed, anthropologists and ethnographers have long worked in a context of persistent and stark power asymmetries between researchers and the people and cultures they investigate. This is unsurprising, given that this discipline emerged in a context of imperial relations, often marked by racism, condescension and exploitation. But it is precisely this distressing history that positions – perhaps even obliges – anthropologists to critically examine their discipline's problematic foundations and find more reflective ways of dealing with unequal power relations that were also so uncomfortably experienced by some of the artists and designers discussed earlier.

Certainly, the classic formula for ethnographic work, consisting of 'fieldwork' (primarily participant observation) followed by the 'writing up' of texts, was not seriously scrutinized for a long time. By the 1980s, however, the 'ideology claiming transparency of representation and immediacy of experience' (Clifford 1986: 2) was definitively exposed as such – as an ideology, rather than an authoritative, scientific account as previously assumed. The publication of *Writing Culture* in 1986, edited by James Clifford and George E. Marcus, proved to be a watershed moment in anthropological thought, generating lively debate that continues to this day.[5] In the introduction to this volume, appropriately entitled 'Partial Truths', Clifford argues that we must comprehensively acknowledge the unsurpassable partiality of ethnographic accounts and accept that 'ethnography is always caught up in the invention, not representation of cultures' (Clifford 1986: 2). In Clifford's paradigm, ethnography is no longer assumed to be a scientific description of peoples, cultures, their customs and habits, but reconceived as a literary construction, shaped by conventions of rhetoric and genre. He thereby manages to bring into focus the 'constructed and artificial nature of cultural accounts' (Clifford 1986). This might sound like it is drifting alarmingly close to the relativism Haraway steered us away from a few pages ago, but I read this as a recognition and reminder that there are no transparent or neutral modes of documentation and representation. When Clifford suggests that the aim is to generate 'coherent ethnographic fictions' (1986: 6), the word fiction has lost its connotation of falsehood and instead become an acknowledgement of the partiality of truths. The acknowledgement that plain factual signification is impossible does not give us licence to listlessly slump towards the banal claim that all truths are constructed and therefore of equal quality.

And indeed, this self-reflexive reorientation has had an invigorating impact on anthropology. It has given rise to a plethora of experimental writing practices that underscore how language, writing and regimes of representation, despite their biases and partialities, can be creatively mobilized to generate and deepen our knowledge of the world. Recent ethnographic publications, such as *Crumpled Paper Boat* (Pandian & McLean 2017) and *The Ends of Kinship* (Craig 2020), continue to address and animate the tensions surrounding the appropriate means to convey an ethnographic encounter with other people's experiences and concerns. These publications remind us that we can strive for truthfulness, while simultaneously accepting that all forms of documentation and representation are constructed. Reflexive ethnographic practice is aware of and continuously reflecting on power dynamics, while also taking into account the subjectivity and partiality of ethnographers themselves. This way of working foregrounds the fact that knowledge (or indeed illustration) can be an intersubjective production that arises from the interplay of researcher (or illustrator), participants and place.

[5] There is seemingly no escape from the epistemological dilemmas caused by research practices that seek to describe groups of people, their everyday practices and cultures: *Writing Culture* (1986) was succeeded by two further edited volumes that continue to explore the myriad of richly detailed but ultimately somewhat circular questions that arose from Clifford and Marcus' original set of claims. See Allison James, Jenny Hockey and Andrew Dawson's *After Writing Culture* (1997) and Olaf Zenker and Karsten Kumoll's *Beyond Writing Culture* (2013).

Mitch Miller picks up this theme when he describes how he originally attempted to capture the everyday flow of things when working on one of his dialectograms at a health and community centre in Edinburgh. However, he soon realized that '[his] presence was actually creating a new social situation; users made a point of coming in on days [he] was going to be there, activities were changed or devised around [him]'. Ultimately, Miller concluded that 'the dialectogram contributed to the social fabric it intended to read' (2015: Booklet 4, 9–10).

Similarly, Nina Sabnani's work *Tanko bole chhe/The Stitches Speak* (2009) navigates this complex territory with great sophistication. Her collaboration with the Kala Raksha Trust takes as its starting point a number of (pre-existing) large narrative embroidery panels that tell the story of the community's displacement in the aftermath of the 2001 Gujarat earthquake. In the course of the project, these were scanned and animated by Sabnani, with supplementary elements added from other embroidery pieces made by the trust's craftspeople. The resulting film is structured by a soundtrack of recorded conversations, in which four key members of the community recount their life stories in overlapping, multilinear narratives. Thus, the work is both an account of real events, as presented and narrated by the community's textile artists (and associates), and equally a record of another type of real event: the encounter between Sabnani and the members of the trust.

Sabnani explained to me that the Kala Raksha Trust initially proposed that *they* would take pictures of the panels and send her the photographs to work on, sparing her the need to travel to visit them. But she protested: 'This would not work – you can't just read an image just because you can see it. [...] One has to talk! [...] When I started talking to [the members of the trust], I realized there were many more stories, not just a narrative of an earthquake – the work was telling other stories of forced migration and displacement' (Sabnani 2023). Notably, these conversations were at least partly facilitated by Sabnani's knowledge of Sindhi, a language she learned from her parents, which has reasonable overlaps with the textile artists' native language of Kutchi. And even though Sabnani's voice is not heard in the final edit, the stories narrated in the film are nevertheless bound up with her presence: they emerged out of the relationships she formed and the conversations she had during her visits.

Sabnani recounts how discussing the panels with the textile artists drew her attention to many details in the work that she otherwise would not have noticed. Moreover, spending all this time talking triggered memories for the two elderly textile artists, which had not been included in the original piece. And the conversations also meandered from the embroidered panels on to other topics, such as the textile artists' transformative journeys of self-discovery: they went from being refugees with a caste-based identity to craftspeople, before ultimately becoming artists. Sabnani was struck by the richness of these conversations and eventually decided to use them as the structuring device for the whole film:

> We came back with a lot of data – lots of recorded conversation and lots of scans of their textile work. We transcribed everything. Sometimes we didn't understand a word and we had to call P. and ask him. It was a lot of work. There was so much material. It occurred to me that, in India, when we speak, we do not allow people to finish their sentences. So, I decided to use the conversation structure as a way to move from one topic to another. One person is talking, and then another person cuts through and talks about something else. This way we could include a lot of things they wanted to talk about.
>
> (Sabnani 2019, 2023)

As I wrap up this chapter, Sabnani's work feels particularly relevant to consider. She describes herself as a filmmaker who works only with found material – she is someone who puts things together in order to help others tell their stories. But by doing so, she inevitably tells aspects of her own story too. Her work grows out of a series of encounters that inevitably add new layers to the found material. One might even say that this particular film is as much a documentation of her encounters as it is an account of the trust members' lives. The 'partial truths' (Clifford 1986) and the 'situated knowledges' (Haraway 1988) materialized in this film compellingly express an intricate set of experiences and connections that – I hope – will continue to elicit new bonds in times to come.

At the start of this chapter, I discussed the tensions I felt while working on the Enter/Entrar illustration (part of *Walking the Elephant*). My attempts at producing a synthesized piece obscured the very liveliness I was seeking to portray. Meanwhile the maps that resulted directly from the workshops communicated their vitality directly through overlapping lines and a multiplicity of notes. I eventually realized that Enter/Entrar failed in its attempt at *re*presenting. I had been trying to visualize and encode a complex enactment of routes and routines, a nimble set of relations and kinship *after these had taken place* – but as an outsider, it was close to impossible for me to retrospectively create coherence and fill the gaps. Looking at the maps resulting from the workshop again, I came to see the possibility of a different strategy: rather than pursuing adequate means for representing community – an approach that assumes community to be something pre-existing, with at least some degree of consistency – perhaps collaborative illustration projects could aim for something else: create the conditions for people to meet and make something new together.

While reflecting on these questions concerning ways to adequately represent community, it dawned on me that the notion of representation itself might be the problem. Illustration is often casually assumed to be a representational practice, where 'something out there' is represented, i.e. shown again, in visual form. The very 're-' in 'representation' suggests that something exists prior to its pictorial rendering. But this is not always the way illustration works, as I will go on to explore in detail in the remaining chapters of the book. Indeed, in his essay 'The Age of the World Picture', Heidegger highlights the presumptions that underpin a representationalist world view, where 'the world is set out before oneself and set forth in relation to oneself', where 'man [*sic*] becomes the masterful subject standing apart from the world he is endeavouring to know' (Heidegger [1950] 1977: 132–3).

Translation studies and ethnography do go part of the way in addressing this dilemma. The much higher levels of self-reflexivity demanded by both of these disciplines have (at least partially) dismantled the idea that subjects can separate themselves from the world they want to know. Ethnography's sense of 'writing about, against and among cultures' (Clifford 1986: 3) has obvious overlaps with the kinds of projects I discuss in this book, where practitioners illustrate about, among and with people, rather than from a detached point of observation. Likewise, ethnography's acknowledgement that it can only bring forth 'partial truths' (Clifford 1986) and its subsequent experiments with more self-conscious forms of writing have been helpful for thinking about the kinds of illustrative documents that result from these projects. But I soon realized that producing 'coherent ethnographic fictions', which are generally created to communicate something about existing cultural practices, was not what primarily interested me; rather, I was curious about the possibility of working with groups of people to self-consciously make something *new* together, to weave together multiple, singular articulations in an attempt to make novel worlds.[6] This collective adventure is what awaits us in the next chapter.

[6] Ethnographic practice and scholarship have, of course, continued to evolve, and there are some forms of experimental ethnography that could be described in similar terms to what I use here: see, for example, Pink (2013) or Pandian & McLean (2017). While there might be overlaps, the project and goal-oriented nature of the participatory illustration projects I am writing about (e.g. 'Let's make a book together!') does make for a different emphasis, compared to ethnography's focus on 'experiencing, interpreting and representing experience, culture, [and] society' (Pink 2013: 34).

5 WORLD-MAKING

What does it mean to 'make a world'? And how can one be made through illustration? In this chapter I address the use of the word 'world' in this book's (sub)title and explore how such a thing might be 'made'.

I start this chapter with a focus on those types of projects that prompt participants to record their personal memories or experiences, to give accounts of a particular time of their lives, or a place they are familiar with. Being asked to do this, after all, gives rise to reflective acts of sharpened attention. *Cracks in the Pavement* and Billy Ash Sakula's project *Rest* occasioned participants to give greater attention to subjective experiences and phenomena of everyday life (such as going for a walk, residing in a particular neighbourhood, drinking a cup of tea, falling asleep to the TV) – things that would usually not receive that level of reflection. In turn, for the women in the writing group, working on *Write Women into History* enlivened some of the memories that are usually overlooked in the course of the everyday – this was also the case for contributors to Sabnani's project with the Kala Raksha Trust. On a more general level, Mitch Miller's dialectograms too are focused on everyday life, and the habitual ways in which people inhabit, experience and remember a place. What does it mean for participatory illustration projects to illuminate and record our experience of the everyday? To think this through I decided to draw on ideas from phenomenology, an area of philosophy that concerns itself with the subjective world of experience.

I noticed that recording these individual acts of attention goes beyond bringing awareness to a pre-existing world. This is because, as we explored in the previous chapter, most acts of documentation do not simply serve to represent a pre-existing reality. After all, there is no way to directly capture what one thinks or feels about one's environment – there is no unmediated, direct method for recording your environment or thoughts. And assembling impressions from a number of different individuals, as often happens in participatory illustration projects, pushes things further still. In their fragmentary accumulation lies great generative potential. The illustrative documents that emerge from these processes, do not show us a distilled, synthesized, agreed translation of what people had imagined previously, but rather an altogether new picture that has emerged through interlocking articulations of many.

Thus, in this chapter, I develop one of this book's key claims: because illustration can 'make a world', it can be described as a performative mode of knowledge production. To put it another way – I believe that illustration is not necessarily a representational practice. In the process of its creation, it can produce the reality it refers to.

Reflective acts of attention

What do participants themselves say about their involvement in community illustration projects? In a feedback session[1] the group who participated in *Write Women into History* spoke about how both *producing* the artwork and *seeing* the finished cover conjured up memories of being involved in feminist campaigns during the 1960s, 1970s and early 1980s. Indeed, several of them commented on how using Letraset (for the placard designs) animated memories of making pamphlets and other feminist publications. I was thrilled to learn that our creative sessions not only brought up memories but also reanimated past passions. When reflecting on working on placard designs for the cover, one woman described a renewed emotional response to the campaigns she had been involved in:

> It seemed authentic to how the [placards] were originally done at the time. The one I did was for the National Abortion Campaign. It was quite an experience to do that, really, because it was as if I was doing it for that purpose, as [the women in the past] would have, so I felt engaged with it – with the campaign and the mood of the time. It was great, really.
>
> (2022)

In short, designing a placard pulled distant actions and convictions that had become dulled by the passing of time back into sharp focus at the forefront of the mind. This experience was echoed by other women – when contemplating the project as a whole.[2] For example, one woman commented: 'It has been a moving experience to participate in a collective writing project with women who were active feminists, as I was' (Hackney HOWLers 2021: 6). These memories and campaigns had been part of the women's lives all along but had lost their enlivening presence in the perpetual unfolding of everyday concerns.

Nina Sabnani also reported this stirring of otherwise shadowy memories in her work with the Kala Raksha Trust. As she spoke with the trust members about their experiences of displacement due to an earthquake (that were depicted in the original textile panels), this ultimately brought up memories of their *previous* experiences of exile. In many ways, a prompt that asks

[1] This was attended by approximately two-thirds of the women.

[2] For the women, the project was, understandably, primarily a writing and publishing project. Creating the communal illustration was just one aspect for them, and far from the most important.

participants to focus on one thing is like tugging at a thread – it unravels many adjacent recollections too. While these memories are always present, they often lie dormant amid the clatter of the day-to-day, until something stirs them back into life.

For their part, Billy Ash Sakula tried to bring the sensorial texture of everyday life to the fore in their piece *Rest*: participants were prompted to first write, then illustrate and ultimately animate accounts of their experiences of taking a break. The young mothers who took part in this project wrote perceptive and detailed descriptions of their individual experiences of rest and renewal, which were then selected, edited and arranged by the group as a whole. The resulting communal poem includes lines such as 'I can smell fresh air from my window, inhale peppermint from my cup' and 'I hear laughter from my own mouth, I drift off to voices murmuring from the TV'. Meanwhile, though my project *Cracks in the Pavement* was not deliberately oriented towards recording sensory impressions, it is striking that one of the main theme emerging from project participants' feedback was an elevated sense of mindfulness towards their surroundings: many reported discovering new details about their area and feeling a greater attachment to their neighbourhood.[3] What to make of all this attention on experiences of the everyday?

In European philosophy, this subjective world of experience came into focus in the first half of the twentieth century as a new branch of theory called phenomenology. In contrast to the perceived fragmentation of everyday life, particularly in the context of modern science and the 'mathematisation' of the world, as well as the onset of industrial capitalism and the corresponding bureaucratic apparatus, phenomenology concerns itself with the way the world appears to the person experiencing it. Philosopher Edmund Husserl, a key figure in the advancement of these ideas, developed the concept of *Lebenswelt* (lifeworld) to express these ideas during the late 1910s. He describes it as a 'framework within which [...] this life is carried on' ([1936] 1970: 143), a 'realm of subjective phenomena' (1970: 111) and the main arena we can draw on for making sense.

Although it was Husserl who coined the term *Lebenswelt*, philosopher Martin Heidegger and philosopher and social scientist Alfred Schütz[4] played a key role in

[3] After I had delivered the final thank-you packs to the walkers, I asked them to complete a short online questionnaire; approximately two-thirds of participants responded.

[4] Schütz took up Husserl's *Lebenswelt* from the 1940s onwards. His work was concerned with the integration of phenomenological ideas into the social sciences in order to understand how people through their individual, conscious experiences and actions co-constitute the social world. He refines and differentiates Husserl's term, changing it to *Alltagswelt* (world of everyday life) (Schütz 1945: 533–4), and further distinguishing *Umwelt* (the directly experienced social reality), *Mitwelt* (the broader world of contemporaries), *Vorwelt* (the world of predecessors) and *Folgewelt* (the world of successors) (Walsh in Schütz 1972: xxvii).

the development of this concept. Like Husserl, Heidegger believed that the world's true mode of existence lies not in the idealized sphere of modern science, with its endless space and time and precise causality. Instead, he argues that the world is something we find ourselves in through our interaction and involvement with it. In his view, we come to know the world not through our interpretive tendencies, which just get in our way (says the man who wrote 400 pages on being!), but in its disclosure to us through our practical behaviours and habitual activities (Heidegger [1927] 1962: 96).[5]

Interestingly, Husserl, Heidegger and Schütz all comment on the fact that the presence of the *Lebenswelt* is usually taken for granted and goes unnoticed in day-to-day life. Husserl writes that '[c]onsciously we always live in the life-world, [but] normally there is no reason for making it explicitly thematic for ourselves universally *as* world' (Husserl 1970: 379, emphasis in original). For his part, Schütz writes that '[i]f I wish to observe one of my own lived experiences, I must perform a reflective act of attention' ([1932] 1972: 102). Similarly, Heidegger comments that a pre-existing world can be 'lit up in certain ways of dealing with our environment' (1962: 114).

Many of the walkers' comments on their experiences participating in *Cracks in the Pavement* chime with these statements about the usually unnoticed character of the lifeworld. It seems that the project operated as a catalyst for people to perform a 'reflective act of attention' that 'lit up' the neighbourhood for them. One walker explained: 'It was different to other walks because we tried to be more conscious and observant of our surroundings, knowing that we would later be updating the map based on what we had seen and experienced along the way.' As another put it: 'It was a very familiar walk, but I looked at things [...] with a more searching eye and that was good.' A third walker commented: 'On this walk, I recorded thoughts, memories and associations much more than I usually would, and I suddenly realized how I really feel about my local area. Sort of made me contemplate all the small everyday things that I usually take for granted – usually you've always got other stuff at the forefront of your mind!' Yet another stated: 'Columbia Road especially was incredibly rich in beautiful details we hadn't noticed before. We had never really stopped to look at each of the mosaic murals properly' (Anonymous 2021).

In a similar vein, participants in Sidney Mann's *Bordando Tierra del Fuego* also opened up to new perceptions of their everyday environments. As one embroiderer put it: 'For me, it was about becoming more aware of what we usually take for granted, reinforcing the sense of belonging, the connection with nature and the richness of its biodiversity.' Another explicitly described how the project helped her generate new knowledge:

[5] Even though Heidegger didn't use the term 'lifeworld' as such, his philosophical work had many overlapping concerns. For example, in *Being and Time* (originally published in 1927) Heidegger reflects on 'The Worldhood of the World' (1962: Pt One, ch. III).

I had to research the area I was assigned, and it was a whole process of discovery; although I had heard of Península Mitre, I had never seen images and only knew it was difficult to access. From pictures, I discovered there was a lighthouse (which I embroidered) and a navy post. I also watched two documentaries. I think it helped us rediscover our landscape, to make it our own. And it gives us identity.

(Quoted in Mann 2025a)

These environments, memories and experiences had been part of participants' life all along, but the details of one's neighbourhood or province can easily be overlooked and undervalued, old memories fade, and the invigorating smell of fresh air (*Rest*) can so easily be taken for granted. Taking part in these projects brings the richness of the everyday rushing back to the forefront of your mind.

Singular spaces, plural worlds

Nonetheless, I would like to go further than simply say that participatory illustration projects have the capacity to bring the pre-existing world of the everyday into renewed focus. French philosopher Jean-Luc Nancy builds on but ultimately departs from Husserl and Heidegger in his theory on how we exist in the world. Indeed, he introduces the idea that contemporary experience of existence (what he calls 'being-in-the-world') has to contend with the 'end of sense' and the 'end of the world' (Nancy 1997: 4–5). By that, he means our individual experiences no longer have any unifying divine or teleological framework and order. In this fragmented scenario, a different kind of sense and world become possible – namely the world as praxis. Practices of sense-making in the form of art, writing or philosophy become the basis of a new, pluralized world-forming. Nancy thus argues that creative, generative acts of *mondialisation* (world-forming) stand in opposition to the horrors of globalization, which is leading us, through social disintegration, misery and injustice, towards *l'im-monde* (the un-world) (Nancy 2007).

Importantly, Nancy links these creative, generative acts of world-forming to images. In his view, images do not represent reality – they create (a) reality. As such, he is not interested in thinking of the image through symbolic structures or functionalist semiotics – interpretive theories that are frequently brought to bear on images. Instead, he views images performatively: in their act of existence they create the world they refer to. As Nancy puts it, '[a] work of art "says" or "announces": yes, there is a world and here it is' (Nancy 2005, quoted in Janus 2016: 3). Therefore, according to Nancy's philosophy, the process of creating an artwork does not merely help us to pull into focus a pre-existing world that generally goes unnoticed in day-to-day life. Rather, it is the act of creating an artwork that engages us in a process of world-forming. Put simply: worlds are made, not found.

This is a significant departure from the widespread view of images as representational. It also adds a new perspective to the ostensibly fixed binary of 'fiction' and 'documentary' forms of sense- (or image-) making. Here, images are conceived of as a performative form of knowledge creation – they generate and announce a new world, rather than representing something pre-existing. The image is not a system of signs, waiting to be read and decoded. Rather, its sense lies in the praxis of its making. This holds true for participatory illustration too. As Mitch Miller says, in reference to his dialectogram practice, '[it] is the phenomenon it illustrates' (2015: Booklet 4, 28). I will argue in detail in the next chapter that the image in participatory illustration projects presents a praxis of collective sense-making, a space of human relations and of new meaning held in common.

Another key point of departure for Nancy centres on the notion of unity and fragmentation. Both Husserl and Heidegger's work was informed by a concern about what they perceived as the fragmentation of experience through modern science (Husserl) and Cartesian philosophy (Heidegger). And while they were not attempting to return to a lost (imaginary?) unity, they were interested in investigating what made the experience of a common world possible, which is perceived and understood as singular.[6] Schütz similarly conceives of a singular world in his conception of the lifeworld as 'not the private world of the single individual, but an intersubjective world, common to all of us' (Schütz 1945: 534). Nancy, by contrast, finds in the fragmentation of the world a profound possibility of its renewal through creative acts of sense-making. For Nancy, there is no pre-given world that we can all access and share. Instead, we may 'without delay, reopen each possible struggle for a world' (Nancy 2007: 54). In the Nancean paradigm, art is one of the primary world-creating activities, where the sketching of multiple singular spaces can result in plural worlds (Roney 2013: 345).

It was always my instinct that we harbour the possibility of coming together to make plural worlds – and that illustration holds a special capacity to draw these out. To say that there is no pre-given and singular, common world does not mean that our only option is to return to an individual, privatized self. There *are* meaningful possibilities for intersubjective connection, and we do have the ability to create temporarily shared worlds. The projects discussed in this book offer tangible manifestations of the possibility of meaning held in common.

[6] Although Husserl occasionally speaks of lifeworlds in the plural, he ultimately stresses that there is only one world for which a plural makes no sense (Husserl 1970: 143). His philosophy posits the lifeworld as a 'universal horizon' (Husserl 1970: 281). Incidentally, Husserl's universalism played a role in his exclusion from public life in Germany in the 1930s. The National Socialists rejected Husserl, who was Jewish, in part because his universalism implicitly included *Unmenschen* (brutes) such as Jews and non-white ethnic groups (Moran 2000: 88).

But how can a constellation of individuals be gathered together to form a coherent world? As discussed in the previous chapter, the question of how to arrange such a nexus visually became a key methodological challenge in my work. The tension between the individual and the community, the singular and the plural plays itself out in some form or another in all participatory creative projects. I lived through it most acutely in my difficulties in *Walking the Elephant*, where I struggled to devise appropriate organizational and illustrative methods to draw individual contributions together into a coherent, shared world. The tension manifests itself formally in the seemingly opposite demands of producing a visually unified and coherent illustration while also allowing for individual and necessarily heterogeneous elements to remain distinct and recognizable. Moreover, these heterogeneous elements risk clashing with one another visually – and in turn their discrepancies may render the illustration incapable of 'pulling itself together' to actually constitute a 'world'.

The reason why the Enter/Entrar illustration in *Walking the Elephant* does not live up to its potential to present an overlapping, intersubjective world of the project participants is not because it strives for unity per se. It fails because of the way this unity was achieved, namely through the obliteration of individual experiences and contributions. However, to add another level of complexity here, I must stipulate that experiences and contributions are also not the same thing. It would be naïve to argue that people's drawings and inscriptions about Elephant and Castle *directly* correspond to their experience of the place – too many other factors play a role here, such as drawing skills and participants' situations when they are invited to draw, alongside many other circumstantial details. Still, the activity of creating these drawings and inscriptions also constitutes an experience in and of itself which registers in people's consciousness. By redrawing the illustration in its entirety, I removed the possibility of people recognizing material evidence of their subjective experience – the experience of creating a drawing – as part of a larger, collective whole.

By comparison, the cover artwork for *Write Women into History*, which is also a synthesized and formally coherent illustration, contains the visible traces of individual contributions and thereby allows participants to perceive and remember the creation of their own drawings. They can recognize their contribution as part of a bigger whole. One woman expressed this very sentiment: 'I feel so proud that this was my placard, this is my drawing of [name]. And I really like that nobody would know that. I feel proud of it, but I don't feel a need for it to be recognized by anyone that *I* did these bits. It really feels like a collective thing.' Another woman chimed in: 'Yeah, I find myself, like you, [thinking] "Uh, yeah! I did that one!"' (2022). The result is the appearance of a world that has 'pulled itself together' but is still clearly made up of the multiple traces and fragments of its contributors' creations.

FIGURE 5.1 A selection of ceramic pigeons from The Portland Inn Project, crafted with local residents in the Portland Street area of Stoke-on-Trent. The same basic pigeon shape is individually painted by members of the community. Photograph by Glen Stoker.

FIGURE 5.2 Rebecca Davies, Anna Francis and other members of The Portland Inn Project, Stoke-on-Trent (2017). Photograph by Glen Stoker.

This is the case for nearly all of the projects under discussion in this book. I shall introduce yet another example to illustrate this point. The Portland Inn Project[7] in Stoke-on-Trent, a hugely inspirational creative arts community organization, decided to produce a 'flock' of ceramic pigeons. The organization developed the pigeon in collaboration with community members. Now, The Pigeon Club, led by team member Alice Thatcher, work to create a handcrafted series of table-top sculptures and ridge tiles, made using two basic pigeon shapes. Individual members of the community paint the birds, resulting in a coherent 'flock' that is nevertheless made up of multiple, individual birds – all of them unique and different. The same is true of Sidney Mann's *Bordando Tierra del Fuego*, Nina Sabnani's *Tanko bole chhe/The Stitches Speak* or Ash Sakula's communally written, spoken, illustrated and animated poem *Rest*. In all of these pieces, it is possible to discern singular, individual expressions forming part of a polyphonic whole. In the case of *Cracks in the Pavement*, with its multiple layers of individual inscription, the effect is especially pronounced. Reflecting on this convergence of the singular and the plural, one of the walkers said: 'I love [the finished map]! Especially the observations of the other walkers. It makes that favourite walk of mine have many more dimensions, observational and emotional.' Another participant commented in even greater detail (and intensity!):

> When I opened [the finished map] up, I was curious to see how it had developed, and then studying it in more detail somehow made me really happy, I couldn't stop smiling. It's so lovely seeing other people's thoughts and responses to places we all know so well and share as a neighbourhood. Looking at the other maps – all of which are very familiar routes and part of what I'd describe as 'home' – did instantly fill me with joy too. I'm not sure why – perhaps the fact that using simple means, people have collaboratively turned these shared (but separate) everyday experiences into interesting, curious, beautiful objects. A small, personal celebration of an area, something that belongs to all of us.
>
> (Anonymous 2021)

There were similar comments regarding the finished artwork of *Write Women into History*:

> The diversity – you know – that every drawing is a different style, yet it fits together as a whole. I think you did a fantastic job, and I really do think it's amazing that we are all there, [...] these are pictures of us, and this is me by

[7] The Portland Inn Project, co-founded and co-directed by artist Anna Francis with artist and illustrator Rebecca Davies, provides an ongoing programme of creative activities and community events with the aim of achieving greater social cohesion, wellbeing and cultural expression for a community on the outskirts of Stoke-on-Trent, an area that has been marginalized by years of political mismanagement and economic decline.

> [name], although now I'm not even sure if that was me, but it doesn't matter, you know. It doesn't matter at all.
>
> (2022)

Indeed, as this particular participant expressed, the output of the project resulted in the specific connection between an individual and their contributions becoming partially forgotten. But to echo her, it does not matter at all: it is still abundantly clear how individual contributions play a part in making a plural world in this piece.

So, where do we stand now? Over the last four chapters, I have elaborated in some detail on the various questions that emerged while working on participatory illustration projects. I have broken the process down into four parts: including others in the work (Chapter 2), eliciting inscriptions (Chapter 3), assembling the contributions (Chapter 4) and reflecting on the finished piece (Chapter 5). In each chapter, I have drawn on cognate literature to illuminate the respective challenges and insights. This last chapter, which begins to philosophically reflect on the results of the work, paves the way for the next chapter, where I deepen my observations on participatory illustration projects and interweave these with theory pertaining to our sociality and the political. This will set me up to present the central hypothesis of this book: over the following pages, I will argue that participatory illustration projects offer an opportunity to reveal and record expressions of community. Here we go!

6 TRACING EXPRESSIONS OF COMMUNITY

To put it succinctly, this book's central argument is that participatory illustration projects have the capacity to assemble community and constitute the political. It is in this chapter that I make my case in detail, bringing conceptions of community into relation with the possibilities of illustration practice.

In doing so, I draw on ideas around community that came to the fore in twentieth-century European philosophy: this was when philosophers such as Jean-Luc Nancy first argued that our sociality and multiplicity are not just a pleasant or interesting addition to our existence but fundamental to our being. To be is always already to be in the communal world – to be with others and to respond to it and them. From this standpoint, others play a necessary role in the constitution of one's own self. Or, to put it in even plainer terms: as individuals, we do not simply exist within ourselves; we *become* ourselves in our exposure to others. In this chapter, I discuss how participatory illustration projects allow us to (quite literally) draw this out – illustration allows us to reconsider, record and reflect on our interrelation with one another.

The word 'community' has a powerful affective dimension. In contemporary vernacular, the notion of community is often used by players on both the political left and right to conjure up a romantic dream. To 'live in community' is projected as a normative ideal, something to be reclaimed in opposition to forces that have supposedly interrupted the natural way of life. On the left, the idea of community is held up as an alternative to the competitive and alienating individualism of capitalist society. On the right, meanwhile, the term carries ugly overtones of ethnic identitarianism; it is used in opposition to the intrusion of supposedly disruptive alien bodies into what is believed to have been a hitherto harmonious unity. On both sides, the term is tinged with nostalgia for an unspecified bygone era, when society was ostensibly structured in more 'organic' clusters of small face-to-face groupings.

Often, to invoke the idea of community is to express a longing for something that is experienced as lost. Reflecting on the term, Jean-Luc Nancy writes that speaking of community 'is like referring back to a lost love' (Nancy 2017: 51).

While the word 'community' continues to be used colloquially as a positive albeit nostalgic term without much consideration, it has garnered more complex debate among philosophers over the years. Especially in the aftermath of the Holocaust and the various repressive and murderous totalitarian regimes of Europe and Soviet Russia, the idea of community – as an essentialist or collectivist 'we' – took on an unpalatable dimension. After the demise of communist rule in Eastern Europe, the liberal primacy of the individual seemed unstoppable. And indeed, the idea of the autonomous subject, which is self-sufficient and self-realizing, continues to dominate our understanding of ourselves and others today. However, the spectre of 'community' continues to haunt and entice.

In Chapter 2, I discussed examples of participatory art and design practice, whereby 'social' or collaborative projects offer a counter model to the individualistic striving of single authorship. According to this line of reasoning, art can serve as an arena in which to oppose the neoliberal ascent of the individual. However, when taken further, these ideas quickly run into trouble. Feminist and political theorist Iris Marion Young (1990) highlights the shortcomings of this argument, explaining that, in a binary where each term is defined by its inverse relation to the other (such as individual vs community), simply flipping the estimation of their value does not accomplish much at all. Upon reflection, both concepts rely on the same ideal of a unified whole: those who support the primacy of the individual think of people as self-sufficient and fully realized within themselves, while those who advocate for the ideal of community see this as a unifying fusion that draws its members into a harmonious unity. And as Young reminds us, mobilizing the idea of community in this manner brings us into uncomfortable proximity to ethnocentric and identitarian ideologies.

How might one move beyond this impasse? Many participatory art and design projects (and people in general) take the existence of 'community' (or specific communities) as a given. They therefore overlook some of the more fundamental questions about the nature of community itself. What does it actually mean to think of our existence in terms of multiplicity rather than singularity? How can we sidestep the traps set by the word's romantic and nostalgic overtones without throwing out the term completely? How might a creative practitioner relate to the idea of community while remaining conscious of these pitfalls? And what role can illustration play in these debates?

When wondering how to respond to these questions, I found some resonant ideas in the work of Nancy and Hannah Arendt. They both sought to rethink the notions of sociality, multiplicity and coexistence while wrestling with European history's dark shadow. In fact, I draw on these philosophers precisely because they demonstrate a heightened awareness of how appeals to a unified 'we' can result in distasteful and murderous consequences. Nancy's detailed and painstaking examination of human sociality on the most fundamental level has been particularly influential for me. His book *The Inoperative Community* (1991) invites us to think of community as something without essentialist foundations (a people, a race, etc.). In other words, Nancy establishes an idea of community that is not predicated on a shared essence or identity.

In this chapter, I primarily draw on Nancy's work on these questions, while also engaging with Arendt's writing on plurality and difference. When we intertwine these thinkers' nuanced ideas on coexistence with collaborative illustration practice, it becomes clear how such projects can serve as an arena that reveals, crystallizes and documents expressions of community.

Arendt's notion of plurality and Nancy's thinking on community both build on the groundbreaking work of Martin Heidegger. It is, of course, well known that Heidegger colluded with and even explicitly supported the Nazi regime in Germany during the 1930s and 1940s. There is much debate about whether his detestable political alignment has influenced or connects with his philosophical work. However, his radical rejection of the self-contained Cartesian subject in favour of a socially grounded conception of existence remains a crucial contribution to twentieth-century thought – and it creates the basis for Arendt's and Nancy's political philosophy. So, for better or worse, Heidegger continues as a guest in this chapter; I hope you can accept his presence.

In Chapter 1, I discussed the associations people generally attach to the term 'political illustration', namely illustration that deals with political subject matter. In reference to William Morris's Kelmscott Press, I raised the question of whether illustration could be considered political not by virtue of its subject matter but rather by the way it has been produced. Notably, Kelmscott Press's small group of professional workers (designers, printers, illustrators) operated in a flat hierarchical structure. By contrast, the projects I discuss in this book take in larger and looser groupings of mainly non-professional participants who contribute to the given project as interested citizens, not creative professionals. So, what does it mean to think of this coming together as political?

Nancy links his detailed thinking on community directly to the idea of the political. He proposes that exploring the nature of the social body is inherently political. The ways in which we perceive the relationality of society must be the basis for all other forms of political theory. It is in this regard that I conceive of participatory illustration projects, including the ones I am discussing in this book, as political. As I will argue in this chapter, they act as a site of ontological disclosure, where we can expose the nature of our being, as well as test and reveal a Nancean understanding of community and the political.

Nancy's fragmentary writing, characterized by an active grappling with language, can feel vague and esoteric at times – I have certainly struggled with it for this reason. But he offers us a way of handling difficult notions such as community without either mythologizing them or inadvertently demolishing them with overzealous critical deconstruction. With his complex and occasionally guarded trains of thought, he sidesteps the traps of a 'deluded proposal of a "solution"' (which he also calls 'myth') on the one hand and 'the pure abyss of nihilism' on the other (Librett in Nancy, 1997: xii–xiii).[1]

In the first section of this chapter, I explain some of the principles of this philosophy by introducing relevant ideas from the work of Heidegger and Nancy in greater detail. If you are feeling impatient, you can skip this part. However, even in the following three sections, philosophical discourse continues to occupy a prominent place. Each segment offers a discussion that blends together ideas from Heidegger, Arendt and Nancy with aspects of community illustration projects. Overall, I am laying out the idea that collaborative illustration projects create space for individuals to encounter one another in expressions of community. This tends to play out in three different ways or stages: illustrations which refer to joint matters of concern act as catalysts for an encounter, serve as focal points for the duration of the interaction and then function as a record thereafter.

No human self in the absence of another

As we set out on this journey, I wish to tackle a few key questions: What are the fundamental principles of the philosophy that I am building on here? How exactly is community theorized by Nancy and Heidegger? Interestingly, Nancy starts from the same place as Young: he expresses discomfort at the way the term 'community' is used nostalgically. Nancy traces this back to the writing of Jean-Jacques Rousseau in the eighteenth century (Nancy 1991: 9) – from this time onwards, perhaps prompted by the experience of modern society and statehood, the idea of community began to be tinged with a sense of loss and nostalgia, which meant that community became something to be *re*gained and *re*constituted. However, writing in the shadow of totalitarianism and its genocidally destructive manifestations, Nancy rejects such nostalgic yearning for community, often conceived of as 'organic communion with its own essence' (Nancy 1991). Instead, he proposes to completely rethink the question of social body's relationality at the most fundamental, ontological level.

Nancy advances this line of inquiry in a series of joint essays with philosopher Philippe Lacoue-Labarthe, which were published under the title *Retreating the Political* ([1981] 1997). The central argument put forward in this book is that we should turn to philosophy, rather than political science or political theory, to find new ground from which to think future possibilities of human association (Lacoue-

[1] As a sidenote, the hasty lurch towards a 'deluded solutionism' feels all too familiar to me as an illustrator – and perhaps even more so as a designer.

Labarthe & Nancy 1997: 109). Indeed, Nancy and Lacoue-Labarthe assert that it is necessary to unpick assumptions surrounding the nature of the human subject and human relations before reflecting on questions of statehood or power, as it is this relationality which underpins political formations (Lacoue-Labarthe & Nancy 1997:117). Their essays present philosophical reflections on historical conceptions of 'the human' and how these ideas underpin notions of political community.

Nancy and Lacoue-Labarthe make a marked distinction between our being in common – which they call *le politique* (generally translated as 'the political') – and the toing and froing seen in the everyday arena of power relations – which they call *la politique* (generally translated as 'politics') (James 2006: 158). If you find this distinction, along with their sustained focus on questions of social coexistence, to be indicative of unnecessary philosophical pedantry, you are not alone. Nancy and Lacoue-Labarthe's work has indeed been criticized for withdrawing from a more direct engagement with empirical politics and specific struggles. American philosopher Nancy Fraser, for example, was noticeably frustrated by the two thinkers' refusal to 'step into politics to which the logic of their own hopes and thought would otherwise drive them' (Fraser 1984: 148).

As I try to parse questions about our fundamental relationality *through* communal illustration, I cannot help but notice how the practical engagement of specific projects braids together *le politique* and *la politique.* While I am using these pages to discuss the potential of participatory illustration to expose us to the possibilities of 'the political' – the relationality of subjects at a fundamental level – many of the illustration projects themselves are intimately involved in the conflictual space of everyday politics. This is because they address political topics, whether that be the spatial injustice wrought by processes of gentrification and other insensitive planning procedures (thematized by Mitch Miller's dialectograms and my project *Walking the Elephant*), the historiography and general (in)visibility of overlooked communities (Nina Sabnani's *Tanko bole chhe/ The Stitches Speak* and my project *Write Women into History*) or the importance of local connections and attachments in the face of escalating global catastrophes triggered by the climate and ecological emergency (Sidney Mann's *Bordando Tierra del Fuego* and my project *Cracks in the Pavement*). Illustration practice does not have the capacity to speak in purely abstract or metaphysical terms; it is, on one level, always about something specific outside of itself. So, while writing this book has propelled me to think about more abstract notions of the political, the projects themselves assuredly step into the 'everyday arena of power relations'. To my mind, this in itself constitutes a compelling reason to hold up illustration as a sophisticated visual practice capable of bridging diverse realms of action and bodies of knowledge.

Nancy's work on relational subjectivity builds, in large part, on his reading of Heidegger's *Being and Time* ([1927] 1962). Heidegger is often credited as being the first contemporary Western philosopher to put forward the now familiar idea that existence is essentially social and relational. In doing so, his work departs from the philosophical tradition of the Cartesian subject who is complete unto themselves and stands separate from an external world. These previous philosophical theories of the individual struggled to convincingly account for intersubjectivity: if you are a unified individual how do you connect to another? Heidegger gets around this by moving away from the idea of an isolated self who must then extend themselves outwards. Instead, he proposes a radically new characterization of selfhood, arguing that there is no human self in the absence of another. In his own words: 'When *Dasein*[2] directs itself towards something and grasps it, it does not somehow first get out of an inner sphere in which it has been [...] encapsulated, but its primary kind of Being is such that it is always "outside" alongside entities which it encounters [...]' (1962: 89). In short, Heidegger proposes that human existence is always already enmeshed and dispersed among other people and things in the world, and so our relation to others in the world is a primary, ontological condition of being per se. He goes on to write that '*Dasein* is essentially Being-with' (1962: 156); being with others is an existential characteristic of our own existence. This is still valid even if we are momentarily on our own, because the experience of being alone can only take place in the knowledge that others exist.

Nancy subsequently picks up on the ideas that Heidegger developed in *Being and Time*, but distances himself from his pronouncements on the heroic futural authenticity of a people (*Volk*) in the latter part of the book, which many read as a prelude to his more explicit turn towards Nazism a few years later. Still, rather than rejecting Heidegger altogether, Nancy proposes a return to and radicalization of his original thought. He holds fast to the idea that our fundamental ontological condition is to be in relation to each other and the world – Nancy calls this being 'singular plural' (2000). He proposes that our coexistence is a fundamental given, that is to say, we do not need to do anything in particular to 'activate' this aspect of our selves. To be sure, there are myriad practices and conventions through which we can express and experience our sociality. However, it is my contention that collaborative illustration has the capacity to initiate, frame and record those processes in particularly compelling ways. I will examine this in depth in the next three sections.

Gathering – Illustration as a catalyst for community

So, how might illustration illuminate aspects of our coexistence? How can reflecting on these projects help us understand how we co-constitute each other?

[2] Human existence, literally 'being-there'

Heidegger certainly laid the philosophical foundations of these ideas through his concepts of *Dasein* (being-there) and *Mitsein* (being-with), but there are some significant limitations to his thought. For one thing, despite his repeated assertion that the fundamental nature of our existence is *co*existence, his philosophy has been characterized as solipsistic and monadic – in other words, concerned with sociality only as a feature of an individual life (see, for example, Schatzki 2005: 236). He also foregrounds what he seems to believe is a fundamental sameness between oneself and others.[3]

I had to look to another thinker for a different way forwards: notably Hannah Arendt offers an alternative perspective. Indeed, Arendt, unlike Heidegger, foregrounds relationality, plurality and *difference* in her political philosophy. On the opening pages of *The Human Condition* she writes that '[...] men, not Man, live on the earth and inhabit the world' (Arendt [1958] 1998: 7) – Arendt argues that it is actually our plurality that constitutes the essential condition of all political life. She adds that '[...]we are all the same, that is, human, in such a way that nobody is ever the same as anyone else who ever lived, lives or will live' (Arendt [1958] 1998: 8).

Plurality and a free public realm are key concepts for Arendt. For her, the political is something that arises between humans in the space of the common world where we can appear to one another and experience our plurality through the simultaneous presence of innumerable perspectives (1998: 52–7). The experience of our mutual presence is key: we see and hear each other and are seen and heard by others. The public realm gathers us together, while also preventing us from falling over each other (1998: 52). This is made possible by a 'world of things [that] is between those who have [the world] in common, as a table is located between those who sit around it' (1998: 52) – I will take the time to parse this citation in detail.

First and foremost, Arendt's repeated use of the word 'things' in this context is intriguing. Today, 'thing' is an informal expression that is used to refer to an otherwise unspecified object. However, this word grew out the Old English *þing*, signifying 'assembly' or 'gathering'. Drawing on this forgotten meaning of the term, various thinkers have reflected on the capacity of 'things' to draw people together and put them in relation to one another.[4]

[3] For example, in his description of 'Others' he writes that: 'By "Others" we do not mean everyone else but me – those over against whom the "I" stands out. They are rather those from whom, for the most part, one does *not* distinguish oneself – those among whom one is too' (1962: 154, emphasis in original).

[4] Arendt seems to allude to this prior meaning when she writes of her hopes for 'the world's [...] transformation into a community of things which gathers men together' (1998: 55). Bruno Latour is more direct. In his 2005 essay 'How to Make Things Public', he explicitly reminds us of the etymology of the word 'Thing', explaining that, in the past, it stood for a 'certain type of archaic assembly' (2005: 12, capitalization in original), or an 'issue that brings people together' (2005: 13). Rather than focusing on our many political disagreements, Latour suggests we should concentrate on the 'hidden coherence

However, Arendt's image of a table that gathers us up while simultaneously preventing us from falling over each other is probably most resonant here – and it provides a compelling metaphor for the projects under discussion in this book. After all, a table performs a number of important functions at the same time: it draws us in, while also holding us at a suitable distance, thus enabling us to interact. It sets us in relation to one another and provides a neutral surface – or a kind of arena – on which to display, share and elaborate on common concerns.

Each of the projects I explore in this book similarly assembled a group of people with a shared interest or overlapping experiences. Miller's dialectograms, Mann's *Bordando Tierra del Fuego* and my own project *Cracks in the Pavement* all bring people together who inhabit overlapping or shared spaces. Sabnani's *Tanko bole chhe/The Stitches Speak*, Ash Sakula's *Rest* and my project *Write Women into History* assemble groups who share similar experiences. Either way, for each project, people were gathered up by the emerging manifestation of their shared concern on pieces of paper or cloth; at the same time, those surfaces (the paper or the cloth), alongside the project framework, kept them at an appropriate distance and prevented them from falling over one another. I would argue that Miller's dialectograms create the most literal image of a group of individuals being drawn towards a large piece of paper that invites them to contribute their individual perspective to an emergent, polyvocal manifestation of their common world. In other projects, such as *Bordando Tierra del Fuego* or *Write Women into History*, the pieces of cloth or paper were much smaller and the participants occasionally dispersed to work separately; still, despite this dispersal, the images and inscriptions, when taken together, created an arena for the presentation of a world in common, drawing participants together and orienting them towards one another. In *Cracks in the Pavement*, the gathering was staggered across intervals of time, but once again the paper map was the 'thing' that enabled the walkers' (in this particular case deferred) encounters, the arena 'where humans can appear to one another and experience their plurality' (Arendt 1998: 52).

This ability to facilitate gathering but prevent collision is the first way in which participatory illustration projects, as I see them, initiate and illuminate experiences of community. Collaborative illustration projects have the potential to transform privately held interests and experiences, scattered among individuals, into a common, public 'thing' that assembles these individuals in their plurality and difference. The basic outlines of a common world – a lightly sketched contour of a shared neighbourhood or territory, the invocation of a shared experience

in what we are attached to' (2005: 5). In an expansion of Arendt's point, Latour's 'Things' appear as complex socio-material assemblies that allow 'matters of concern' to occasion the gathering up of relevant parties. Taking things (!) further still, contemporary Swedish scholars of participation design Bjögvinsson, Ehn and Hillgren propose the term 'design Things' which they define as 'Things that are modifying the space of interactions and performance and that may be explored as socio-material frames for controversies, opening up new ways of thinking and behaving, being ready for unexpected use' (2012: 12). I am grateful to Mitch Miller for drawing my attention to this rich vein of thinking.

– exert a gravitational pull through a common concern and a mutual sense of attachment. And while it is this pre-existing sense of attachment that initially orients individuals towards one another, it is the emergent rendering of these concerns as collaborative, illustrative documents that then really draws people in.

In Chapter 2, I invoked the image of a climbing frame to describe project structures that are explicitly designed to help participants engage, while also putting them in new relationship to one another. In Arendt's vision, those metaphorical climbing frame rungs could be reconstrued as supportive and well-proportioned furniture that allow everyone to have a seat at the table and enable participants to get involved in processes of inscription. By drawing (or stitching) themselves into an emergent common world, individuals are gathered up. Thus, collaborative illustration has the capacity to act as a catalyst for a public encounter.

A politics of communication – Illustration as an enactment of community

While one of Arendt's rallying cries is the importance of a free public space, in which people can speak and act in their plurality, Nancy focuses on the possibility of rethinking the notion of community as such. Building directly on Heidegger's ideas of human existence, Nancy sees a fundamental directedness towards others as our basic ontological condition. Thus, Heidegger's concepts of *Dasein* and *Mitsein* become Nancy's 'being-toward' and 'being-with'.

In *The Inoperative Community* (1991), Nancy suggests that community is not something that has been dislocated due to modern subjects being separated or ripped apart, but that our very separation or rupture is precisely the condition that makes community possible in the first place. He thereby rejects the nostalgic idea that 'community' is something that we have lost and must recover, emphatically distancing himself from an understanding of community as an organic, unifying fusion of individuals predicated on a shared essence or self-realizing identity (what Nancy calls 'immanence') (1991: 15). Instead, he suggests we need to rethink the concept on wholly new terms. Community, according to Nancy, becomes possible in the very moment of our dispersal and rupture. It is only through fracturing and separation that subjects are exposed to one another in their singularity and finitude.[5] In Nancy's own words: 'What this community has "lost" – the immanence

[5] 'Singularity' is Nancy's preferred expression, as opposed to 'individual' or 'subject' which implies an atomized absolute (1991: 4). 'Finitude' is a key term in Nancy's thinking on community. Heidegger had proposed that, for each individual human, their existence stands in relation to their own death, and Nancy (by way of Georges Bataille's work on sacrifice) develops this into a crucial cornerstone in his thinking on community. He proposes that we can only come to understand our own death (and birth) by witnessing this in others (Nancy 1991: 15). Nancy scholar Ian James gives a good summary of this discussion (2006: 179–86).

and the intimacy of a communion – is lost only in the sense that such a "loss" is constitutive of "community" itself. It is not a loss: On the contrary, immanence, if it were to come about, would instantly suppress community, or communication, as such' (1991: 12).

And so, in a move that overlaps with Arendt's conception of a 'table in the public realm', Nancy proposes to think of community as an encounter between singularities which are exposed to one another through their separation. This separation is key, as it allows us to see and recognize one another. In his own words, '[t]he being of community is the exposure of singularities' (1991: 30), 'a socially exposed particularity' (1991: 74). Without being separated, or 'spaced out', as he also calls it, we would be fused in a 'socially imploded generality' (1991: 74). He clearly rejects accounts of community that are based on an essential unity or totality.

This focus on the experience of community as 'a space itself', on what lies beyond the self is key. Indeed, this scenario makes communication essential; Nancy accordingly celebrates 'the being-communicating (and not the subject-representing)' (1991: 24).[6] Communication is central to Nancy's conception of community (and the political more broadly) – and becomes a major theme in his work. In *The Sense of the World* (1997), he writes about community as an incessant tying up of singularities with each other, which happens through a '"seizure of speech" that would include all of the "singular decipherings" that comprise the "wandering labour of sense"' (1997: 115). In other words, as opposed to a conception of community that reduces us to a common essence, he proposes community as a social formation that entails an ongoing process of communication, which connects us as individuals. Precisely what is communicated is less important than the existence of communication itself, because 'each communication is, above all, communication not of something held in common but of communicability' (1997: 114). Being in community is expressed through repeated attempts at making sense together.

This image of singularities exposed to one another, engaged in the 'wandering labour of sense' is another fitting description for many of the projects I am discussing in this book. In Miller's dialectograms, Sidney Mann's *Bordando Tierra del Fuego* and my own project *Cracks in the Pavement*, the 'singular decipherings' of particular neighbourhoods or territories become intermingled and amalgamated with each other on shared pieces of paper or cloth. Similarly, in drop-in sessions for *Walking the Elephant*, I noted how spontaneous conversations emerged: when various people were contributing to the project maps at the same time, they often chatted about their overlapping and divergent views of Elephant and Castle. What's more, new arrivals were keen to study how previous participants had marked up the map and would then add their own view in relation to what was

[6] I will discuss this crucial difference between communicating/presenting and *re*presenting later in this chapter, as well as in Chapter 7.

already there. In Heideggerian terms, this recalls the image of a common world: 'the world is always the one that I share with Others' (1962: 155). Nancy's more nuanced thinking takes this a step further to suggest a slightly more complicated picture: there is no world, bar the sense we make in our collective consideration of something.

Cracks in the Pavement also picks up on this idea of separated singularities trying to jointly make sense of something. Here, due to pandemic restrictions, individuals communicated with each other across intervals of time via the emergent maps. As they were (in principle at least) walking the same routes, it was precisely those intervals that prevented them from falling over one another (to use Arendt's terms). But it was also those temporal deferrals that accentuated the separation which, according to Nancy, is necessary for the experience of community. Furthermore, the social rupture, which Nancy sees as key to experiences of community, was emphasized and exacerbated by the lockdown restrictions. In this scenario, our fundamental inclination towards one another was materialized on the shared pieces of paper that were passed from one walker to the next. But beyond the piece of paper, participants continued to sense each other in additional ways. They knew that each of them would be preceded and followed by various others and that these others would touch what they were touching now – both hands on the paper and feet on the shared pavement. The sense of the world, and the sense of

FIGURE 6.1 Luise Vormittag, *Walking the Elephant/Recorriendo Elephant* (2017–2019) for Latin Elephant. Participants at a workshop in the Elephant and Castle shopping centre in April 2017. Photograph by Cristina Errea.

FIGURE 6.2 Luise Vormittag, *Walking the Elephant/Recorriendo Elephant* (2017–2019) for Latin Elephant. Participants at a workshop at the Draper Residents' Association's Great British Summer Day Fair, July 2017. Photograph by Daniel Hopkinson.

one another, then, went beyond the ocular to encompass touch, smell and sound. One walker commented: 'I loved doing the walk and the thought that other people were also going to do the walk. I wondered what other people's responses to the sights, sounds, smells of the walk might be. It was mysterious in a way because we didn't meet each other on the walk' (Anonymous 2021).

Nancy's insistence on the centrality of communication for being in community in his writing is mainly centred on linguistic expression: he evokes 'the cry, the call, and the complaint as much as the theoretical discourse, the poem, and the song, along with the gesture and silence' (1997: 115), although he does at one point stretch to include 'the sumptuous graphic singularities and fleeting semantics of graffiti' as a 'crude and desperate [!] mode' of collective sense-making (1997: 116). Leaving aside this rash characterization of graffiti as 'desperate', it must be said his focus on acts of communication, including graphic communication, as a way to connect singularities to each other bears out in all of the projects I am discussing here.

The discipline of illustration is, of course, intimately linked to communication. In *The History of Illustration*, the authors describe illustration as 'visual communication through pictorial means' (Doyle, Grove & Sherman 2018: xvii); meanwhile, in *Illustration Research Methods*, the desire to communicate is posited as one of several key principles of illustration (Fauchon & Gannon 2021: 16). However, these general definitions refer to a finished piece of work. To be sure, the outputs that emerge from the participatory illustration projects I am discussing have their own communicability (I will delve into this further in Chapter 7), but the point I wish to make here relates to the communications that take place *during* the processual emergence of the pieces. The various frameworks (climbing frames), alongside the material manifestations of encounters on pieces of shared paper and cloth, occasion the 'incessant tying up of singularities with each other'. On the maps in my and Mann's projects, the lines or stitches overlap. In Miller's dialectograms, multiple accounts of a shared space bump up against each other. It becomes clear that 'my' domain is enmeshed with 'yours': this space between us appears on the pictorial surface that we share. I see and acknowledge your neighbourhood and understand and position my version in relation to yours. Similarly, the portraiture task in *Write Women into History* communicates first and foremost that we have observed each other and thereby 'made' each other, however imperfectly, a part of a shared world. Likewise, even though the narrative embroidery panels in Sabnani's *Tanko bole chhe/The Stitches Speak* were primarily worked on by only two artists, other members of the trust contributed additional elements that were integrated into the animation. Overall, this project speaks of a shared past and a mutual set of concerns that become meaningful through the act of holding them in common. Similarly, Ash Sakula's animation *Rest* brings together multiple 'singular decipherings' that together give rise to a communal world.

Thus far, I have considered how participants expose their singularities to one another in the process of collective sense-making. However, the illustrator-facilitator clearly also has a part to play in these processes. I too was intertwined in my projects, albeit in a set of roles that differed from those of the other participants. While discussing the task of assembling various contributions in Chapter 4, I noted how different projects are designed with varying levels of interventions by the illustrator-facilitator. Nevertheless, our involvement is obvious and undeniable in all of the work. Communal acts of sense-making do not only emerge and manifest in the space between participants, but also in the space that appears between them and us. In the projects I have worked on so far, I certainly revealed aspects of who I was in that moment in time in my encounters with the group in question.

What this discussion shows is that collaborative illustration projects have the capacity to manifest and materialize our ontological condition of being towards one another. They highlight our shared social ontology, our fundamental structure of being, which, as Heidegger and Nancy highlight in their respective ways, is intrinsically relational. Illustration thus becomes a form of ontological disclosure. But, in fact, I believe that the projects I have highlighted go beyond this: they do not solely expose but also subtly amplify the conditions and processes of being towards one another. Nancy occasionally uses the term 'clinamen' to describe our fundamental inclination towards one another (1991: 3) – this word is usually used to describe the unpredictable swerve of atoms. Likewise, these projects demonstrate how participatory illustration, by crystallizing and materializing our ontological inclination towards one another, can indeed increase or change the swerve of those atoms (or people). In other words, they modify our interactions.[7] It turns out that the material presence of an emergent illustrative document can have an effect on the groups and publics in which it emerges. It acts like a magnet, pulling us together – and it even has the potential to reconfigure the social fields in which it appears. By taking part in the projects, illustration materializes and simultaneously subtly redefines the participants' relationships to each other.

This swerving of social atoms is clearly visible in *Cracks in the Pavement*. Prior to the project, individual participants might have passed each other on the street without knowing, despite living in the same neighbourhoods. Of course, given that the project partly worked through word of mouth, many of the walkers did know the person directly preceding and following them. But through participation in the project, they were rearranged into a string of social connections that included people previously unknown to them. Sidney Mann's *Bordando Tierra del Fuego* similarly reconfigured the social sphere. Over time, a new constellation of people crystallized around the regular gatherings and the expanding cloth map – or, to use other terms, a community emerged in the process of stitching their shared territory into being.

These considerations establish the second facet of participatory illustration projects that I want to highlight in this chapter. The overall project design, alongside its material manifestation in the form of emergent illustrative documents, does not just gather people up, but also creates an opportunity for participants to draw each other out – to co-appear and thereby co-constitute each other. Community is not found in the elimination of difference, the merging of identities and the collapse of distance. Instead, community is enacted through the exposure of our individual selves to each other via the 'seizure of speech'. Through (graphic) communication, community can be drawn out. Taking part in these projects becomes an enactment of community.

Collective sense-making – Illustration as a trace of community

So, I have established that acts of communication are central to the enactment of community, as they give rise to a practice of collective sense-making. But what are the key qualities of this 'sense' that is being made together? In this section, I will discuss the nature of communal sense-making in greater detail and consider how

[7] This recalls Bjögvinsson, Ehn and Hillgren's recommendation to 'design Things that modify the space of interactions' (2012: 102).

this manifests itself in the illustrative documents that emerge from these projects. I intend to highlight two main attributes of these documents: how they depict a non-totalizing multiplicity and how they present (rather than *re*present) events.

First and foremost, as indicated above, Nancy believes that plural sense-making unfolds in its most lucid and unambiguous form through linguistic modes – either in different forms of speech acts or in what he terms 'literary writing' (1991: 64).[8] He emphasizes literature as an exemplary mode of sense-making, because it is 'the practice of a sharing of voices' (1991: 80) and because he believes it can offer resistance to simplistic closure. In other words, Nancy finds in literature a form of writing that maintains an openness towards plurality and heterogeneity. And it is certainly true that, as a genre, literature has the ability to convey other people's subjective experiences particularly well. It also less frequently slumps towards oversimplified or mythic culmination compared to most political rhetoric.

However, I would assert that the resistance to closure that Nancy locates in literary writing is mirrored in the processual nature of drawing (see my discussion in Chapter 3). Tim Ingold, for example, describes drawing as a process that operates with a continuous deferral of closure and resolution. The lines of drawings, of which there could theoretically always be more, express a continuous history of becoming (2011: 221). Ingold uses these meditations on drawing to ponder the discipline of anthropology: like drawing, anthropology ought not to try to 'enframe others, to paint them into a picture, and thereby bring closure to their lives' (2011: 221). After all, lives are not lived as 'enframed'; rather, all life is social, as Ingold argues, since it is fundamentally multi-stranded, 'intertwined' and emergent.

It is surprising, given Nancy's focus on 'co-appearance' and Ingold's writing about 'intertwined' life, that neither consider collaborative or dialogic forms of praxis to a greater extent. The more I think about it, the more convinced I am that participatory illustration projects, such as those I have been reflecting on, are perfectly poised to highlight and document our co-appearance or our multi-stranded, intertwined existence – perhaps more so than literary writing or drawing. After all, these participatory illustrative projects manifest and materialize the exposure of singularities to one another, they open up and record the appearance of an in-between. And by doing so, they allow new narratives and vistas of places and times held in common to emerge. Because all of the projects under discussion are

[8] While expounding on this aspect of Nancy's thought, the philosopher Ian James repeatedly attempts to mitigate against the bewilderment that he imagines his readers might experience upon learning that an extended reflection on the political and community results in a celebration of literature (2006: 200–1). Somewhat defensively, he repeatedly points out that this is indeed a coherent and compelling conclusion. He argues that literature is, after all, 'where the sharing of human voices and community occurs; it is where the new and the different can be affirmed' (2006). I did not think that this swerve towards the literary was all that surprising, as I suppose it would not be for most people who read novels or are more generally involved with and invested in the arts. One of the most exciting things about an artwork is that it allows you to get a sense of other ways of being.

assemblages of multiple contributions, they are by their very nature open-ended. There is always room for one more, things might always take a new direction or bent. Thus, their outputs can be aptly described as a non-totalizing, intertwining manifestation of the participants' common concerns, as exposed and revealed at the moment of their sharing.

This is an important point to make, because plural, open-ended heterogeneity is not normally thought of as a quality of illustration, especially commercial illustration practice. To be fair, I did start this book with Michele H. Bogart's account of illustration as a 'collective, negotiated enterprise' and 'collectively generated material culture' (2018). From her description, you might assume she is referring to the types of projects I have been discussing. But Bogart actually has a different collectivity in mind. Her scholarship is concerned with North American advertising imagery of the early to mid-twentieth century; indeed, this type of illustration can also be described as having been collectively produced. Bogart works in the tradition of social art history, and therefore focuses on the external figures and forces that impact the creation of an illustration. As such, while only one pair of hands produced the images of a jolly 1950s Santa Claus drinking a bottle of Coca-Cola (illustrator Haddon Sundblom), a much larger number of people and systems shaped their appearance. Bogart points to 'art directors, "layout men", copywriters and clients', alongside more general systems of production, circulation and reception, all of which play a role (2018). However, these images do not speak of open-endedness and plurality, quite the opposite. They conceal their collective authorship and present a narrow declaration of normative ideals, which are typically inscribed in these types of pictorial regimes. Bogart's scholarship prises open these seemingly innocuous images to reveal not a singular illustrator working in isolation, but a complex enmeshment of forces and intentions.

In contrast to these kinds of images, participatory projects do not pretend to speak of singular authorship – instead, they pull in the opposite direction. They work hard to disclose and emphasize the relational processes of their creation. Instead of putting forward a definitive message or a declarative statement, they suggest 'that community is coming about, or rather that something is happening to us in common' (Nancy 1991: 69). They present a tessellation of singular utterances around a shared concern.

In addition to this open-ended, plurality, illustrative documents that emerge from collaborative projects have another feature – one that took me quite a long time to fully understand. Looking at the outcomes of these projects, it occurred to me that they did not show a *re*presentatio*n* of a pre-existing reality; rather, it was something more akin to a *presentation* of something new and different – something that had emerged in the process of creating the work. And because it had grown out of the interlocking articulations of many, it was always open-ended and to some degree unforeseeable. I began to see that the combination of multiple utterances facilitated by participatory projects makes the emergence of something new more likely, compared to work that is created by a single author.

I have already touched on the seemingly minor differences between *re*presentation and presentation in Chapter 5. Although I primarily leaned on Nancy for his nuanced work on community, it is interesting to note his thinking on images here too. Nancy, as it turns out, is averse to representationalist conceptions of visual culture. In his view, images do not reframe anything pre-existing, nor do they point to something 'real' beyond their 'mere' appearance. He seems less occupied with the question of what an image is, focusing instead on what an image does, its performativity, its generative act of world-forming and its capacity to act as an 'announcement of a world' (Janus 2016: 2).[9]

Performative knowledge creation is often exemplified by J. L. Austin's notion of performative utterances (1962): these are speech acts that do not describe reality but create it. Austin most famously cites sentences spoken during marriage ceremonies ('I do … hereby take you as my lawfully wedded wife'). Another example of language's performative power, which perhaps has a more direct relation to some of the projects I am discussing here, comes in the form of geographer Yi-Fu Tuan's assertions that language is crucial in processes of world-making and place-making: 'Words have the […] power to call places into being' (1991: 686).

How, then, might illustration be performative? In addition to Nancy's work on images, artist and academic Barbara Bolt's writing provides several detailed responses to this question. In her numerous publications (2004, 2007, 2011, 2013), she proposes that art has the capacity to transcend a representationalist relation to the world, already decried by Heidegger in his essay 'The Age of the World Picture' (see Chapter 4). She explains how, for Heidegger, understanding and knowledge emerge relationally through being in the world, being involved in it, handling things and relating to others. The world is never objective – it is not separate, rigid and settled. It cannot be known in advance and we cannot master or take hold of it through representational practices (Bolt 2011: 64). Rather than *re*presenting – presenting again – a reality that is already out there, Bolt suggests that art can be 'the unconcealment of that which has never before been revealed' (2011: 68). She ultimately asserts that art is a performative practice, a mode of poetically revealing what is. 'It produces rather than represents reality' (2004: 136).

These philosophers and theorists convincingly argue that it is more productive to think of art in general, and images in particular, as performative – that they have the capacity to make worlds, rather than show us something already known and settled. I believe that this capacity is only compounded when multiple contributors find themselves working together. Nobody can know in advance

[9] See also my article 'Illustration as an Announcement of a World', where I discuss the idea of performativity and illustration in greater detail (Vormittag 2024b).

what might emerge when we spend time drawing each other out. As we disclose ourselves to each other, as we act towards one another, our singular expressions jointly outline a new perspective on our shared neighbourhood, our shared histories and our shared concerns. For example, the five neighbourhood maps of *Cracks in the Pavement* do not represent anything pre-existing – nobody saw or imagined their neighbourhood like *this*! (See Figure 1.5, p.27) Instead, they present the repeated intertwining of singularities, as the lines of the walkers' routes intersect and overlap. They (literally!) show us the 'wandering labour of sense' (Nancy 1997: 115) that took place in between a specific group of people, in a particular place and at a particular time. So, to put it simply, the maps do not *re*present; they present, both to the walkers and to subsequent audiences, the possibility of a world. Sidney Mann's *Bordando Tierra del Fuego* likewise presents us with a tapestry of encounters, expressing how the 'chicas del mapa' came to a joint, new understanding of their region and the possibilities of inhabiting it more meaningfully and intentionally. Similarly, the cover of *Write Women into History* does not *represent* the group, instead it *presents* the group *as group*, as singularities coming into sight of each other and 'tak[ing] control of narrating their own history', as the women explain in the postscript of the book.

These discussions lead me to the third and final facet of participatory illustration projects that I wish to highlight in reference to the main argument of this book. Collaborative illustration projects do not only gather up individuals and provide opportunities for them to draw each other out and to co-constitute each other in an expression of community. They also exemplify a particularly resonant form of performative knowledge production, where an open-ended collection of singular utterances gives rise to a new world.

Certainly, we enact our sociality through innumerable everyday conventions and processes. We do not need participatory illustration projects to bring about our connection, to prompt us to co-constitute each other. We are, as Heidegger would say, always already in the social world, in constant relation with others. Still, the strength of these projects is not that they provide a radically new way of being in community, but that they provide a particularly resonant manifestation of these processes. In these projects, the process of enacting community and conjuring worlds is not transient, but rather captured on pieces of paper, cloth and other materials. As a result, they can document processes that are otherwise ephemeral and dispersed. The work can act as a trace of community, (semi-)permanently inscribed on paper – I will further elaborate on this point in the next chapter.

Taken as a whole, this chapter highlights how collaborative illustration has the capacity to assemble, enact and record community. I have argued for collaborative illustration projects to be recognized as an arena for ontological disclosure, a space to reveal our being as 'singular plural'. It is primarily on this account that I propose that this work constitutes the political. With all this in mind, let us now turn to what happens after the work is completed – what constitutes the project's afterlife.

7 AFTERLIVES

And so now we face the (almost) final act. This chapter is concerned with the afterlives of collaborative illustration projects. Thinking about an afterlife while you are in the midst of something does not always come naturally – at least it does not for me. I have tended to let myself get swept up in the immediacy of the encounters, as well as the urgent practical pressures that arise in this type of work. It was not until I had completed a number of projects that I started to wonder if there was not something else I might do with all the material I had amassed over the course of the years, beyond organizing it into folders in my cupboard. These had been such lively projects. Might there be a way to promote their *future* vitalities, too? Besides the participants themselves, what other publics might the projects' outputs be able to communicate with? Could Nancy's idea of the 'community of communication' (Chapter 6) extend beyond those who were directly involved in the creation of the work? What was needed for that to happen? Is some form of longevity possible or even desirable?

In this chapter, I continue the discussion I initiated in the final pages of the previous chapter on the nature of the illustrated outputs that emerge from this work. I believe that reflecting on (and caring for) the illustrative documents that emerge from these projects lends the work additional dimensions. It opens up new perspectives for thinking about the nature of illustration (as an indexical trace! as a document!) and prompts us to consider what role these documents could play in future. I explore how they record and hold on to the liveliness that gave rise to them and consider how they might journey beyond the group that worked on them into other realms.

Quite rightly, there has been a lot of attention on the aftermath of participatory art projects (Foster 1996: 196; Kwon 2002: 97; Matarasso 2019: 114, 118–20). Various writers correctly point out that drawing these projects to a close and concluding the complex social situations that they often involve can be awkward and disappointing for participants, if it is not done with sufficient planning and care. I too found this when I spoke to participants for a case study that I considered early on as part of this research: they described experiencing the end of a project as bewildering and abrupt. After all, it is not always easy to know how best to wind things down. The Portland Inn Project in Stoke-on-Trent, England, is confronting this challenge head-on by working on a hundred-year plan (!) with and for the community they are embedded in.[1] This plan seeks to put in place structures that could lead to lasting change, but it also functions as an invitation to embrace different time frames in this kind of work. As Anna Francis, one of the founders, put it: 'Perhaps the work you are doing is not always about the immediacy of what you might be able to achieve, but instead is about the longer term and the bigger landscape?' (Davies & Francis 2023).

This kind of long-term commitment, however, is not always possible. In my own work, I tend to work with clearly defined project outputs which, among other things, function as an indication of the finite nature of the work. To mark an ending and bring closure, I often reproduce and distribute copies of those outputs to everyone involved in the project. Other practitioners handle the conclusion of their projects differently – sometimes with public exhibitions (for example, Miller's dialectograms and the touring exhibit of Sidney Mann's *Bordando Tierra del Fuego*) or screenings (for example, Nina Sabnani's *Tanko bole chhe/The Stitches Speak* and Billy Ash Sakula's *Rest*). What unites these examples is the impulse to galvanize the group around a clearly articulated, shared goal from the start, and then to find a way to mark and celebrate its realization.

This chapter, however, is not about the care and thoughtfulness required to navigate these complex social scenarios; others have written insightfully on this topic (see, for example, Goldbard & Matarasso 2021 or Helguera 2011) and I am enormously grateful for their work. I will, however, focus on the materials that result from participatory projects – because even a clearly articulated output as collective goal does not necessarily spell out what to *do* with the work once it has been completed. As I was cycling around East London distributing thank-you packs to contributors to *Cracks in the Pavement*, I started thinking about how the contents of the packs would end up tucked away in shelves and drawers, while the original maps and supplementary materials would be stored in a cupboard in my studio. There is nothing inherently wrong with this, but it still felt like something of a muted ending to what had otherwise felt like a vibrant project. As I dropped

[1] The Portland Inn Project started in Stoke-on-Trent's Portland Street neighbourhood in 2015, when artist/illustrator Rebecca Davies and artist Anna Francis hosted a number of individual short-term projects in the area. When residents told them that they wanted something more permanent, Davies and Francis joined forces to respond to this request. Over the following years, a series of successful funding applications supported them to gradually build a community arts organization with a permanent base. This orientation towards long-termism has helped Davies and Francis work with the community to address some of the more deeply rooted problems they face in their neighbourhood through a range of hugely inventive and inspiring creative initiatives. Establishing themselves as an organization has also prompted them to focus actively on succession planning – putting in place structures to enable the work to continue with other people in leadership roles.

FIGURE 7.1 Sidney Mann and 'las chicas del mapa', *Bordando Tierra del Fuego* (2017–2024) on show at the Casa de las Artes in Tierra del Fuego National University, Ushuaia, Argentina. The piece is touring to different museums throughout the country.

off the packs, a number of participants suggested organizing an exhibition. While I could see how such an event would be a great opportunity for a social gathering and might indeed provide a meaningful moment of celebration, I believed that organizing such an event would ultimately only postpone the questions I had begun asking myself. Where does this work belong? Where should I put it?

Cracks in the Pavement is characterized by having 'original' outputs – the physical paper maps that participants used and worked on directly. Quite naturally, these original maps acquired a certain patina that distinguishes them from the reproductions that I was distributing to the walkers. However, my dilemma of where to 'put' the work did not really grow out of a concern for the storage and preservation of rarefied objects. In fact, I also experienced similar questions around other projects I worked on where the 'original' was much less clearly identifiable. For example, *Walking the Elephant*, my project with a Latin American community organization in South London, existed primarily as a webpage; meanwhile, *Write Women into History* was a book with multiple print editions. In both cases, talk of an 'original' did not make much sense. And yet, I was still unsatisfied with the idea of tidying away the project material and being done with it. After much rumination, a realization started to take hold: I had been thinking of the outputs as 'illustrative documents'. And a document wants to be *filed*.

So, where might I file them? Ultimately, I decided to deposit outputs of projects I worked on in publicly managed and accessible repositories. In its final format as a webpage, *Walking the Elephant* is filed on *Layers of London* – a crowd-sourced, map-based history website developed by the Institute for Historical Research

FIGURE 7.2 *Cracks in the Pavement* original map.

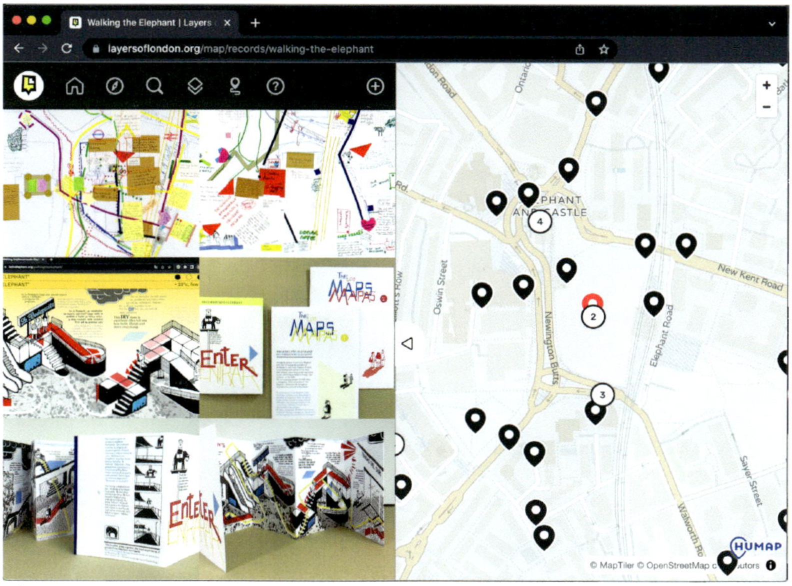

FIGURE 7.3 Luise Vormittag, *Walking the Elephant/Recorriendo Elephant* (2017–2019) for Latin Elephant, filed on the Layers of London website.

(SOAS, University of London). Copies of the book *Write Women into History* – in addition to being distributed through various feminist networks and sold in some local bookshops – were submitted to a local library. And the original maps of *Cracks in the Pavement*, alongside a variety of accompanying documents, were donated to the Hackney Archives in East London, where they were presented and exhibited during an event, before being filed in their archival storage system.

It was the notion of the public sphere (and public record) that felt pivotal in these decisions. All these projects present the experiences of a group of people in a specific geographical place at a particular moment in time. The outputs – or illustrative documents – are a record of a specific set of geographical, historiographical and social configurations. By submitting these outputs to publicly accessible archives, I realized I could inject them with additional spatial and temporal dimensions. Placing them in these repositories would at least create the *possibility* of future encounters with these materials.

Thus, in this chapter, I draw out points of discussion on the nature of these documents and the possibilities they hold when they are inserted into the public sphere. I will be focusing primarily on my own projects in this chapter, as I do not have much relevant information on the afterlives of other people's work. In the first section, I reflect on the formal and material qualities of the illustrative documents resulting from collaborative illustration projects. What enables them to record and, to some degree, subsequently replay the enactments of community that created them? To answer this question, I reflect on their indexical, documental

FIGURE 7.4 Storage facilities in the Hackney Archives, where *Cracks in the Pavement* has been filed.

and suggestive qualities. The outputs can be seen as evidentiary records of a series of social acts. As such, they carry traces of the process of their creation; that is to say, they can attest to the communal moments of their creation. I further Nancy's argument about community being enacted through communication in this section by referencing Italian philosopher Maurizio Ferraris, who argues that it is not merely communication but inscription and registration that are fundamental to society (2013: 176). Acts of inscription create a fixedness and stability that enable transmission – or *relay* – of ideas to other times and places.

Once we have ensured that illustrative documents are indeed able to transmit the vitalities they carry, where do they go? In the second section of this chapter, I offer reflections on surrendering project outputs to public repositories in the hope that they may encounter other audiences, generate new 'communities of communication' and perhaps even contribute to the continuation of the public sphere itself.

Then, in the third and final section of this chapter, I discuss *why* we should offer these documents up to the public record. I question what value these acts might hold for contemporary as well as future audiences. As illustrators, we are often in the habit of regarding our work as insignificant and trivial. The idea of being able to contribute to the preservation of cultural expression and articulations of 'worlds' in the face of looming extinctions might not come easily to us. But I believe that these (admittedly small!) projects demonstrate an important principle: illustration has a capacity to safeguard unique perspectives against oblivion. It can register and transmit visions of collectively articulated common ground.

So, overall, I propose three things in the pages that follow. Firstly, collaborative illustration projects can serve to mediate and bind us together over periods of time around shared concerns. Secondly, they can provide a 'space of appearance' for marginalized groups. And finally, these projects have the capacity to contribute to the structuring and endurance of a shared and plural public realm.

Indexicality, documentality and suggestiveness

For projects to exist beyond the duration of their unfolding between the participants and the illustrator, the outputs need to have permanent form. Indeed, it is rather exciting to think about enactments of community becoming an enduring configuration. Our gestures and our conduct towards one another are often ephemeral and generally do not leave a trace. This speaks to the core of why I believe illustration in its immutability can play such an integral role in helping us think through ideas about community. In the previous chapter, I wrote about how illustrative documents emerge in the course of these projects as an arena for collective sense-making. The paper or cloth substrates record moments of multiple individuals acting towards one another in an expression of community. But the outputs do not just register these moments of time; they preserve and, to a certain extent, replay them in the future. What is it about these illustrative artefacts or documents that makes this possible? And how can examining the qualities of these documents challenge our common understanding of what illustration is or does? How does this move us towards a vision of illustration as a form of performative knowledge production, as discussed in previous chapters?

Throughout this book I have referred to outputs as 'documents' and the act of marking the various sheets of paper, cloth or other materials to generate these documents as 'inscription'. Why have I used this language? 'Inscribe' or 'inscription' is loosely understood as the permanent alteration of a surface with a meaningful mark. It is precisely the word's free-wheeling openness that I was initially attracted to. On a practical level, I thought that inviting participants to 'inscribe' a piece of paper would be less intimidating than asking them to 'illustrate' something. Although I did not actually utter the word 'inscribe' directly – I preferred to use words such as 'mark', 'sketch', 'add', 'draw', 'stick' and 'scribble' – it acted as my internal indicator as to what I was inviting people to do.

Beyond the enabling breadth that attracted me to the word, 'inscription' has other conceptual facets that proved meaningful in my thinking. Notable among these is the way it combines discursive and material qualities. Bruno Latour, for example, introduces the idea of the 'immutable mobile' in his discussion of the scientific revolution: he uses this concept to explain the sudden progress in modern science that, according to him, occurred because 'anything and everything was transformed into inscriptions' (1986: 4). The 'immutable mobile' is an object that is immutable, presentable, readable and combinable (Latour 1986: 7), essentially any kind of image, writing or diagram on paper. In its light-footed potential for circulation, amalgamation and reorganization, it gives rise to new combinations of ideas, perspectives and knowledge. Inscriptions need to be both immutable and mobile to acquire their power. And both qualities outlined by Latour are of critical importance for the afterlife of the participatory illustration projects I have been discussing: they must be simultaneously durable (immutable) and transmissible (mobile).

If we edge a little closer to the field of illustration, artist and visual theorist Johanna Drucker also reflects on the concept of inscription. Drucker reminds us that an inscription 'always has a physically material indexicality to it, linking the change to the action and its effect on the substrate' (2009). I alluded to the indexical quality of my projects in the previous chapter, when I wrote about illustration as a *trace* of community. Acts of communal sense-making are materially captured at the time of their creation, producing a record of those acts. The inscriptions thus refer us back to the moment of their origin, namely the singular-plural encounters that produced them in the first place. So, 'inscriptions' can be defined as durable, mobile and indexical markings – and to think of illustration as consisting of inscriptions opens up exciting new perspective. I shall elaborate on this further.

Indexicality

Both illustrators and audiences often focus on the subject matter of an illustration – what it refers to, what it represents. But I became intrigued by the possibility of looking at the marks in illustrative documents in a different way. Instead of seeing them as predominantly pointing outwards to an external referent, I wondered what might happen if we were to acknowledge that they are also pointing in another direction, namely backwards in time. What if we think of them as signs that refer back to the event or process that produced them? Acknowledging that these documents carry indexical traces is particularly relevant in the scenarios that I have been discussing, where the work emerges from a communal encounter. But thinking of an illustration as an index will introduce a new outlook on any kind of work that acquires at least part of its significance through the process of its creation.

The concept of indexicality was originally introduced by Charles Sanders Peirce in the second half of the nineteenth century as part of his semiotic theory. American art critic Rosalind Krauss then built on these ideas in her discussion of

North American art practice in the 1970s. Indexical marks, writes Krauss, acquire their meaning due to a direct, physical relationship to their referent: 'They are [...] traces of a particular cause, and that cause is the thing to which they refer, the object they signify' (1986: 198). An index therefore functions as a 'pointing gesture [that] isolates a piece of the real world' (1986: 216). Like Drucker, Krauss calls attention to the fact that indexical inscriptions are not encoded. Instead, 'drawing is converted from its formal status of encoding reality to one of imprinting it' (1986: 216), making the surface of the drawing a 'repository of evidence' (1986: 216).

The idea of a drawing as a 'repository of evidence' was revelatory for me. From this perspective, an illustration acquires an additional layer of signification: it no longer just refers to its subject matter but also evokes its moment of creation. This rings true for several of my project outputs. On the face of it they might each speak of different themes – the intricately woven social networks of a migrant community in South London in *Walking the Elephant*, the concerns of the Women's Liberation Movement in *Write Women into History* and a reorientation towards hyper-locality during the COVID-19 pandemic in *Cracks in the Pavement*. However, their vitality is largely derived from the process of their creation, making them just as much – or perhaps even more – 'about' the encounters that gave rise to them, rather than the subject matter they ostensibly refer to.[2] Future audiences will come to acknowledge the encounters that led to the documents' creation by noticing the heterogeneity of the participants' contributions that are present in the final project outputs and that have obviously been produced a range of different people. These diverse inscriptions function as indexical traces of the communal acts of sense-making, reminding us of the moment when people gathered around a shared concern and collectively manifested a new vision of the places and times held in common.

Krauss goes on to describe how an indexical trace is experienced as 'physically present, temporally remote', giving rise to a 'presence' that 'fills the work with an extraordinary sense of time-past' (1986: 217). This continuous 'presencing' of an event at a temporal distance is particularly palpable in *Cracks in the Pavement*. In this project, it is not only subsequent audiences who encounter indexical traces connected to prior events. The internal logic of the project itself rested on 'physically present, temporally remote' material inscriptions. The maps were set up to emphasize the temporally staggered co-presence of fellow participants and there is every reason to believe that future audiences who access the original documents in the Hackney Archives could have similar experiences of remotely sensing the presence of those walkers. In their storage box in the archives, these original documents retain the verve and vitality that arose from the project's

[2] This is another inflection of the point I made in the previous chapter when I argued that my projects animate both 'politics' – issues relating to the everyday political contestations of power – and 'the political' – considerations of our fundamental relationality. The work is always functioning on two levels simultaneously.

connective materiality and accumulative inscriptions in the absence of actual embodied encounters. And the indexical quality – a 'pointing gesture' that refers to a past event – is retained, even when we move away from the original paper that was worked on by participants.[3] In *Cracks in the Pavement*, scanning and printing copies of the maps for all participants produced outputs that obviously lack the battered quality of the original maps, but still have, to a significant degree, the evocative power to conjure up the process of their creation.

Compared to *Cracks in the Pavement*, the final output of *Write Women into History* contains fewer of these indexical inscriptions. But each printed edition of *Write Women into History*, of which there are several, still points back to the polyvocal moment of its origin, as a range of vastly different portraiture styles is evident in the final version. I took care in my intervention not to obscure these differences and thereby preserve the indexical qualities of the drawings. Meanwhile, *Walking the Elephant*, as previously discussed in Chapter 4, suffered precisely because its indexical qualities were eroded in the process of my intervention.

Another compelling aspect of the indexical trace is its relationship to (or its undermining of?) artistic style – a central and occasionally fraught topic for many illustrators. Krauss highlights how artworks made up of indexical traces sidestep questions of style because of the limitation, or even removal, of artists' formal intervention in creating the work (1986: 208). This in turn reanimates a debate on the nature of authorship. In this scenario, an artist's task is not one of making or creating, but one of framing, selecting and presenting, thereby undermining a history of aesthetic convention and expressivity. Feminist media scholar Mary Anne Doane eloquently summarizes how indexical traces function in an artwork: 'Things speak for themselves, they are not spoken' (2007: 3).

Working with the affordances of the index is an exciting prospect for expanding the scope of illustration. Thinking of illustration as a practice that creates evidentiary documents that emerge from a specific set of conditions or events opens up a whole new avenue of possibilities. This does not mean that other modes or methods are outdated or wrong. An illustrator who is more strongly attached to their personal expressive style, and perhaps more generously imbued with a knack for observational drawing than I am, would pursue a project on the intersection of illustration and community in a radically different way to me – and with equal validity and substance. One might think, for example, of the highly observant work of Olivia Twist, who depicts people interacting in their everyday cultural environments, such as the upper deck of a London bus, the

[3] Krauss herself uses the process of photography as a model in her elaborations on the index. She argues that 'the ghostly traces of departed objects' are not dependent on the continuity of the material substrate of their inscription for their evocative power. Rather, the process of 'physical genesis' which 'disallows processes of schematization or symbolic intervention that operate within the graphic representation of most paintings' is what produces the indexical quality of the inscriptions (1986: 203).

market, the chicken shop or the kitchen. Twist represents gatherings of people she knows and observes, encoding and schematizing what she sees in her distinct and highly impactful graphic language. By contrast, I create frameworks for letting community articulate itself. This is not to make claims of superiority, far from it. I am a huge admirer of Twist's work. The contrast simply serves to draw out the distinction.

But my position stretches even beyond the idea of letting 'things speak for themselves'. In my work, I feel community *becomes* community in these very acts of articulation. We can become ourselves by showing the world who we are. This type of illustration has the capacity to produce the reality it refers to.

Documentality

So, how might this performativity play itself out? Indexicality in its very nature is oriented towards the past, towards a prior event or presence that is fixed and framed for subsequent recall. If we frame the artefacts that contain those performative indexical marks as documents, we are able to take the analysis a step further.

Documents, such as certificates, contracts or records of a meeting, do not just record and replay a past event; they also contribute to the construction of social reality. This point is made at length (and with some occasional pomp and grandiosity) by Italian philosopher Maurizio Ferraris in his book *Documentality* (2013), where he argues that the social world fundamentally relies on systems of registration and inscription. According to him, societies depend on documents that record and store various acts and facts for future reference. In other words, social reality draws from the sedimentation and re-elaboration of traces (Ferraris 2013: 175).

It is Ferraris's description of documents as stable objects that can register and thereby *produce* social realities that is most relevant here. I have been arguing that, via participating in collaborative illustration projects, individuals enact community – they become community in the process of inscribing themselves on a shared document around a common concern. Ferraris's work, then, shines a light on the mechanics of this process, explaining how community becomes community in the act of inscription. Every social role or agreement depends on the society's shared memories of a relevant series of acts and events – and it is in the form of inscribed documents that these acts are registered, their memory materialized and their meaning amplified. By framing my projects' outputs as 'documents', I therefore draw attention to their role as evidentiary records of a series of social acts, an attestation of a social reality.

In the previous chapter, I discussed Nancy's conviction that communication is central to the being of community, as it forms the basis of collective sense-making. Reading Ferraris's book, I subsequently saw how this point can be pushed further. Ferraris argues that 'a system of communication that was unable to keep traces and to register the communications would be ruinous, because it would lead to the dissolution of society' (2013: 176); therefore, as he contends, '[t]he act of communicating is not sufficient on its own but turns out to be a function subordinated to something more essential, namely registration' (2013: 179). Although Ferraris is being somewhat dramatic here (and he also fails to account for the existence of sophisticated societies that rely or relied predominantly on oral systems of communication), the argument did resonate with me. The idea of registration is indeed central to many of the projects I have been discussing. Since they involve working on material substrates such as paper or cloth, expressive articulations in these projects are always already a form of permanent registration (allowing for obvious limits to this due to the possible erasure of some marks and the eventual disintegration of the substrate). Framing these project outputs as documents highlights their status as a public registration of a social act.

Nina Sabnani, for example, has reflected on how the film *Tanko bole chhe/The Stitches Speak* became a historical document. When the film first premiered in Kutch (where the Kala Raksha Trust is based), members of the community expressed how impressed they were with the result. 'It's not a story,' they said, 'it's our *history*!' (quoted by Sabnani 2019). Sabnani affirmed how important it was for the community to recognize the animated film and the stories it contains as their own: 'It's an acknowledgement of a life. Of an existence. That you have been duly acknowledged' (Sabnani 2019). However, much has changed since the film was completed. One key contributor has died, another has left the region. With more money, the lifestyle of the community has also been transformed. 'Everything is different,' said Sabnani more recently, 'so the film is a document of how things were in a particular time and place' (Sabnani 2023). The piece thus acts as a record of a specific geographical, historic and social configuration. It registers a particular period of time, when things were a certain way – it has become a historical document that can offer a stable point of reference for a community in the otherwise transient passage of time. Building on this, if we think of participatory illustration project outputs more generally as documents, we cast them as part of a system of registrations and inscriptions, which contributes to the structuring of society and the public realm.[4]

[4] I should probably add a greater degree of exactitude to this claim: there is clearly a superabundance of different types of documents in existence. I shall spare you the painstaking system of differentiation drawn up by Ferraris, offering just a few clarifying remarks in its place. For example, a marriage certificate and the illustrative project outputs I have been discussing are both documents that attest to a social bond. But there are clearly significant differences too. Besides the obvious legal distinctions, which I do not need to spell out here, a marriage certificate has a different relationship to time and duration. Its effects on social (and legal) affiliation are intended to extend themselves into the future continuously. This is to say, people remain married until an event (usually death or divorce) puts an end to it. By contrast, the illustrative documents I am discussing here attest to the fact that something, in this case an enactment of community, has taken place at some point in the past. They are a form of documentation, attestation and substantiation, rather than a licence, certificate or contract. Sabnani's

One of the types of documents described by Ferraris is the so-called 'strong document'. This 'is not descriptive but performative, [...] it aims to produce effects'. In other words, these documents contain 'inscriptions of acts, which would not exist without the inscriptions' (2013: 268–9). These performative documents operate in the same way as J. L. Austin's performative utterances, in that they produce the reality they refer to. Even the examples Ferraris offers – marriage or degree certificates – are similar to the instances of performative speech Austin named in his work.[5] So, how does this map on to illustration? When I was discussing performativity in Chapter 5, I argued that it is more appropriate to think of illustrative documents as performative, rather than representational. The projects' outputs put forward a 'presentation of a world', they render worlds that would not exist were it not for the communal acts of inscription that created them. They are thus performative in respect to the world they refer to – but they are also performative in another sense. While the projects outputs put forward a 'presentation of a world', they also render those presenting it as a community.[6] Jaleen Grove recently highlighted illustration's capacity to help us empathetically conjure a different future when we find ourselves mired in a problematic past (Grove 2023: 17). Building on that, I suggest that illustration can remake us right here in the present too. It can announce and present who we are, as well as who we have become in the very act of making the illustration.

Suggestiveness

In addition to their indexicality and 'documentality', the outputs of collaborative illustration projects have a third quality that enables them to reach future audiences in meaningful ways. In many cases, the final pieces (documents!) are not solely made up of indexical traces of the participants' inscriptions. As I have already outlined, in the projects I worked on, my own interventions, my processes of assembling and consolidating the contributions, resulted in varying degrees of illustrated and designed input from me (see Chapter 4). After all, indexicality

film attests to the community's existence and substantiates their life stories; it does not contractually bind them into some perpetual union. This distinction is important. I have, after all, been arguing for a conception of community that is generative and active and does not rely on any form of essentialist constancy. The permanent registrations of the enactments of community which are recorded in these documents are important for what I term the 'endangerment sensibility' that surrounds the communities and their concerns – I will cover this in the final section of this chapter. Taking note of these on a public record marks them out as having value and significance, rather than the documents being a legitimizing seal of approval for the permanent existence of a particular community.

[5] One of Austin's most famous examples is the kind of sentence spoken during marriage ceremonies: 'I do [hereby] take this woman to be my lawful wedded wife' (Austin 1962: 5). These utterances are linguistic actions that alter the reality in which the speaker exists.

[6] I have written in greater detail about this in my article 'Illustration as an Announcement of a World' (Vormittag 2024b).

is not the only way to visually communicate experiences and encounters. The choice of materials, the use of graphic design and a thoughtful engagement with processes of reproduction can clearly enhance future audiences' experiences by offering up suggestive clues and tactile experiences. In Chapter 4, I wrote that one of the major tasks of the illustrator-facilitator is to make the work travel-ready, to prepare it for its onward journey towards other audiences and publics. That includes the integration of suggestive design and production elements that underscore and enhance the themes of the work.

These considerations resonate particularly loudly in the case of *Write Women into History*, where every design and production decision was taken with due consideration. This book has seen a variety of print runs (using different processes), and so now exists in a variety of different iterations, but the first 200 copies were printed at local riso-print shop on uncoated paper using specialist inks. The main colours (purple, white and green) were chosen as a tribute to an earlier wave of feminists in the UK, the suffragettes. In addition, the risograph printer is a piece of Japanese technology released in the 1980s, but the imperfect look and feel of riso prints is suggestive of earlier DIY print publications and graphic ephemera, seen in activist pamphlets and fanzines of the 1960s and 1970s. The typographic design of the book's title also came from one of the women in the group, who submitted this as her placard design. She made the design using one of the Letraset sheets I sent out as part of the pack of materials for participants. I subsequently scanned and used this without altering her design, maintaining the slight unevenness of the letter placement. Letraset, which came into widespread use during the 1960s, was a dominant force in self-published fanzines and student newspapers in the 1970s and '80s. During the workshop I ran with the women, it was clear that many of the women were very familiar with the dry-transfer lettering, with one loudly exclaiming that this reminded her how much she had always hated using it, much to the bemusement of everyone.

I am unable to retrospectively determine exactly which typeface the title is rendered in, but it is similar to the Rooney typeface used for headlines inside the book. In fact, I chose Rooney for its general retro feel, vaguely gesturing towards the 1960s, 1970s and 1980s, without being overtly connected to any particular decade. Together with the jumble of other typefaces that were employed for the various placard designs on the cover, it lends a distinct DIY aesthetic to the overall design. This, alongside the book's tactility, print quality and the overall design, was intended to conjure the spirit of 1960s, 1970s and 1980s counterculture in general, and the Women's Liberation Movement in particular.

I do not have access to feedback from other audiences and readers of the book, but many women from the group felt that the cover artwork's design and production does suggest a particular style and culture to its viewers. One woman said: 'I think it speaks of the time – the colours were just brilliant. The style of it is very in keeping with second wave feminism, somehow. [...] It really does conjure up what we were.' Another commented: 'I showed it to my partner, I didn't say anything, just showed it to him, and he said: "Oh, that is so of the Women's Liberation Movement!" It just did exactly what it was designed to do' (HOWLers 2022).

Cracks in the Pavement presents another scenario in terms of the suggestiveness of its print design. The project's central output is, of course, the maps themselves, and they consist nearly entirely of inscriptions by the participants. The reverse sides of the original maps, however, do contain some print design: a range of illustrative and graphic elements combine with text to explain the project's rationale and rules of engagement. In contrast to *Write Women into History*, these illustrations and designs were produced in the initial stages of the project. Rather than communicating the results of a participatory phase, they were intended to invite people to enter into the project – they showcase different types of drawing and mark-making styles in an attempt to make the project feel accessible. The illustrative vignettes are very obviously made up of different pieces of paper arranged together. Their composite character is further emphasized through the inclusion of paper clips and tape in the illustrations and the emphasis on shadows that appear between the different elements. Overall, they do not conjure a particular place or time but are generally suggestive of improvised convergence and temporary assembly.

All in all, the presence of indexical traces in my projects' outputs, the hand-rendered inscriptions of my participants and, in the case of *Cracks in the Pavement*,

FIGURE 7.5 Luise Vormittag, *Cracks in the Pavement* (2020–2021), illustrative vignette.

the battered quality of the original maps combine with the suggestiveness of my illustrated and designed additions to produce communicative documents that have the capacity to speak to other audiences beyond the participants themselves. The indexical elements in the outputs also refer us back to the singular-plural moments of their creation, showing that individuals came together in a collective process of sense-making around a shared concern. The resulting documents manage to attest to the enactments of community that have taken place in their creation, while also speaking of the particular concern at hand. Thus immutable but mobile, they could be cut loose.

The public sphere – A space of appearance

All things must end. But once the project is finished – with the outputs completed and furnished with qualities that (one might hope!) give them the possibility of onward travel – how does one see them off? Nancy offers us some thoughts on these moments of completion. He asserts: 'the work […] must be offered up for communication[…], that is to say, presented, proposed, and abandoned on the common limit where singular beings share one another. The work, as soon as it becomes a work, at the moment of its completion […] must be abandoned at this limit' (1991: 73).

As I mentioned above, when I was planning and carrying out my projects, I did not thoroughly consider how or to whom I was hoping to offer or present the projects' outputs, and where exactly I wanted to 'abandon' them. While I was focused on producing an output, I did not really think beyond delivering them as a coherent and satisfying token of achievement for the participants and myself. For example, I initially imagined that the *Write Women into History* booklets were simply intended for the women in the group and their friends and families – after all, we originally planned for a very small print run of only sixty copies. Similarly, while I was working on *Cracks in the Pavement*, I had no particular publication ambitions. Beyond the intended distribution of copies to participants, there was every chance that, without further intervention, the various outputs and documents that resulted from these projects would end up stored in a cupboard in my studio at home.

Nonetheless, over time, this came to appear a somewhat stymied fate for this kind of rich work. In its form as a webpage, my project *Walking the Elephant* did have a certain public profile, but after the Elephant and Castle site was ripped out and I saw the gaping hole where there had once been an intricately woven web of relations, I felt compelled to register the project on a more general public record. In this, I was propelled by a desire to contribute a historic record, to make it known that something else had once existed on this spot. In other words, I came to understand that I wanted to offer these documents to the public sphere.

The idea of the public sphere is of critical importance to Arendt's political philosophy. Indeed, the public sphere is a place where 'everything that appears [...] can be seen and heard by everybody and has the widest possible publicity', which is crucial because '[f]or us, appearance – something that is being seen and heard by others as well as ourselves – constitutes reality' (Arendt 1998: 50). So, in Arendt's view, the public realm is of much greater importance than private thoughts, experiences or feelings. Private experiences need to be translated into a form that is fit for public display for them to acquire greater meaning. When Arendt subsequently goes into greater detail about the possibilities of translating private experiences into public ones, it almost seems as if she is writing about the kind of work that I have been discussing in this book: 'The most current of such transformations occurs in storytelling and generally in artistic transposition of individual experiences' (Arendt 1998: 50). For Arendt, the public space offers us a 'space of appearance', a kind of stage where human beings in their plurality can co-constitute a shared world.

Illustrator and arts facilitator Jhinuk Sarkar echoes the importance of the 'artistic transposition of individual experiences' and how the materialization and public display of previously private concerns can have a powerful impact. Describing her work with a group of mothers whose children are or have been mental health service users she says:

> 'Working through illustration, they get to process their ideas more deeply [...]. If we were doing similar [reflective work on motherhood] just through a conversation, it would feel more like therapy. With this, it has an external, material form that can be evaluated. You are capturing something that's inside your head for somebody else to look at and interpret'.
>
> (Sarkar 2023)

As Arendt develops this line of thought, she comes to write about how the 'human artifact' structures and organizes our public realm (1998: 52). This then leads her to 'the world of things [that] is between those who have it in common [like] the table [which] is located between those who sit around it' (1998). I have already discussed Arendt's metaphorical image of the table which gathers us up and puts us in relation to one another in some detail in Chapter 6, where I argued that the ability to assemble while simultaneously preventing a collision is one of the key affordances of collaborative illustration projects. Interestingly, designer and academic Carl DiSalvo makes a similar argument. He relates Arendt's invocation of the 'human artifact' that organizes the public realm specifically to design, suggesting that the metaphor of Arendt's 'table' could be transferred to any manner of made items, including communications, events, environments and systems, as these things can also serve to mediate and bind us together (2020: 261). In turn, DiSalvo also helped me see how this idea can be taken further. When I was writing about Arendt's 'table' in Chapter 6, I was thinking of the process of projects – how they assemble and configure people, materials and ideas. But DiSalvo alerted me to the possibility of conceiving of project *outputs* as potential structuring devices for future publics. He writes: 'In addition to being a means to gather and stage the public, the stuff of design also enables the *endurance* of the public. It provides a continuity of relations, and while these relations can and do change, there remains a means of ongoing orientation' (2020: 261–2) (my emphasis).

Inserting – or, as Nancy would say, 'abandoning' – the outputs of my projects in publicly accessible repositories then adds another facet to the work. In the previous section, I demonstrated how these outputs act as documents that attest to enactments of community. Having been subsequently filed on the public record, these attestations acquire value and esteem for those communities and their concerns – they are offered up to the 'space of appearance', where 'everything that appears can be seen and heard' (Arendt 1998: 50). Thus, these illustrative documents now stand a chance of extending Nancy's notion of a 'community of communication', offering the possibility of a 'continuity of relations' and suggesting an 'ongoing orientation' towards a similar set of concerns to future audiences.

Future worlds

It is, of course, impossible to predict if and how these projects' outputs perform the noble function of enabling the endurance of the public (DiSalvo) – or even if they simply reach others in an extended 'community of communication' (Nancy). In many ways, neither I, the participants, nor anybody else has that much influence over how the work will actually be encountered or experienced by spectral future audiences. And imagining ever-expanding periods of time stretching forth into the unknowable future (one year, ten years, 100 years, 1,000 years?) gives this feeling of powerlessness a vertiginous quality. In the face of this, it was a sort of relief to abdicate responsibility and give it all away.

Arendt's work, for one, underscores the 'miraculous openness and desperate contingency' (Canovan in Arendt 1998: xvii) that underpins any kind of action in the public sphere. Arendt writes about how our plurality, combined with the fact that new people are unceasingly coming into this world, makes for a situation where we are all continually starting new things and setting off chains of potentially unexpected events. On the one hand, this gives rise to hope, as new beginnings cannot be ruled out even when society appears ensnared in disastrous dead ends. However, this also means that 'one cannot foresee even the effects of one's own initiatives, let alone control what happens when they are entangled with other people's initiatives in the public arena' (Arendt 1988: xviii). Notably, designer and philosopher Tony Fry modifies this outlook to remind us that 'the future is never a blank slate, it is already colonized by whatever the past and the present have sent to it' ([1999] 2020: 10).

So, in the final pages of this chapter, I wish to discuss why we should be offering these kinds of documents up to the public record. What shall we send into the future? What value might be lost if the perspectives that are recorded in these illustrative documents are not conveyed to contemporary or potential future audiences? Ultimately, I believe that the projects I have been discussing in this book speak to themes relevant to our times – and beyond. They propose an orientation which I feel is worthy of preservation.

In one sense, it is the very act of offering these illustrated documents up the public that holds the most value: it does not matter what actually happens to them after that. Even if nobody ever looks at them again, depositing them in a publicly accessible repository inscribes the work in a new, more expansive temporal framework. Their storage in temperature-controlled rooms (or on a publicly funded website) makes their continued (material) existence for longer periods of time more likely, compared to their potential fate in more hazardous and uncertain private settings. Their enrolment in systems of classification also enables them to be positioned in relation to other records. The addition of keywords and digital metadata markers such as hashtags further support cross-referencing and accessible search protocols. So, overall, these preservation and filing practices give the documents future-making capabilities that they would not possess in a studio cupboard. Whether these possibilities of contributing to future worlds are realized or not, the orientation towards possible futures bestows an atmosphere of value, anticipation and hope, which is experienced and felt in the present – I have been happy to share this atmosphere with my project partners and participants. For example, at the end of the event celebrating the transfer of the *Cracks in the Pavements* maps to Hackney Archives, I overheard one of the participants excitedly say to another: 'We are part of history now!'. Likewise, one of the women taking part in *Write Women into History* commented on the value of the project: 'It has validated my life and all my struggles' (Hackney HOWLers 2021: 6).

When I look at *Walking the Elephant* as a record on *Layers of London*, it is interesting to note how this project now stands in relation to other records on the site that share its geographical location (See Figure 7.3, p. 139). The current cluster of entries around Elephant and Castle include a compilation of photographs of the shopping centre from 2011 and photographs of the centre and its construction in the 1960s posted by the Metropolitan Archives, alongside a few brief historical notes on the architects and quotes from its sales brochure. There are also entries on the general strike of 1926, including a photograph of mounted police containing protesters at the time, as well as other entries from further back, such as an image of the Elephant and Castle pub from 1760. It is to be expected that these relational connections – to other records, if not so much to people – will continue to propagate as *Layers of London* grows in complexity and abundance.

Meanwhile, *Write Women into History* lives on in various London libraries. Much like *Walking the Elephant*, cataloguing and tagging it with keywords has embedded it in these repositories' collections, enabling the book to be seen alongside other publications and documents exploring similar themes. Notably, even though feminism remains an urgent area of activism and campaigning, its establishment as an academic focal point and general topic of concern is now largely uncontroversial. There are, thankfully, a number of organizations, initiatives and individuals that concern themselves with the history of feminism and as such I am confident that this book will continue to meet future audiences alongside other historiographic feminist documents.

Happily, *Cracks in the Pavement* is well looked after in Hackney Archives – at the moment, it is being cared for by an archivist who is keen to host future events that bring the project to new audiences. For me, this project is particularly resonant in terms of what it has to offer us as we face increasingly uncertain futures and reassess many of the assumptions and tenets of our current way of life – and so it deserves closer attention. I will elaborate on this a little later.

FIGURE 7.6 *Write Women into History* on display at Hackney Central Library, London, during Women's History Month, March 2025.

Rodney Harrison, professor of critical heritage studies, pointedly describes how today's heritage practices emerged in the context of modernity's temporal framework (2020: 21). He maintains that modernity's emphasis on rapid progress generates a sense of moral obligation to create systems that will reliably capture and organize the past in order to render it accessible to an imagined future. Furthermore, Harrison argues that this moral obligation has recently intensified thanks to the situation of endangerment and threat we find ourselves in today. Thus, the perception of our own vulnerability, the risk to and likely loss of numerous natural as well as cultural assets, and a sense of looming extinction and destruction contribute to an 'endangerment sensibility', which creates a strong, affective impulse towards preservation and perpetuation (2020: 28).

This 'endangerment sensibility', which emotively prompts acts of preservation for the potential benefit of 'future generations' (a term with complicated histories of its own – see Harrison 2020: 21), is certainly at work in many of the projects I have discussed in this book. Both Sabnani's *Tanko bole chhe/The Stitches Speak* and *Walking the Elephant* have become historical documents, capturing a way of life that has ceased to exist. Meanwhile, *Write Women into History* and Miller's four Red Road dialectograms (*The Concierge Station*, *The Nivens from S(i)even*, *The Mecca Bingo* and *The Brig Bar*) are probably the most self-conscious projects in terms of their own historiographical relevance – they explicitly set out to capture and secure people's stories for posterity while this is still possible. Indeed, Miller was directly commissioned to produce work that would preserve the legacy of the flats, at a moment in time when they had already been scheduled for demolition and were starting to undergo a slow decanting process. In turn, the express intention of *Write Women into History* was to record the group of women's experiences for future generations. In the introduction to the book, two of the group members write about the importance of the Women's Liberation Movement of the 1970s and 1980s: '[t]hose of us involved in that exciting period are now ourselves getting old. Many of us have already died. [...] [T]his is an ideal time to record our own stories and [...] pass[...] on our experiences of struggle and hard-won understandings to a new generation' (Burgess-Macey & Chester in Hackney HOWLers 2021: 5). Thus, they clearly articulate a sense of endangerment and the moral imperative of preservation.

Cracks in the Pavement is a particular case, in that it emerged in the midst of an exceptional period in history, with a sense that the project might somehow, in an as-yet-undefined way, be important for the future. As such, it relates slightly differently to this 'endangerment sensibility', as it was neither conceived of (by me) or entered into (by participants) in a spirit of wanting to preserve something precious. Instead, it was a response to finding oneself in the midst of a crisis, a disorienting scenario that disrupted our social, spatial and temporal experiences. The various COVID-19 lockdowns and restrictions, as well as anxieties about the virus itself, generated an atmosphere that can be characterized, in the anthropologist Rebecca

Bryant's terms, as an 'uncanny present' (Bryant 2016). She argues that a crisis can 'bring the present into consciousness, creating an awareness or perception of *present-ness* that we do not normally have' (emphasis in original, 2016: 20). Bryant's 'uncanny present' is certainly an apt description for the experience of lockdown. The stark temporal and spatial interruptions of this period meant that the reflective acts of attention I was hoping to encourage through participation in my projects were perhaps already part of people's everyday experience. Lockdown made us look at our everyday environments, experiences and companions afresh. And *Cracks in the Pavement* provided a framework to amplify and register that moment, when many of us were walking around our immediate neighbourhoods somewhat aimlessly, with no particular destination in mind.

Indeed, *Cracks in the Pavement* suggested that we trace each other's footsteps and see if we could discover new things about our neighbourhoods, each other and ourselves. Looking through the finished maps, I note observations, memories, thoughts, occasionally some historical knowledge on the area and, as previously mentioned, a surprising amount of sensory data that goes beyond the visual – 'sweet jazz music plays on the corner of the road' (Map 2: Chatsworth Road), 'sounds of rustling leaves in plane trees' (Map 4: London Fields) and 'my hands are feeling really cold' (Map 5: Newington Green to Butterfield Green).

When I was planning this project, I was not particularly thinking of these sensations. Rather, in the context of increased levels of anxiety, isolation, restrictions and the near-total digitization of everyday life, I wanted to develop a project that foregrounded materiality, embodiment and being in common. My central concern was how it might be possible to be alone, but still in active relation to others. And the resulting maps do indeed show our bonds and attachments; they record how we connected to our shared neighbourhoods during the lonely and unsettling period of the pandemic. For example, on Map 1: Walthamstow Wetlands, walkers focused on the natural environment and its textures. Looking at the accumulation of drawings, photographs and inscriptions on this map, it soon becomes clear that the sheet of paper and art supplies are not the only materials that were shared. Rather, the ground, the path and the 'pavement' of the project's title are other examples of materiality held in common. Our common ground is rendered as heterogeneous, verdant and shimmering.

Other projects I have covered treat similar themes. As previously outlined, *Bordando Tierra del Fuego* and the dialectograms invite participants to look around and pay attention to how they are intertwined with each other and their environments. In other words, they materialize experiences and expressions of place-based community. After all, encouraging participants to reflect on and share their perspectives on a place is important, because it makes them more aware of relationships that have developed over a period of time, but that on any given day are probably not at the front of people's minds. The invitation to record them makes us see them afresh. Similarly, *Write Women into History* and *Tanko bole chhe/The*

Stitches Speak awaken our senses to the presence of companions with overlapping life stories and rekindle memories of life-defining experiences. In their own ways, all these projects make us aware of and articulate our interdependence with one another and the everyday environments in which our encounters unfold.

Today, the Red Road Flats are no longer standing, the community at the Kala Raksha Trust has evolved, the Women's Liberation Movement has morphed into other forms of feminist practices and lockdown is over. But preserving the outputs of the projects confirms the work itself as well as the people, places, times and the networks of relations that link them together, to be of collective value and concern. The preservation of the particular experiences recorded therein protects these different standpoints from oblivion.

Collectively, the projects propose that examination of and engagement with place, everyday life and others is constitutive of who we are. By filing them in publicly accessible repositories, we can make these illustrative documents part of a network of touchpoints in ongoing and emergent chronologies and orientations. This becomes particularly apparent when viewing *Walking the Elephant* on *Layers of London* and seeing this piece of work in relation to multiple other histories that have unfolded on the site. But the other projects, too, take up their place as points of reference – whether that be in histories of feminist practices or South American cartography, as well as other possible future narratives that are not yet conceivable today.

If we come to appreciate illustration's wide-ranging capabilities, if we begin to think of it as a performative method of knowledge production, where the existence of an illustration generates the world it is referring to, the process of illustrating community and its relation to place offers dynamic possibilities for local reinvention. Rather than just documenting what is already there and/or what happened, illustration can conjure hopeful visions of collectively articulated common ground. This approach staves off nostalgic temptations to cling to a picturesque past and creates potential to embrace the opportunities inherent in uncertain futures.

CONCLUSION: COMMON GROUNDS?

I started this book with a question about how illustration practice could more thoroughly engage with notions of community, attempting to move away from the casual manner in which this term is typically used. For the purposes of this book, I have focused on illustrations as co-produced, visual documents, which foreground the multiplicity of perspectives and forces that led to their creation. These documents can function as evidence of geographical, historiographical and relational (re)configurations. And after a journey through several theoretical realms and a range of projects that emulate these principles, the main claim at which I have arrived is that participatory illustration projects have the capacity to *enact* community by drawing people together and by prompting, revealing and recording our fundamental nature of 'being with'.

As a reminder, Nancy characterizes enactments of community as 'the exposure of singularities' (Nancy 1991: 30). He maintains that his philosophical considerations regarding the fundamental nature of our sociality are 'political', even though his writing is distinct from what is more generally understood as political philosophy. His work maintains a focus on the fundamental, ontological conditions of our sociality, rather than proposing a set of principles of governance or advocating for a particular political orientation.

Like Nancy, in this book I have primarily concerned myself with how we relate to others and have refrained from explicitly offering guidelines or instructions for illustrators wishing to work with communities. My focus has been on outlining the potential of participatory illustration projects as a site for ontological disclosure, showing how they can draw out and delineate aspects of our coexistence, demonstrating how our being is fundamentally constituted by our relations with others. In this regard, my work mirrors Nancy's idea of 'the political' in its interest in the underlying nature of our sociality.

Nonetheless, because I did not pursue this research in the abstract, but rather through staging and studying collaborative illustration projects associated with particular people, places and issues, the book does in fact spill over into what is more conventionally understood as the political – the everyday wrestling for power and influence in the public sphere. Some of the projects I discuss deal with obviously political concerns, ranging from the callous eviction of well-established migrant traders from a neighbourhood they had helped build up (*Walking the Elephant*) to more general struggles against the disregard for intricately woven community networks in many urban development schemes (Miller's dialectograms) or women's stories and memories (*Write Women into History*, Sabnani's *Tanko bole chhe/The Stitches Speak*). And while other projects (such as *Cracks in the Pavement* or Mann's *Bordando Tierra del Fuego*) do not engage so combatively with such causes, these projects too have a political aspect. *Cracks in the Pavement* quietly encourages hyper-local larking about, in opposition to modern society's default imperatives of individualistic striving, efficiency and economically driven toil. Similarly, *Bordando Tierra del Fuego* prompts people to connect with their local landscapes in ways that go beyond the instrumentalist and anthropocentric attitudes that tend to dominate contemporary discourse.

So, in contrast to theoretical writing that adopts abstract language in the establishment of an argument, it seems that practice-led illustration research cannot help but operate on two registers simultaneously. So this work is 'political' in the Nancean sense, in that it explores ontological questions of our being in common and the manner in which society is produced, and it is also political in the more conventional understanding of the word, in that it engages with and orients itself towards specific power dynamics between people, events, places and histories. As a result, the knowledge that is produced through this work also falls into two categories: the illustrator-facilitator draws out specific knowledge about each project's topic, while at the same time using the work as a site for considering more general questions on the nature of community. To follow this thread even further, I would also see the beneficiaries of these kinds of projects as residing in two camps: the work should serve the communities in question by producing an output that relates to their needs and interests; however, at the same time, I hope that the work involved in researching and writing this book about participatory illustration practice offers something new to my fellow illustrators and academics in the form of new thinking about the affordances of our discipline.

On this note, I wish to briefly recap a number of practical principles that crystallized for me as I was working through this book's material. While these are not universal edicts, some of them might prove useful for other practitioners. Furthermore, their emergence highlights the value of situated methods for illustrators working in complex social settings more generally – methods that take into consideration the specific context of each project. Firstly, in Chapter 2, I explained why I prefer to construct responsive 'climbing frames' for my project participants, rather than performing extensive acts of authorial renunciation. I argued that postulating a definitive and communicative output as a shared goal for a group of participants can have the effect of propelling a project towards an anticipated and satisfying conclusion, since everyone walks away with a tangible result that can be kept and shared with others. Then, in Chapter 3, I reflected on various methods of persuading participants to inscribe or otherwise contribute to the shared documents that form the central focus of these projects, including preparing enticing art materials, offering the option of using stickers, implementing prompts that undermine the repressive ambition to produce a 'good drawing' and inviting participants to draw a route (which cannot really be drawn 'badly'). Chapter 4 contains my reflections on synthesizing participants' work, which led me to the conclusion that it is best to harness the vitality of their original inscriptions as much as possible, rather than reinterpreting their contributions.

In these more practical chapters, a variety of explanations emerged as to why illustration is an apposite discipline for this kind of participatory work that seeks to recount and record everyday realms of experience and interaction. Firstly, illustrators are trained in the procedures of a creative service discipline, and so are well disposed to synthesize the needs and requirements of other people (traditionally clients) with their own creative vision – this is invaluable for projects that call for sensitivity towards a participating group as well as ambition for visual impact. Secondly, inviting participants to annotate, draw or otherwise inscribe aspects of their lived experience elicits reflective acts of attention which bring the usually unnoticed everyday 'lifeworld' to the front of people's minds. This happens regardless of whether people are engaged in observation or recollection as a catalyst for their contributions: in both cases, the task of having to draw things on a sheet of paper (or stitch them into fabric) enlivens the situations and circumstances that are being observed or remembered in the minds of participants, when these situations and circumstances – however interesting and vital they might have once seemed – might otherwise slumber at the peripheries of people's consciousness, dulled by the corrosive repetitiveness of the everyday. In short, that the act of illustrating makes you look at things afresh. By prompting participants to productively engage with their environments and relationships through the deployment of attention and inscription, collaboratively produced illustrative documents constitute a form of collective 'world-making', as theorized in Chapter 5.

Subsequently, in Chapter 6, I turned to the main argument of this book, asserting that collaborative illustration has the capacity to act as a catalyst, focal point and trace of a public encounter. These kinds of encounters, I argued, enact community, where community is not conceived as a closed group of people fused together through essentialist characteristics, but rather as the process of singularities (Nancy's preferred term for individuals) 'acting towards one another'. Illustration projects can gather people together by focusing them on a shared concern, provide a structure for their communicative engagement (through the collaborative activity of inscription) and record the encounter after it has taken place (thanks to the results of this activity).

Finally, in Chapter 7, I discussed the potential that arises from submitting the results of these projects to publicly accessible repositories: this allows the outputs to act as historical documents that refer back to the moments of their creation. To put it simply, the publication of these documents confirms that these enactments of community did indeed take place – but there is even more to it than this. Through their articulation and public display, thoughts and convictions that were previously privately held are transformed into widely accessible visual artefacts, thus entering Arendt's so-called 'space of appearance'. This is significant because 'something that is being seen and heard by others as well as ourselves constitutes reality' (Arendt 1998: 50). In other words, by appearing as material inscriptions or registrations on the public record, these concerns and articulations achieve a fixedness and longevity that more fleeting forms of collective sense-making, such as spoken conversations, lack. As such, illustrative documents have the potential to reach into the future, acting as touchpoints for ongoing orientations and debates and shaping a polyvocal public realm. They enable the 'community of communication' (Nancy 1997: 114) to extend into times to come.

Overall, I believe that illustration can expose and delineate aspects of our social coexistence. In the form of co-created visual documents, it presents itself as a space where we can reconsider, record and reflect on the relations that occur in our everyday experience of community and practices of collective world-making.

What is illustration (research) good for?

During my work on this book, there have been many joyful moments of discovery alongside the inevitable frustrations, struggles and moments of doubt that accompany a long-term project of this scale. There were times when the limitations of my projects in particular and illustration practice in general loomed uncomfortably large. After all, my main argument centres on the potential of illustration to prompt a creative and generative process of coming together and making a world. But what was I to do when projects threw up failed connections and broken links? What about the affiliations that did not materialize, either because of flaws in the project structure or the unpredictable ebbs and flows of external events? What happens when the work amplifies, rather than overcomes, the many creases and tears of our social fabric? What about the moments when worlds did not emerge or I was unable to make them intelligible to myself and others?

All of my own projects certainly encountered limitations. For one thing, *Walking the Elephant*, besides the shortcomings I have already discussed in Chapter 4, did not realize its initial ambition to support the community organization in question by providing persuasive materials in a timely manner that would bolster its cause. Meanwhile, *Cracks in the Pavement* gracefully connected strangers of many different ages but did not manage to reach beyond a circle of white, middle-class residents, despite my attempts to include a broader range of perspectives.[1] And although *Write Women into History* largely 'worked' insofar as it delivered on my ambition to gain the trust of a group of older, local feminists and support them in their efforts to present themselves to external audiences, this project remains by all accounts a relatively modest undertaking involving just fourteen participants and a slim, self-published booklet.

Still, I wonder if these kinds of limitations are tolerable, or sometimes even productive? While the projects have some limitations in and of themselves, their success as projects does not stand in direct relation to their generative capacity for research insights. *Walking the Elephant* and *Cracks in the Pavement*, for example, had obvious flaws, but these two projects proved to be the most productive in prompting me to develop my thinking, compared to *Write Women into History*. In fact, the difficulties I encountered during *Walking the Elephant* are precisely what pivoted me towards thinking of illustration as a performative (rather than representational) knowledge creation practice.

During my years of work on this book, I was propelled by the belief that, despite inevitable limitations, illustration is filled with moments of profundity and there is value and significance in the contributions illustrators can make to questions that reach beyond our discipline. After all, illustration is a method of making sense of the world. In *The Creation of the World* (2007), Nancy writes about how the praxis of making sense creates the possibility of a world as such. In his eyes, the sense of the world is never given but must be made, necessitating a struggle that, in one of his typically labyrinthine paragraphs, is described as 'effervescence of thought [...] transformed into contagious communication as propagation of an enjoyment' (Nancy 2007: 55). In other words, sense-making is a world-creation practice which ought to be communicative and ultimately joyous.

Interestingly, Grove recently voiced similar sentiments – and tied them explicitly to illustration: 'Conjuring is the imaginative act at the heart of illustrating' (Grove 2023: 17). She continues: 'Let us remember that an illustration is a theory of what something *is* or could be' (Grove 2023, emphasis in original). Although Nancy speaks of 'world-making' and Grove of 'conjuring', both invoke creation rather than representation of something pre-existing. And by describing illustration as

[1] Prominent sociologist Susan Wessendorf describes Hackney, the London borough where the majority of *Cracks in the Pavement* participants (including myself) are based, as a place where 'diversity is acknowledged and sometimes talked about, [but] actual engagement with difference remains limited and people rarely explore cultural differences more deeply' (2014: 394). *Cracks in the Pavement* appears to confirm this characterization of the neighbourhood.

a 'theory of what something *is* or could be', Grove confirms that it is indeed a method of making sense.

Grove accordingly goes on to explain the power that lies at the core of illustration. Reflecting on some of the seemingly insurmountable challenges in the world today, she writes:

> Changing the future is imperative [...]. This is where illustration conjuring comes in: if we can't see where we're going, we'll never get there. If we can't agree on where to go, we'll never start. If we leave our problems unseen, we won't know how to begin. Illustration sets ideals, attracts and bonds collaborators, and documents applications, failures and solutions—illustrating is always at the start of any meaningful human action. And every illustration begins with a conjuring act, turning nothing into something [...].
>
> (Grove 2023: 17)

I share Grove's views and could not have formulated this sentiment more eloquently. The challenge in participatory illustration projects is to entice groups of people to partake in this conjuring and documenting of worlds. But I am confident that the projects I have worked on and studied have resulted in illustrations that do indeed conjure hopeful visions of polyvocal worlds. Plus, through various forms of publishing – whether that be exhibiting, screening or submitting them to publicly accessible repositories – they have the potential to continue to 'bond collaborators' oriented towards more optimistic futures.

In the Introduction, I wrote that the methodological advancement of illustration practice was of crucial importance, especially in the face of recent developments in AI image creation practices that can mimic the results of many run-of-the-mill illustration commissions. I believe that this book sets out one of the many *other* things that illustration can do, beyond quickly filling a gap on the page. As I have argued, illustration can act as an innovative and imaginative creative practice that illuminates, records and amplifies constellations of interdependence. But what, you may ask, about illustration *research*?

Much has happened in the past few years to solidify and legitimize illustration as a serious academic discipline. However, establishing a 'serious discipline' is not an end in itself. What do we need it for? Illustrators are increasingly realizing that our talents can be applied much more broadly than many people give us credit for – perhaps including ourselves. But in order to secure new and exciting possibilities for illustration as a nuanced cultural activity that can creatively respond to opportunities within the private, public and third sector, while also defending our roles as 'public intellectuals'[2] by using our work to contribute to

[2] 'The Illustrator as Public Intellectual' was the tantalizing theme for the 6th International Illustration Research Symposium (2015), which was organized by Susan Doyle, Rob Brinkerhoff and Jaleen Grove at Rhode Island School of Design (RISD), Providence, USA.

broader debates in society, we need more than our illustration practice alone. We also need scholarship, theory and spoken and written language to enable us to back up and amplify our argument convincingly. Theoretical concepts allow us to see and frame what is around us but we might otherwise overlook. Convincing arguments can help us recruit allies to our cause, empowering them to create opportunities where illustration can thrive. This recalls Bolt's distinction between 'artwork' and 'the work of art' (2007: 34). In short, 'artwork' can be understood as the ways in which illustration practice puts forward claims, makes worlds and conjures new visions. However, in order to live up to the potential that is inherent in our practice, we also need 'the work of art', which Bolt locates in the written 'exegesis' that articulates the effects and significance of practice.

Thanks to my work on this book, the importance of combining periods of practice with periods of reflection – which encompass the study of cognate theory and practice as well as the sometimes laborious interweaving of theory and practice – has become superabundantly obvious to me. I have come to prize the process of writing for a number of reasons. As Bolt suggests, through writing, one is able to draw out knowledge that may remain dormant in practice but can be more fully activated (including for the practitioner!) in its alliance with linguistic ideas, concepts and narratives. In addition, writing helps make knowledge claims more generalizable beyond the specifics of an individual project. And lastly, spoken and written language aids us enormously in advocating for ourselves as illustrators, for the concerns and causes we take on in our work, and for illustration practice more generally. However, it is not universally accepted that illustration practice and scholarly research can support and nourish each other. Indeed, having spent considerable time teaching in and visiting various higher education illustration courses in the UK, I can state that many of them encompass no significant written components at all, and in those that do, students often struggle to appreciate their significance.

To return to one of the theoretical realms we visited in the book, there are a considerable number of parallels that can be drawn between the development of translation studies and the gradual growth of scholarship in/on/through illustration. Firstly, like illustration, translation is a creative discipline that is practised commercially through a series of commissions, mainly by freelance practitioners, who are embedded in various economic and regulatory systems which shape key parameters, such as budgets, deadlines and copyright. In addition, illustrators, like translators, have often felt overlooked and undervalued: see Venuti (1995: 8) for a chronicle of translators' marginalization and Male (2019: 8) for an account of illustrators' historic 'low-rank' status. Both have also grappled with the general perception that their creative practice is characterized by subservience to an 'original' or primary text. Happily, translation scholarship has done much to challenge this perception and gradually led to a much broader and nuanced understanding of and reflection on translation practice.

Illustration is at an earlier stage of academization and so is still contending with the challenges associated with the establishment of scholarly research around a commercially practised creative discipline, which seems to provoke some suspicion and reticence on the part of some practitioners. Grove discussed this scepticism in an article for the *Journal of Illustration*, which was published in 2011 (Grove 2011) – and my experience working in higher education illustration environments confirms that this feeling is still very much alive today. So, even while illustration has made great strides to establish itself as a more academic discipline, there is more work to do with regard to articulating and demonstrating the value of illustration scholarship.

Still, although I believe that illustration practice can benefit greatly from scholarly research, it is vital to emphasize that I am not advocating for scholarship on its own. Once again, translation acts as a useful precedent. Translation studies and translation practice, which have made great strides by informing and enriching one another, also do not always intertwine in mutual support and harmony. Bassnett describes how academic theory has separated itself from the practice of translation in some university departments, resulting in an awkward and unnecessary chasm between the two (Bassnett & Bush 2006: 2) – undoubtedly a resonant warning for all of us illustration scholars.

Nonetheless, I am confident that the steadily growing number of people and organizations dedicated to the thoughtful evolution of illustration practice and its associated realms of scholarly exploration and exchange will continue to collectively advance the possibilities and reach of our discipline. I am proud to be contributing to these inspiring conversations and networks.

A world without an outside

In this book, I have braided together illustration practice and theory to reveal and record aspects of our coexistence. I have thought through how participatory illustration projects can act as a site of ontological disclosure, where we can enact, record and reflect on our experiences of community. And I have also advanced the idea of illustration as a performative method of knowledge creation, where the act of creation establishes the reality it refers to. All these ideas have emerged at the intersection of illustration with other forms of knowledge – including philosophy, translation studies and anthropology.

I have repeatedly referred to the fact that this work overall operates on two levels simultaneously: it is political both in the sense of being invested in the nature of the social body at its most fundamental level, while also – through the individual projects and initiatives – getting involved in everyday power struggles and activist contestations. In this book, I have (I hope) shared insights that contribute to illustration as a discipline, while also presenting projects that express specific local insights about the experiences of groups of people at a particular time and place. In the previous section, I reflected on the nature and merits of scholarly knowledge that flows from practice. Here, I wish to add a few more reflections on the mode of knowledge production in the practice itself.

My practice as an illustrator is broadly concerned with coming to know the world in the companionship of others. In Chapter 5, I wrote about Heidegger's insistence that we can only know about the world through our relational involvement in it. Bolt transposes these philosophical insights into creative arts inquiry, where 'praxical engagement with tools, materials and ideas produces its own kind of [in] sight' (2004: 187). My own practice complicates these statements, as I do not set out to learn about the world by practising on my own, but rather by setting up groups of other people to collectively generate and express a version of a world. Anthropology and ethnography have offered some methodological guidance for this, in particular with regard to the necessity for continuous self-reflexivity. However, unlike anthropologists who, after years of painstaking self-reflection, arrived at the difficult conclusion that studies *of* people almost inevitably involve a process of 'othering' (Ingold 2011: 226), I designed my projects from the outset as events that got people involved in creating something new with me. Rather than assuming the position of an observer in an attempt to generate knowledge about existing cultural or social practices, I was always an obvious actor – or even ringleader – setting up encounters, situations and activities in an attempt to study *with* people. Ingold optimistically refers to this orientation as 'a process of togethering' (2011).

And this 'process of togethering' resulted in the production of newly articulated, shared worlds. In Chapter 5, I reflected in detail on processes of collective world-making, drawing on Husserl's concept of the 'lifeworld' to explain how, from the early twentieth century onwards, the subjective experiences of everyday life were reconceived as unifying worlds, as opposed to the perceived fragmentations brought about by modern science, technology and industrial capitalism. Nancy, characteristically, offers a slightly different perspective. Just as he argues that it is our very separation into 'singularities' that makes community possible, he suggests that it is precisely the world's fragmentation that offers a profound possibility for its renewal. Thanks to processes of creative sense-making which produce new meaning, we have the capacity to collectively make and enact new worlds.

From the point of view of the illustrator, the process of world-making sounds, initially at least, relatively straightforward. The process of drawing and or designing worlds seems to fall squarely within our remit – illustration is, after all, a practice of 'conjuring' (Grove 2023). On closer examination, however, perplexingly complex questions emerge. Representing a world implies a vantage point from outside, from where the world can be seen and represented. But this stands in direct opposition to the idea that the world reveals itself through our involvement with it. Viewing the world from outside reduces it, in Heidegger's words, to a conquered object in front of the supposedly masterful subject ([1950] 1977). Indeed, Heidegger decries 'the world becoming picture' (1977: 132) and man's [*sic*] concomitant transformation into 'subiectum' – a supreme individual bestowed with powers for the 'calculating, planning and moulding of all things' (1977: 135). Nancy elaborates on the same problem when he writes that '[a] world "viewed", a represented world, is a world dependent on the gaze of a subject [who] cannot itself be within the world' (2007: 40).

The difficulties I experienced while working on *Walking the Elephant* – my struggle to find adequate means to synthesize and *re*present the contributions the participants had produced during the workshops – were in essence born from my inability to fully grasp the limitations of an outside perspective at the time. Like some anthropologists, who assumed that writing necessitates a turn away from observation (see Clifford 1988: 52), I had designed my project around two discrete phases of observation or data gathering, followed by subsequent illustrative rendering. However, once I was back in the studio, separated from the world I was trying to represent, I was paralysed by my inability to conjure anything that felt adequate. The only way I found to salvage the project was to reinject workshop elements back into the final package of outputs, including the maps and the photographic documentation that revealed the process of their creation.

The challenge, then, is knowing how to draw a world without an outside. How can illustration articulate something as elusive as the everyday world which discloses itself through our immersion in it, through our actions, involvements and relationships?

Rather than attempting to step outside of our worlds to look back on them I have, in my projects, set up the possibility for new circumstances, actions and relationships that illuminate our pre-existing identities and experiences afresh. People found themselves sitting around a sheet of paper, and then had to work out collectively, who they were here, now, with this, and in relation to each other. The ensuing 'lifeworlds' resulted from the interlocking articulations of many perspectives, rather than a pre-existing imaginary shared by all. In this paradigm, creating collaborative illustrative documents becomes a generative rather than a representational process. Rather than engaging in a form of 'data collection' about a community and the worlds they make and inhabit and then grappling with the means to adequately render this information, I created frameworks for people to come together. And indeed, it is through the very process of coming together that the participants become a community, drawing up a plural world.

Blind spots

There are many more avenues to be explored on the themes and ideas that I have set out in these pages. As I write the last few lines of this book, I find myself acutely aware of the many omissions and blind spots[3] in what I have put forward. There is much more work to be done – but one must, of course, finish *somewhere*. So, while my focus has been on the overlaps between illustration and notions of community, and I have done my best to advance a nuanced understanding of these terms, not all concepts have been analysed in such depth. The word 'encounter', for example, which I have used many times in this book, is ripe for much greater scrutiny. In his book *Meeting Place* (2013), academic Paul Carter positions Australian Aboriginal understandings of meeting in contrast to the Western enthusiasm for public encounter. He explains that Australian Indigenous societies would understand their territories and societies '[...] relationally, as expressions of a web of reciprocated responsibilities whose well-being depended on maintaining the tonos [tension] of the distances in between, as if space were composed [...] like a string figure, and psychological as well as material prosperity depended on keeping the strands of the figure taut' (Carter 2013: 2). It left me questioning how illustration practice can help us think about systems of interdependence more generally, while taking into account that a 'web of reciprocated responsibilities' might involve a host of different types of meetings – or perhaps, on occasion, no direct encounters at all? How might illustration be able to interpret other forms of relationality which extend over periods of time and/or space – or which might indeed be reliant on us never meeting each other, while still being intimately bonded? I am looking forward to pursuing these questions in greater depth through future projects.

I am also heartened and relieved to find that I am no longer on my own writing about the complex scenarios that emerge at the nexus of illustration, participation, place, identity and history. When I visited Mitch Miller's studio in 2016, he remarked that, as far as he knew, we were the only two people publishing on these themes.[4] Today, as I browse recent issues of the *Journal of Illustration*, I find a delightful abundance of diverse contributions. These include Nina Sabnani's writing on how a community's memories can be captured in materials such as cloth or wood (2024) and Kimberley Ellen Hall's detailed and thoughtful reflections on a recent community mural project (Hall & Masri 2024). Karen Jiyun Sung's contribution to these conversations is also hugely important. Her participatory drawing project *Sketch Circle*, situated in South Korea, illuminates how the interplay between the singular and the plural plays itself out differently in this cultural context, which contrasts markedly with my own Eurocentric understanding (see Sung 2024). Yeni Kim, also working in South Korea, combines heritage studies, ethnography and participatory methods with the communicative

[3] In my use of this word, I am taking inspiration from the 13th Annual Illustration Research Symposium in St Louis, Missouri, 2023, which ran under the theme of 'Blind Spots' – an evocative term for illustrators to consider!

[4] Nina Sabnani had, of course, already been working with communities, blending ethnography, illustration and animation for a while, showcasing and publishing her projects in India and beyond, but we were unaware of her practice at the time.

storytelling practices of picture books in the service of cultural preservation (see Kim 2022) – another significant contribution to these debates. And Pat Wingshan Wong's fearless and unconventional community archiving projects in London and Hong Kong illuminate the complex interplay between economic forces and urban conservation (see Wong 2023, Wong & Chan 2023). I am sure there are others who are also working and publishing in this area, and I look forward to learning from them and their work.

I conclude this book with the firm conviction that illustration – both as a practice and as a field of research that is prompted and propelled by the practice – has much to offer. As a form of sense-making, it can help us situate ourselves and draw out our relationships to our environments, experiences and each other. Illustration can elicit and articulate our interdependence on one another and our overlapping worlds. It can also bring into focus that which otherwise recedes in the business of the everyday and can contribute to the structure of the public realm. And above all, it can sketch out patches of common ground on which we may assemble, however briefly, and provide an orientation for where we might want to go next.

REFERENCES

Adorno, T. ([1958] 1991) 'The Essay as Form', in Tiedemann, R. (ed.) (1991) *Notes to Literature*, Vol. 1, New York: Columbia University Press, pp. 3–23.

Alsaraji, A. (2023) Conversation with the author, The Passmore Edwards Library artists' studios, East Ham, London, 7 December 2023.

Anonymous. (2021) Anonymous online feedback questionnaire for *Cracks in the Pavement*.

Arendt, H. ([1958] 1998) *The Human Condition*, introduction by Margaret Canovan, Chicago: Chicago University Press.

Arnstein, S. (1969) 'A Ladder of Citizen Participation', *JAIP*, Vol. 35, No. 4, pp. 216–24.

Ash Sakula, B. (2023) Conversation with the author, The Waiting Room café, Deptford, London, 17 November 2023.

Ashbrook, S. & Syme, A. (2018) 'Chapter 15: Beautifying Books and Popularizing Posters in Europe and America, 1855–1910', in Doyle, S., Grove, J. & Sherman, W. (eds) *History of Illustration*, New York: Fairchild Books, pp. 232–47.

Austin, J. L. (1962) *How to Do Things with Words*, Cambridge, MA: Harvard University Press.

Bahri, D. (2003) *Native Intelligence: Aesthetics, Politics and Postcolonial Literature*, Minneapolis, MN: University of Minnesota Press.

Baker, E. (2025) *Make Your Own Job: How the Entrepreneurial Work Ethic Exhausted America*, Cambridge, MA: Harvard University Press.

Bakhtin, M. ([1934-35] 1981) 'Discourse in the Novel', in Holquist, M. (ed.) *The Dialogic Imagination: Four Essays*, Austin: University of Texas Press, pp. 259–422.

Barad, K. (2007) *Meeting the Universe Halfway*, Durham, NC: Duke University Press.

Barthes, R. ([1967] 1977) 'The Death of the Author', in Heath, S. (ed.) *Image Music Text*, London: Fontana Press, pp. 142–8.

Bassnett, S. (1998) 'The Translation Turn in Cultural Studies', in Bassnett, S. & Lefevere, A. (eds) *Constructing Cultures: Essays on Literary Translation*, Clevedon & Bristol: Multilingual Matters Ltd, pp. 123–40.

Bassnett, S. & Bush, P. (eds) (2006) *The Translator as Writer*, London: Continuum.

Bassnett, S. & Lefevere, A. (eds) (1998) *Constructing Cultures: Essays on Literary Translation*, Clevedon & Bristol: Multilingual Matters Ltd.

Benjamin, W. ([1923] 2021) *The Translator's Task*, in Venuti, L. (ed.) (2021) *The Translation Studies Reader*, London: Routledge, pp. 89–97.

Bennet, J. (2010) *Vibrant Matter*, Durham, NC: Duke University Press.

Berger, J. (2007) *Berger on Drawing*, Cork: Occasional Press.

Berlant, L. (2011) *Cruel Optimism*, Durham, NC: Duke University Press.

Bermingham, A. (1986) *Landscape and ideology – The English Rustic Tradition*, London: Thames and Hudson.
Bhabha, H. (1994) *The Location of Culture*, London: Routledge.
Bishop, C. (2012) *Artificial Hells*, London: Verso.
Bjögvinsson, E., Ehn, P. & Hillgren, P. A. (2012) 'Design Things and Design Thinking: Contemporary Participatory Design Challenges', *DesignIssues*, Vol. 28, No. 3, pp.101–16.
Black, S. (2012) 'Rear View Mirror', *Varoom*, Vol. 18, pp. 54–9.
Black, S. (2014) 'Illumination Through Illustration: Research Methods and Authorial Practice', *Journal of Illustration*, Vol. 1, No. 2, pp. 275–300.
Blaiklock, D. (2019) 'What Is the Nature of Illustration Expertise', in Male, A. (ed.) *A Companion to Illustration*, Hoboken, NJ: John Wiley & Sons Inc, pp.185–98.
Blundell Jones, P., Petrescu, D. & Till, J. (eds) (2005) *Architecture and Participation*, London: Taylor & Francis.
Bogart, M. (2018) 'Making Meaning of Illustration', *Rockwell Centre for American Visual Studies*, online. Available at: https://rockwellcenter.org/essays-illustration/making-meaning-of-illustration (accessed 9 March 2026).
Bolt, B. (2004) *Art Beyond Representation: The Performative Power of the Image*, London: I. B. Tauris.
Bolt, B. (2007) 'The Magic Is in the Handling', in Barrett, E. & Bolt, B. (eds) *Practice as Research: Approaches to Creative Arts Enquiry*, London: I. B. Tauris, pp. 27–34.
Bolt, B. (2011) *Heidegger Reframed*, London: I. B. Tauris.
Bolt, B. (2013) 'Introduction', in *Carnal Knowledge: Towards a 'New Materialism' Through the Arts*, London: I. B. Tauris, pp. 1–13.
Braund, S. (2011) 'Slowing Time Down: Correspondences, Ambiguity and Attendance', *Journal of Illustration*, Vol. 4, No. 3, pp. 427–43
Bruinsma, M. (2018) 'Unicorns in the Geometrical Park', in Horton, I. & Furnée, B. (eds) *Hard Werken*, Amsterdam: Valiz, pp. 212–16.
Bryant, R. (2016) 'On Critical Times: Return, Repetition, and the Uncanny Present', *History and Anthropology*, Vol. 27, No. 1, pp. 19–31.
Burke, K. (1941) *The Philosophy of Literary Form*, Baton Rouge, LA: Louisiana State University Press.
Burrows, N. (2024) Presentation at Camberwell College of Art, University of the Arts London, 22 May 2024.
Carter, P. (2013) *Meeting Place: The Human Encounter and the Challenge of Coexistence*, Minneapolis, MN: University of Minnesota Press.
Chute, H. (2010) *Graphic Women: Life Narrative and Contemporary Comics*, New York: Columbia University Press.
Clifford, J. (1986) 'Introduction: Partial Truths', in Clifford, J. & Marcus, G. (eds) *Writing Culture: The Poetics and Politics of Ethnography*, Berkley: The University of California Press, pp. 1–26.
Clifford, J. (1988) *The Predicament of Culture: Twentieth Century Ethnography, Literature, and Art*, Cambridge, MA: Harvard University Press.
Clifford, J. & Marcus, G. E. (1986) *Writing Culture: The Poetics and Politics of Ethnography*, Berkeley: University of California Press.
Coe, S. & Metz, H. (1983) *How to Commit Suicide in South Africa*, London: Knockabout Comics.
Craig, S. R. (2020) *The Ends of Kinship*, Seattle: University of Washington Press.
Cross, N. (ed.) (1972) *Design Participation: Proceedings of the Design Research Society's Conference, Manchester, September 1971*, London: Academy Editions.

Cross, N. (1982) 'Designerly Ways of Knowing', *Design Studies*, Vol. 3, No. 4, pp. 221–7.
Crow, D. (2003, 2010, 2018, 2022) *Visible Signs: An Introduction to Semiotics in the Visual Arts*, Lausanne: Ava Publishing.
Daston, L. & Galison, P. (2007) *Objectivity*, New York: Zone Books.
Davies, R. & Francis, A. (2023) Conversation with the author, private residence, Stoke-on-Trent, 11 December 2023.
De Carlo, G. ([1970] 2005) 'Architecture's Public', in Blundell Jones, P., Petrescu, D. & Till, J. (eds) *Architecture and Participation*, London: Taylor & Francis, pp. 3–18.
DiSalvo, C. (2020) 'Publics', in Tassinari, V. & Staszowski, E. (eds) *Designing in Dark Times: An Arendtian Lexicon*, London: Bloomsbury Publishing, pp. 259–62.
Doane, M. A. (2007) 'Indexicality: Trace and Sign, Introduction', *Differences: A Journal of Feminist Cultural Studies; Indexicality: Trace and Sign*, Vol. 18, No. 1, pp. 1–6.
Doyle, S., Grove, J. & Sherman, W. (2018) *History of Illustration*, New York: Fairchild Books.
Drucker, J. (2009) 'Nano-Graphology and Models of Digital Writing as Notation, Inscription, Trace, Code and Attitude', in *Beyond the Margins*, publication following a symposium on experimental typography organized by Anglia Ruskin University in association with the research unit for Information Environments, UAL, Cambridge, 12 September 2009, no page numbers.
Elkins, J. & McGuire, K. (eds) (2013) *Theorizing Visual Studies: Writing Through the Discipline*, Abingdon: Routledge.
Fauchon, M. (2024) *Illustration, Narrative and the Suffragette*, London: Bloomsbury Publishing.
Fauchon, M. & Gannon, R. (2021) *Illustration Research Methods*, London: Bloomsbury Publishing.
Felksi, L. (2015) *The End of Critique*, Chicago: The University of Chicago Press.
Ferraris, M. (2013) *Documentality*, New York: Fordham University Press.
Foster, H. (1996) 'The Artist as Ethnographer', in *The Return of the Real*, Cambridge MA: MIT Press, pp. 170–203.
Foucault, M. ([1969] 1977) 'What Is an Author?' in Bouchard, D. (ed.) *Language, Counter-Memory, Practice*, Ithaca: Cornell University Press, pp. 113–38.
Fraser, N. (1984) 'The French Derrideans: Politicizing Deconstruction or Deconstructing the Political?', *New German Critique*, No. 33, pp. 127–54.
Freeman, J. (1972) 'The Tyranny of Structurelessness', *Berkley Journal of Sociology*, Vol. 17, pp. 151–65.
Fry, T. ([1999] 2020) *Defuturing*, London: Bloomsbury Visual Arts.
Goldbard, A. & Matarasso, F. (2021) *Ethics and Participatory Art, Art and Community Notebook No.1*, Lisbon: Calouste Gulbenkian Foundation.
Goldsmith, K. (2011) *Uncreative Writing: Managing Language in the Digital Age*, New York: Columbia University Press.
Grove, J. (2011) 'Netting jellyfish: A Point of View on Illustration Research from the United States and Canada', *Journal of Illustration*, Vol. 4, No. 3, pp. 287–307.
Grove, J. (2018) 'The "Theoretical Turn" and Pedagogy in Illustration Education', *Journal of Illustration*, Vol. 5, No. 2, pp. 179–90.
Grove, J. (2023) 'The Lacuna's Calling: A Graphic Reckoning with History', *Colouring In: The Past*, No. 3, pp. 15–36, online. Available at: https://www.colouring-in.com/images/uploads/colouring-in-issue-3-the-past.pdf (accessed 9 March 2026).
Hackney HOWLers (2021) *Write Women into History*, London.

Hackney HOWLers (2022) Online conversation with the authors, 18 May 2022.
Hall, K. E. & El Masri, O. (2024) 'Us and Them: We Draw Together: Exploring Inclusivity in a Community Mural Project', *Journal of Illustration*, Vol. 11, No.2, pp. 347–72.
Hall, P. A. & Dávila, P. (2023) *Critical Visualization*, London: Bloomsbury Publishing.
Haraway, D. (1988) 'Situated Knowledges: The Science Question in Feminism and the Privilege of Partial Perspective', *Feminist Studies*, Vol. 14, No.3, pp. 575–99.
Harley, J. B. (1989) 'Deconstructing the Map', *Cartographica*, Vol. 26, No.2, pp. 1–20.
Harrison, R., DeSilvey, C., Holtorf, C., Macdonald, S., Bartolini, N., Breithoff, E., Fredheim, H., Lyons, A., May, S., Morgan, J. & Penrose, S. (2020) *Heritage Futures: Comparative Approaches to Natural and Cultural Heritage Practices*, London: UCL Press.
Heidegger, M. [(1927] 1962) *Being and Time*, Oxford: Basil Blackwell.
Heidegger, M. (1977) *The Question Concerning Technology and Other Essays*, London: Garland Publishing.
Helguera, P. (2011) *Education for Socially Engaged Art: A Materials and Techniques Handbook*, New York: Jorge Pinto Books.
Holliday, G. (2023) Conversation with the author, South London Gallery, 5 December 2023.
Husserl, E. (1970) *The Crisis of European Sciences and Transcendental Philosophy*, Evanston, IL: Northwestern University Press.
IDEO (2009) *HCD Toolkit*, San Francisco: Designkit IDEO.
IDEO (2015) *The Fieldguide to Human Centred Design*, San Francisco: Designkit IDEO.
Ingold, T. (2011) *Being Alive, Essays on Movement, Knowledge and Description*, London: Routledge.
James, A., Hockey, R. & Dawson, A. (1997) *After Writing Culture: Epistemology and Praxis in Contemporary Anthropology*, London: Routledge.
James, I. (2006) *The Fragmentary Demand: An Introduction to the Philosophy of Jean-Luc Nancy*, Standford: Standford University Press.
Janus, A. (2016) 'Introduction', in Giunta, C. & Janus, A. (eds) *Nancy and Visual Culture*, Edinburgh: Edinburgh University Press.
Jost, E. & Whadcock, I. (2018) 'Contested Spaces', *Varoom*, Vol. 38, pp. 58–63.
Kim, Y. (2022) 'Intangible to Tangible: Illustration Practice as a Tool for Safeguarding a Disappearing Culture of Lived Experience', *Journal of Illustration*, Vol. 9, No. 1-2, pp. 239–61.
Kimbell, L. (2011) 'Rethinking Design Thinking: Part 1', *Design and Culture*, Vol. 3, No.3, pp. 285–306.
Kimbell, L. (2012) 'Rethinking Design Thinking: Part 2', *Design and Culture*, Vol. 4, No.2, pp. 129–48.
Kitchin, R. & Dodge, M. (2007) 'Rethinking Maps', *Progress in Human Geography*, Vol. 31, No.1, 331–44.
Krauss, R. ([1976–77] 1986) 'Notes on the Index: Part 1 & Part 2', in *The Originality of the Avant-Garde and Other Modernist Myths*, Cambridge: MIT Press, pp. 196–220.
Kress, G. & Van Leeuwen, T. (1996, 2006 & 2020) *Reading Images: The Grammar of Visual Design*, London: Routledge.
Kunzle, D. ([1973] 1990) *The History of the Comic Strip II: The Nineteenth Century*, Berkley, CA: University of California Press.
Kunzle, D. (2021) *Rebirth of the Comic Strip: A Kaleidoscope 1847–1870*, Jackson, MS: University of Mississippi.
Kwon, M. (2002) *One Place After Another*, Cambridge, MA: Harvard University Press.
Lacoue-Labarthe, P. & Nancy, J.-L. (1997) *Retreating the Political*, London & New York: Routledge.

Lacy, S. (1995) *Mapping the Terrain: New Genre Public Art*, Seattle: Bay Press.
Latour, B. (1986) 'Visualisation and Cognition: Drawing Things Together', *Knowledge and Society in the Sociology of Culture Past and Present*, Vol. 6, pp. 1-40.
Latour, B. (2004) 'Why Has Critique Run out of Steam? From Matters of Fact to Matters of Concern', *Critical Inquiry*, Vol. 30, pp. 225–48.
Latour, B. (2005) 'From Realpolitik to Dingpolitik, or How to Make Things Public', Latour, B. & Weibel, P. (eds) *Making Things Public*, ZKM Centre for Art and Media Karlsruhe, Cambridge, MA: MIT Press, pp. 5–31.
Leeson, L. (2019) 'Our Land: Creative Approaches to the Redevelopment of London's Docklands', *International Journal of Heritage Studies*, Vol. 25, No. 4, pp. 365–79.
Leishman, D. (2018) 'More Eyes, Different Eyes ', *Journal of Illustration*, Vol. 5, No. 2, pp. 191–205.
Lorusso, S. (2019) *Entreprecariat: Everybody Is an Entrepreneur, Nobody Is Safe*, Eindhoven: Onomatopee.
Lovejoy, R. W. (2018) 'Chapter 11: Dangerous Pictures: Social Commentary in Europe, 1720–1860', in Doyle, S., Grove, J. & Sherman, W. (eds) *History of Illustration*, New York: Fairchild Books, pp. 170–83.
Lupton, E. (1998) 'The Designer as Producer', in Heller, S. (ed.) *The Education of a Graphic Designer*, New York: Allworth Press, pp. 159–62.
Lynch, K. (1960) *The Image of the City*, Cambridge, MA: MIT Press.
Male, A. (ed.) (2019) *A Companion to Illustration*, Hoboken: John Wiley & Sons Inc.
Mann, S. (2023) Online conversation with the author, 29 November 2023.
Mann, S. (2025a) Email correspondence with the author, 4 May 2025.
Mann, S. (2025b) Video posted to Instagram, online, translated by the author. Available at: https://www.instagram.com/p/DHG02axtHMv (accessed 9 March 2026).
Matarasso, F. (2019) *A Restless Art: How Participation Won and Why It Matters*, London: Calouste Gulbenkian Foundation.
McCarthy, S. (2013) *The Designer as ... : Author, Producer, Activist, Entrepreneur, Curator, and Collaborator*, London: Laurence King Publishing.
McQuiston, L. (1995) *Graphic Agitation: Social and Political Graphics Since the Sixties*, London: Phaidon.
McRobbie, A. (2001) '"Everyone Is Creative": Artists as New Economy Pioneers?', *Open Democracy*, online. Available at: http://www.opendemocracy.net/node/652 (accessed 9 March 2026).
McRobbie, A. (2011) 'The Los Angelisation of London: Three Short Waves of Young People's Micro-Economies of Culture and Creativity in the UK', in Raunig, G., Ray, G. & Waggenig, U. (eds) *Critique of Creativity: Precarity, Subjectivity and Resistance in the Creative Industries*, London: Mayfly, pp. 119-31.
Miers, J. (2021) 'Conflict or Compromise? An Imagined Conversation with John Hicklenton and Lindsay Cooper About Living with Multiple Sclerosis', *Biography*, Vol. 44, No. 2&3, pp. 25–38.
Miessen, M. (ed.) (2007) *The Violence of Participation*, Berlin: Sternberg Press.
Miessen, M. (2011) *The Nightmare of Participation*, Berlin: Sternberg Press.
Miller, M. (2013) 'Illustrating Space as Collaborative, Socially Engaged Practice: The first report from the DRAW DUKE STREET Residency', *Varoomlab*, Vol. 2, pp. 24–40.
Miller, M. (2015) *An Unruly Parliament of Lines: The Dialectogram as Process and Artifact of Social Engagement*, PhD thesis, Glasgow School of Art.
Miller, M. (2016) Conversation with the author, Wasp Studios, Glasgow, 9 May 2016.
Mitchell, W. J. T. (1994) *Picture Theory*, Chicago: University of Chicago Press.

Mitchell, W. J. T. (2005) *What Do Pictures Want?* Chicago: University of Chicago Press.
Moran, D. (2000) *Introduction to Phenomenology*, London: Routledge.
Morgan, C. (2014a) *A Taxonomy of Deception*, PhD thesis, Royal College of Art.
Morgan, C. (2014b) 'Illustration and Deception', paper presented at *Mokita: 'Style' Illustration Symposium*, London, Somerset House, 10 October 2014.
Morgan, C. (2016) 'The New Canon', *Varoom*, Vol. 32, pp. 36–7.
Morgan, C. & Fauchon, M. (2011) *Phantom Settlements*, London: Ditto Press.
Nancy, J.-L. (1991) *The Inoperative Community*, Minneapolis: University of Minnesota Press.
Nancy, J.-L. (1997) *The Sense of the World*, Minneapolis: University of Minnesota Press.
Nancy, J.-L. (2000) *Being Singular Plural*, Stanford, CA: Stanford University Press.
Nancy, J.-L. (2007) *The Creation of the World or Globalization*, Albany: State University of New York.
Nancy, J.-L. (2017) *The Possibility of a World*, New York: Fordham University Press.
Pandian, A. & McLean, S. (2017) *Crumpled Paper Boat: Experiments in Ethnographic Writing*, Durham NC: Duke University Press.
Pateman, C. (1970) *Participation and Democratic Theory*, Cambridge: Cambridge University Press.
Perloff, M. (2010) *Unoriginal Genius: Poetry by Other Means in the New Century*, Chicago: University of Chicago Press.
Pink, S. (2013) *Doing Visual Ethnography*, 3rd edition, London: Sage.
Poynor, R. (2010) 'Show and Tell: "Illustration Criticism" is Practically an Oxymoron', *PRINT*, June, pp. 30–2.
Pritchard, O. (2016) 'Unicef Utilises the Talents of an International Roster of Illustrators to Raise Awareness of Air Pollution', in *It's Nice That*, online. Available at: https://www.itsnicethat.com/news/unicef-climate-change-illustrators-air-pollution-211116 (accessed 16 March 2026).
Pugh, A. (2024) *The Last Human Job: The Work of Connecting in a Disconnected world*, Princeton NJ: Princeton University Press.
Quito, A. (2019) 'Why Editorial Illustrations Look so Similar These Days', *Quartz*, online. Available at: https://qz.com/quartzy/1728767/why-editorial-illustrations-look-so-similar-these-days (accessed 9 March 2026).
Regan, C. (n.d.) 'Illustrator as Detective: Discovery Through Drawing', *Varoomlab*, Nr 4, 'Visionaries', pp. 73–84. Available at: https://theaoi.com/resources/research-and-insights/varoomlab-4-visionaries/ (accessed 3 March 2022, accessible for AOI members only).
Richardson, L. (1994) 'Writing: A Method of Inquiry', in Denzin, N. & Lincoln, Y. (eds) *Handbook of Qualitative Research*, London: Sage, pp. 516–29.
Ricoeur, P. (1977) *Freud and Philosophy: An Essay on Interpretation*, New Haven, CT: Yale University Press.
Rock, M. ([1996] 2013) 'Designer as Author', in *Multiple Signatures: On Designers, Authors, Readers and Users*, New York: Rizzoli, pp. 45–56.
Roney, P. (2013) 'The Outside of Phenomenology: Jean-Luc Nancy on World and Sense', *South African Journal of Philosophy*, Vol. 32, No. 4, pp. 339–47.
Sabnani, N. (2019) 'Art as Ethnographic Practice', *Mumbai Local*, YouTube, online. Available at: https://www.youtube.com/watch?v=uJJtu3884l0 (accessed 9 March 2026).
Sabnani, N. (2023) Online conversation with the author, 16 November 2023.
Sabnani, N. (2024) '"Fluid, Not Frozen": Assigning Memory to Material', *Journal of Illustration*, Vol. 11, No. 2, pp. 247–62.

Sarkar, J. (2023) Conversation with the author, Kraft café & bar, Dalston, London, 1 December 2023.
Schatzki, T. (2005) 'Early Heidegger on Sociality', in Dreyfus, H. & Wrathall, M. (eds) *A Companion to Heidegger*, Oxford: Blackwell Publishing, pp. 233-47.
Schütz, A. (1945) 'On Multiple Realities', *Philosophy and Phenomenological Research*, Vol. 5, No. 4, pp. 533–76.
Schütz, A. ([1932] 1972) *The Phenomenology of the Social World*, London: Heinemann Educational Books.
Shaughnessy, A. (2011) 'Authorial Practice', in Brazell, D. & Davies, J. (eds) *Making Great Illustration*, London: A&C Black Publishers, p. 195.
Siddall, L. (2015) 'Pick Me Up 2015 Has Arrived and Here's Why It's Totally Great', *It's Nice That*, online. Available at: http://www.itsnicethat.com/articles/pick-me-up-2015 (accessed 9 March 2026).
Su, J. J. (2011) 'Amitav Ghosh and the Aesthetic Turn in Postcolonial Studies', *Journal of Modern Literature*, Vol. 34, No. 3, pp. 65–86.
Sung, K. (2024) 'Sketch Circle: Using Collective Drawing to Illuminate the Personal Identities of South Koreans', *Journal of Illustration*, Vol. 11, No.1, pp. 69–87.
Taylor, R. E. (2024) *Illustration and Heritage*, London: Bloomsbury Publishing.
Till, J. (2005) 'The Negotiation of Hope', in Blundell Jones, P., Petrescu, D. & Till, J. (eds) *Architecture and Participation*, London: Taylor & Francis, pp. 19–41.
Till, J. (2006) 'The Architect and the Other', in *Open Democracy*, online. Available at: https://www.opendemocracy.net/en/architecture_3680jsp (accessed 9 March 2026).
Triggs, T. (2000) 'What Am I?' in Heller, S. & Arisman, M. (eds) *The Education of an Illustrator*, New York: Allworth Press, pp. 48-50.
Tuan, Y. F. (1991) 'Language and the Making of Place: A Narrative-Descriptive Approach', *Annals of the Association of American Geographers*, Vol. 81, No. 4, pp. 684–96.
Venuti, L. (1995) *The Translator's Invisibility: A History of Translation*, London: Routledge.
Vormittag, L. (2014) 'Making (the) Subject Matter: Illustration as Interactive, Collaborative Practice', *Journal of Illustration*, Vol. 1, No. 1, pp. 41–67.
Vormittag, L. (2015) 'Rumor, Legend, Tradition, Fact', *Journal of Illustration*, Vol. 2, No. 2, pp. 223–44.
Vormittag, L. (2021) 'Optical Unconscious', *Varoom*, Vol. 42, pp. 82–93.
Vormittag, L. (2024a) 'Walking the Elephant: Drawing as Enactment of Community', *Migration Studies*, Vol. 12, No. 2, mnad012.
Vormittag, L. (2024b) 'Illustration as Announcement of a World', *Journal of Illustration*, Vol. 11, No. 1, pp. 45–68.
Weizmann, E. (2011) 'Prologue: The Paradox of Participation', in Miessen, M. (ed.) *The Nightmare of Participation*, Berlin: Sternberg Press, pp. 9-11.
Wessendorf, S. (2014) '"Being Open, but Sometimes Closed." Conviviality in a Super-Diverse London Neighbourhood', *European Journal of Cultural Studies*, Vol. 17, No. 4, pp. 392–405.
Williams, Z. (2024) 'Life Inside a Therapeutic Prison: "Look, we've Done Some Terrible Things … "', *The Guardian*, online. Available at: https://www.theguardian.com/society/2024/dec/18/hmp-grendon-therapeutic-prison-psychology-offenders-treatment (accessed 15 December 2024).
Withagen, R. & Caljouw, S. (2017) 'Aldo van Eyck's Playgrounds: Aesthetics, Affordances, and Creativity', *Frontiers in Psychology*, Vol. 8, online. Available at: https://www.frontiersin.org/journals/psychology/articles/10.3389/fpsyg.2017.01130/full (accessed 9 March 2026).

Wong, P. (2023) 'Barter Archive: Reimagining Archival Alternatives Through Participatory Illustration – A Case Study of Billingsgate Fish Market (2019–22)', *Journal of Illustration*, Vol. 10, No.1, pp. 57–65.
Wong, P. & Chan, K. (2023) *Foreseen Property Agency*, online. Available at: https://www.fore-seen.com (accessed 9 March 2026).
Young, I. M. (1990) 'The Ideal of Community and the Politics of Difference', in Nicholson, L. J. (ed.) *Feminism/ Postmodernism*, London: Routledge, pp. 300–23.
Young, R. J. C. (1998) 'Ideologies of the Postcolonial', *Interventions: International Journal of Postcolonial Studies*, Vol. 1, No. 1, pp. 4–8.
Zenker, O. & Kumoll, K. (2010) *Beyond Writing* Culture: *Current Intersections of Epistemologies and Representational Practices*, New York: Berghahn Books.

INDEX